D0915215

ArtScroll Series®

Rabbi Nosson Scherman / Rabbi Meir Zlotowitz
General Editors

Igniting the Power ◆ of Your Tefilla

Praying

Published by

Mesorah Publications, ltd

With Fire

A 5-Minute Lesson-A-Day

Rabbi Heshy Kleinman

FIRST FULL SIZE EDITION
First Impression … August 2005
FIRST PERSONAL SIZE EDITION
First Impression … August 2007
Second Impression … June 2008
Third Impression … September 2008

Published and Distributed by
MESORAH PUBLICATIONS, LTD.
4401 Second Avenue / Brooklyn, N.Y 11232

Distributed in Europe by
LEHMANNS
Unit E, Viking Business Park
Rolling Mill Road
Jarow, Tyne & Wear, NE32 3DP
England

Distributed in Australia and New Zealand by
GOLDS WORLDS OF JUDAICA
3-13 William Street
Balaclava, Melbourne 3183
Victoria, Australia

Distributed in Israel by
SIFRIATI / A. GITLER — BOOKS
6 Hayarkon Street
Bnei Brak 51127

Distributed in South Africa by
KOLLEL BOOKSHOP
Ivy Common
105 William Road
Norwood 2192, Johannesburg, South Africa

ISBN:
ISBN 10: 1-4226-0572-8 / ISBN 13: 978-1-4226-0572-1 (hard cover)
ISBN 10: 1-4226-0573-6 / ISBN 13: 978-1-4226-0573-8 (paperback)

Typography by CompuScribe at ArtScroll Studios, Ltd.

Printed in the United States of America by Noble Book Press Corp.
Bound by Sefercraft, Quality Bookbinders, Ltd., Brooklyn N.Y. 11232

סמואל קמנצקי

Rabbi S. Kamenetsky

Study: 215-473-1212
Home: 215-473-2798

2018 Upland Way
Philadelphia, Pa 19131

בס"ד יום עש"ק ...

לכבוד ידידי, הנכבד והנעלה הרב החשוב וכו'
ר' ... הכהן קלינמן שליט"א

אחדשה"ט בידידות עזה וכו'

...

(718) 436-1133

RABBI YAAKOV PERLOW
1569 - 47TH STREET
BROOKLYN, N.Y. 11219

יעקב פרלוב
ביהמ"ד עדת יעקב נאוואמינסק
ברוקלין, נ.י.

בס"ד יום ראשון ג' לסדר ויגש תשמ"ו

לכבוד, הרב כבוד ועד מכון עלכה, אשר גמרו לעשות האסיפה
הרה"ג ר' לאמשה חתן קלויזנר שליט"א, ברכת שלומים וישע רב.

רצוני לעורר חשיבות הענין הנוגע לצורת ההוראה, לכן כל ישראל לדאוגאת
התקנה לחזקת עדת. וינ"ל בעד לגדל מדרבי מאד הענין, כי כן אבינו
הנקנה השוקים כל מצוה ורחמנות לאלקים אבלה לרבו? שמי אן החשוב
לאותו הישיבה ולאמצלי השלח ישראל. ונ"ל ובראש הענין מצוה רבה
לאשר ולזרוק הדברים השוממות היולון על סיני ק ולקדש את ל'רוך תשמינו ומצוה.
ונא גואה ה' אלו לדבו? אל הנוגעי ולבני? ה' החולה ימיש ומרוח? לגדל הענין
ולעבוד מצוה ה'ה ת"ח, כדעתית, ויקוו? לוקידם להאדר כל מום סאל
וחזק הגולה

מכתב הסכמה מהרב הגאון ר' מתתיהו סולומן, שליט"א
משגיח דישיבת לאקווד

בשבט תשס"א כבר נתתי הסכמתי להחבור החשוב "בכל
דרכיך דעהו" בעניני מדות והשקפות התורה מאת הר"ר
אברהם צבי קליינמאן שליט"א. וכתבתי שהחבור היה חלק א'
מסודר על סידור הלכות והנהגות, וערך בלשון קל וסגנון ברור
אשר גדול וגם קטן יכול ליהנות ממנו.

הנה בא לפני הר"ר אברהם צבי קליינמאן שליט"א, והראה לי
עוד מיגיע כפיו ופרי מעלליו, ספר חדש בשפה האנגלית, בשם
Praying With Fire
ומצאתי בה דברים של טעם ודעת, מתוקן ומסודר, ללמוד
וללמד, דברים שיש בהם תועלת גדול לצבור הרחב. הספר
הזה נחוץ מאד מאד בעת צרתינו, וכדכתיב "ונצעק אל ה'."

ורצוני בזה לתת שוב פעם את ברכתי להמחבר הנ"ל שימשיך
לזכות את הרבים בדברים המועילים, בזה החיבור ובכל
מעשה ידיו מתוך שמחה וטוב לבב.

מתתיהו חיים סולומן

Table of Contents

Chapter 6: Thirteen Practical Strategies to Achieve True Kavannah

Chapter 7: Finding Answers to Unanswered Prayers

Chapter 8: The Spoken Word:
Our Downfall, Our Salvation

PREFACE:
PRAYERS ARE ALWAYS EFFECTIVE

by Harav Mattisyahu Salomon
adapted from the Hebrew
by Rabbi Yaakov Yosef Reinman

*C*hazal present us with a paradox. They tell us (*Berachos* 6b) that *tefillah* is "among those things that stand at the pinnacle of creation," and then they observe that "people nonetheless treat it lightly." We cannot help but wonder, if *tefillah* is indeed so exalted, why do people treat it so lightly?

Rav Chaim Volozhiner, in *Nefesh HaChaim* (2:13), writes that we haven't even the faintest notion of the vast and awesome power of the *kavannos* that the *Anshei Knesses HaGedolah* infused into the *tefillos* they formulated for us, that every word, every letter is fraught with the most profound meaning and value. Furthermore, he writes, all the *kavannos* of the Arizal HaKadosh, which are themselves beyond the comprehension of virtually everyone, are but a drop in the ocean compared to the *kavannos* of the *Anshei Knesses HaGedolah*.

Most people are aware of the extreme holiness and power of the *tefillos*, and yet, unfathomably, they take them lightly. How can this be? Even if they do not understand the *tefillos* fully, shouldn't people at least stand in awe of them? Shouldn't they at least tremble when they utter the hallowed words?

It occurs to me that a sense of frustration may be at the root of the cavalier attitude of some people toward the *tefillos*.

A woman called me after her husband had passed away following a long and excruciating illness. "What about all the *tefillos* that I prayed?"

she asked. "What about all the *Tehillim* that I said? What about the rivers of tears that I shed? Were they all for nothing?"

This good and faithful woman was not questioning the justice of the Almighty. She was not complaining about the terrible fate that had befallen her family. No, she was expressing her frustration and her deep disillusionment. She had been certain that if she prayed with all her might her prayers would be answered and her husband would recover. But it did not happen. And now she was confused. Frustrated and confused. What happened, she wanted to know, to all her prayers? Where did they go? What had she accomplished with all her tremendous emotional efforts?

Most people have similar experiences at one time or another in their lives. In times of crisis, they reach down into the depths of their souls and pray with extraordinary intensity and sincerity, and then, nothing happens. It seems to them as if their prayers were completely futile, and they lose heart. They become frustrated and disillusioned, and they can no longer bring themselves to invest that type of intensity and concentration when they pray. They take the *tefillos* "lightly," in the words of *Chazal*.

So what is the proper response to this kind of reaction? How are we to understand the meaning and purpose of *tefillah* in the proper light? How can we avoid the frustration and disillusionment that come from disappointment?

The first step is to correctly assess the role of *tefillah* in our lives. Some people tend to think that *tefillah* is a device, a mechanism that we use regularly to achieve our needs and wants. But this is not so.

The Mabit writes in *Sefer Beis Elokim* (15) that *tefillah* is a mitzvah in the Torah, as it is written (*Devarim* 11:13), "To serve Him with all your heart." The Gemara states (*Taanis* 2), "What kind of service is in the heart? It is *tefillah*." Consequently, *tefillah* is one of the *Taryag mitzvos* in the Torah, no different from wearing *tefillin* or taking an *esrog*. When a person prays with *kavannah* he fulfills a mitzvah in the Torah. The form of the mitzvah of *tefillah* is to express Hashem's praises and to ask for our various needs, because by doing so, we affirm that the fulfillment of our needs lies in His hands alone.

Therefore, even if Hashem does not grant our request for whatever reason, the mitzvah is in the asking of it. When a person prays he is rewarded just as he is rewarded when he takes an *esrog*, because he has performed one of the mitzvos in the Torah. And what is his reward? It is a share in *Olam Haba*, the next world, just as with any other mitzvah.

The Mabit goes on to say, however, that *tefillah* can also bear an additional reward in this world. First of all, it is possible that his prayers and requests will be granted. Furthermore, even if there is a *gezeirah* and his prayers are not granted, he may receive certain benefits and rewards that at least bear some resemblance to his original request. Moshe Rabbeinu prayed to be allowed to enter Eretz Yisrael. Hashem did not grant this wish, but he did show him the Land and the important events that would shape its future. In the same way, a person who does not accomplish a reprieve from his illness through his prayer may nonetheless gain a reprieve for another family member who might have otherwise fallen victim to a similar illness.

It stands to reason then that just as we embrace the mitzvah of *esrog* with the fullest enthusiasm, giving no thought to what it will accomplish for us in the here and now, so too should we approach the mitzvah of *tefillah*. The goal of the mitzvah is not to fulfill our needs but rather to express our recognition that only Hashem can fulfill those needs, should He choose to do so. And the reward for this mitzvah, as with all mitzvos, awaits us in the next world. As we say every day before *Shacharis*, "These are the things of which a person enjoys the profits in this world yet the principal remains intact for the next world: . . . concentration on prayer (*iyun tefillah*) . . ." It happens sometimes that we are disappointed and our prayers are not granted, but this does not diminish in the least what we have accomplished through our prayers. They were not wasted, and there is really no cause for frustration and disillusionment.

Still, in a certain sense, this is small consolation. True, when we pray for the recovery of a sick person we are performing an import mitzvah by declaring that health and illness, life and death, are in His hands alone. True, we are rewarded in the next world for performing this mitzvah regardless of whether or not the patient recovers his health. But what about the patient himself? Is our only accomplishment that we ourselves have gained another share in the next world? After our prodigious efforts on behalf of the patient, have we accomplished nothing for him if we have not brought about his recovery? These are questions that continue to plague us even if we understand that *tefillah* is a mitzvah like any other.

Let us take a closer look, however, at the efficacy of prayer. Even though we have explained that the value of prayer is not dependent on the results it produces, we all know that prayer very often does indeed produce quite remarkable results. How does prayer accomplish this? If there was a heavenly decree that some calamity should come to pass, is it possible for us to change the Divine mind, so to speak? Can we come before Him and protest that this would not be a good thing to do? Can we convince the Almighty to do something other than what He, in His infinite wisdom, had planned to do? Obviously, this is completely ridiculous; it is outrageous even to suggest it. So how then can prayer produce results?

The *Chovos HaLevavos* (*Cheshbon HaNefesh* 18) writes that the purpose of *tefillah* is not to change the Almighty's mind but rather to bring us to the realization that our fate is completely dependent on His will, that we can only survive through His mercy. The very act of prayer, however, elevates, exalts, and transforms us, so that we are no longer the same people we were before. Consequently, a Heavenly decree against a person, Heaven forbid, can effectively be rescinded through prayer. Since the person has been transformed through his prayer, he is no longer the same person against whom the decree was originally issued. The *Chinuch* (513) also makes a similar point.

But a question remains. If prayer works only because it transforms the one who prays and thereby changes his destiny, how does prayer for other people work? If a Heavenly decree is issued against a person and he falls ill to the point that he is unable to pray for himself, how can the prayers of his family, friends, and community effect his recovery? What connection is there between the transformation of other people through their prayers and the person for whom they are praying?

I asked this question to my rebbi, Rav Eliyahu Lopian, and he gave me a very succinct answer. "When people pray for another person, they become like his *talmidim* in that he is causing them to gain merit."

In other words, whenever a person causes a good thing, whether consciously or unconsciously, he gains merit for causing it. Og gained merit for informing Avraham that Lot had been abducted, even though his intentions were evil.[1] Balak was rewarded for his *korbanos*, even though his intentions were evil.[2] Had not Avraham preceded him, Bilaam would have gained merit for teaching people diligence, even though his intentions were evil.[3] It is clear that a person gains merit for causing a good thing, whether or not he intended to do so.

In the same way, when people pray for the recovery of a sick person and in the process draw closer to the Almighty, it is the sick person who has caused this transformation, and the merit goes to him. And the more people that pray for him and are elevated, the more merit he ac-

---

1. See *Rashi, Bereishis* 14:13.
2. See *Nazir* 23b.
3. See *Rashi, Bamidbar* 22:21.

cumulates. Ultimately, the sick person himself is transformed by all the merit he has accumulated, albeit without his knowledge, and the decree against him may be rescinded.

Moreover, if the sick person is righteous and worthy, if he is someone with fine qualities and accomplishments other people admire, then he gains an even greater measure of merit. Why? Because when people pray for him, they mention all the good he represents and they plead for Divine mercy. And as they contemplate all the good things this person has done and accomplished, they learn from his example and become better people themselves. In this sense, he is their rebbi and they are his *talmidim*. He is, in effect, teaching them how to live and think, albeit unconsciously, and he gains merit from their elevation and transformation.

Sometimes, the merit a sick person accumulates through the prayers of other people is sufficient to tip the scales in his favor and rescind the evil decree. Sometimes, however, the evil decree simply cannot be rescinded. We cannot fathom the intricacies of the Divine plan; we only know that the end result of the Divine plan is completely good. And if the Almighty chooses not to rescind the decree despite the accumulation of mountains of merit through prayer, we accept with full faith that this is the best way to further the Divine plan for the entire world and achieve the ultimate good.

But the prayers have not gone to waste. After all, for what does a faithful Jew struggle his entire lifetime in this world if not to earn a beautiful share in the next world? Prayer for a sick person accomplishes exactly that. The merits accumulated by the sick person, through his own prayers and through the prayers of others, belong to him for all eternity, along with the merit of all the mitzvos he has performed during his lifetime. These merits will raise him to the highest levels of *Olam Haba* and the highest degrees of illumination forever.

FOREWORD

by Rabbi Yisroel Reisman

WHY PRAY?

For most people, prayer is an opportunity to ask *HaKadosh Baruch Hu* for the things which they need. We call this *bakashas tzerachim,* asking for the things we need.

There is another dimension to prayer. When a person prays to Hashem, he recognizes that *HaKadosh Baruch Hu* is the Source of all blessings. This recognition is fundamental to our faith in G-d as an active ruler of the universe. The more we pray, the more we incorporate this belief into our psyche. We call this *avodah,* service of G-d.

As we study prayer, we will find many clues to these two aspects of prayer.

The Gemara teaches that our prayers are modeled after the prayers of our *Avos;* "Tefillah avos tiknum." We are also told that they are modeled after the service in the *Beis HaMikdash;* "Neged temidim tiknum." Although the Gemara appears to bring these as two competing views, the Rambam accepts them both. In fact, each represents one of the two dimensions of prayer. "Avos tiknum" refers to the requests of our *Avos,* the *bakashas tzerachim* part of prayer. "Neged temidim tiknum" is clearly a reference to the *avodah* aspect.

The Rambam cites the Biblical verse, "l'avdo b'chol levavchem," *to serve Him with all your heart,* as the source for our prayer obligation. The Ramban offers a different source: "Ki seitzei lamilchamah al o'yevecha … u'sekatem ba'chatzotzros," *When you go out to battle against your enemies … blow your trumpets (as a call to prayer).*

Here again, we have two verses that mirror the two aspects of prayer. *To serve Him with all your heart* is a clear reference to the *avodah* aspect. *When you go out to battle …* clearly refers to *bakashas tzerachim.*

WHY PRAY FOR EVERYTHING?

There are basic differences between these two reasons for prayer. If *bakoshas tzerachim* were the sole purpose of prayer, it would hardly make sense to *require* that a person ask for everything. A person should be permitted to choose those *berachos* which contain the requests for which he wishes to pray on any given day.

Yet, the middle *berachos* of *Shemoneh Esrei* contain requests for virtually all of a person's needs. The *poskim* rule that if a person misses any one of these *berachos*, he has not satisfied his prayer obligations (*berachos m'akvos zu es zu*). Why should this invalidate the prayer?

If prayer were solely a request from Hashem, *bakashas tzerachim*, it is difficult to see why we are required to ask for everything. However, the second aspect, the *avodah* part, uses prayer to reinforce our faith, requiring us to recognize Hashem's control over those things for which we ask. Thus, we can understand why the requirement to pray for all our needs should cover every aspect of our lives. This explains why we pray for everything, strengthening the *avodah* in all areas of our lives.

In fact, the Satmar Rebbe, in *Divrei Yoel*, teaches that during the time that the *Beis HaMikdash* stood, a person was *not* required to mention all of the *berachos* of *Shemoneh Esrei*. At that time, the *avodah* was in the *Beis HaMikdash*. This left only the *bakashas tzerachim* aspect of prayer, which does not require that every *berachah* be mentioned.

This enables us to understand the Gemara's statement that the order of the middle *berachos* (which had originally been formulated by the *Anshei Knesses HaGedolah*, centuries earlier), was forgotten and had to be reformulated after the *Churban*. It seems difficult to understand how the *Shemoneh Esrei* prayer could be forgotten, if it was uttered by Jews every day. In fact, the order *was* forgotten precisely because it was not used during the time that the *Beis HaMikdash* stood.

A DEEPER LOOK

This insight enables us to explain another difficulty in the laws of prayer.

If a person finds that his mind has strayed during his prayers, to the point that he does not recall which *berachah* he has recited, how should he continue?

Chayei Adam rules that he may continue only from a *berachah* which he is certain that he has not recited. If he is in doubt regarding any *berachah*, he may not recite it, because he would be risking a *berachah l'vatalah*, a wasted *berachah*.

The Steipler Gaon expresses amazement at this ruling. Indeed, our primary concern should be to avoid the risk of a *berachah l'vatalah*. However, since the *Shulchan Aruch* rules that if a person misses any one of the *berachos*, he has not satisfied his prayer obligation (*berachos m'akvos zu es zu*), it would be prudent to ensure that every *berachah* is said (thus avoiding eighteen potential *berachos l'vatalah*). It would therefore follow that the person should recite every *berachah* which he *may* have missed. Although this risks an individual *berachah l'vatalah*, it avoids the greater risk of invalidating the entire prayer!

Given our understanding of the dual parts of prayer, the ruling of the *Chayei Adam* can be explained. It is true that if one *berachah* is missing, the individual has not satisfied his prayer requirement. As explained, this is a failure in the *avodah* aspect of prayer. Still, this does not render the rest of his *Shemoneh Esrei* as wasted *berachos*. The prayer, even when missing a *berachah*, satisfies the *bakashas tzerachim* aspect (similar to prayers during the *Beis HaMikdash* era), and are not *berachos l'vatalah*.

There is an additional source for this insight from the surprising ruling of the *Mishnah Berurah (see Beur Halachah 593:1)* that a person who is traveling and has no *siddur* may recite the *Shemoneh Esrei* by heart, as best he can, even if he knows he will not remember every *berachah*. Clearly, the *Mishnah Berurah* does not view an incomplete *Shemoneh Esrei* as a series of *berachos l'vatalah*!

YOUR PRAYERS

Given this understanding of prayer, the language of *Shemoneh Esrei* takes on new meaning. In fact, if you pay attention as you pray, you will find the dual aspect of prayer in the language of virtually *all* the *berachos* of *Shemoneh Esrei*!

For example, in our prayers for healing, we start with *bakashas tzerachim* ("Heal us …"). Then we add, "For You are G-d, the King, the faithful Healer …" — a statement of faith in G-d, the *avodah* aspect. This form of *berachah* holds true for almost every one of the middle *berachos* of *Shemoneh Esrei*.

As you follow the language of your prayer, you will find that this newfound insight gives you focus. Look for it as you *daven*, and the prayers will take on greater meaning. You will find that the more you understand *davening*, the easier it will be to have *kavannah* when you pray.

❧❧ ❧❧

Prayer may be the service of your heart, but it cannot succeed without the input of your mind.

The more we understand the fundamentals of prayer, the more we apply ourselves to understanding prayer, the more we will succeed in prayer.

The *sefer* before you is a wonderful source for greater insight into your prayers. It contains a breathtaking wealth of information on *davening*, written in a style which is inviting to the layman and informative to the scholar. It is your first step toward a better *avodah b'lev,* and a stronger case for your *bakashas tzerachim.*

May *HaKadosh Baruch Hu* grant us the wisdom and insight to make the most of this wonderful tool toward a better *davening*!

INTRODUCTION: IGNITING THE POWER OF PRAYER

There is no force as central to our lives as prayer. It is the most powerful vehicle for spiritual growth, material success, health, security — everything that really matters to us. In times of crisis, when Hashem's mercy and protection are so clearly all that stand between us and the forces of hatred and chaos in the world, *tefillah* is our only truly useful weapon, and our only reliable source of comfort as well.

For far too many people, however, it is an inadequately understood vehicle. We pray each day, but without a full awareness of what our prayers really are, how to bring out their full potential, and where they can take us.

When we are first introduced to *tefillah* as children, we are taught only what we are capable of learning: the mechanics of praying and some simple concepts. As adults, we must go much farther if our *tefillah* is to be the meaningful, life-sustaining endeavor it is meant to be. In these pages, we hope to give the reader a cogent and inspiring foundation upon which will stand a lifetime's worth of pure, focused, effective *tefillah*. We will explore:

  (a) What we are praying for — and why;
  (b) the effect of each prayer in the Heavens and on our daily lives;
  (c) how to find Hashem and feel closer to His Presence through prayer; and
  (d) the meaning of *kavannah* and how to maintain it during prayer.

With these tools, we will find within our hearts a greater appreciation for the Divinely granted privilege of addressing our Creator three times a day. Our prayers will be vastly strengthened as we imbue ourselves with heightened awe and respect for the One Who hears our *tefillos*.

Rav Shimshon David Pincus, author of *She'arim B'Tefillah*, explained, "The basis for success and the pillar of our work is to know that *tefillah* is one of the foundations on which everything [in this world] rests. Just as the study of Torah is a pillar of this world that everything stands on, similarly, *tefillah* is a foundation in the construct of mankind and the world."[1]

You may ask: Can an ordinary person unleash the power of *tefillah* to enable it to function as "a foundation in the construct of mankind and the world?" It is much easier to accept that great *tzaddikim* can change the world with their powerful prayers than to comprehend the potential of ordinary people like ourselves — who are immersed in the everyday activities of home, family, and livelihood — to do likewise.

In truth, however, the very fact that a person is exploring ways to make *tefillah* more meaningful shows that he has taken a serious approach to prayer, which will, in itself, enable him to access this powerful tool. In fact, the simple act of picking up this book is an important step on the road to meaningful *tefillah*.

Rabbi Elie Munk wrote in the preface to his classic work, *The World of Prayer*:[2] "Vague philosophizing about the nature and idea, origin and form of expression of the prayers is of little help. A more direct method of approach is required. Whoever has succeeded in penetrating the external shell of the formal prayer to its innermost core will comprehend the world of thought and feeling hidden deep in its central sphere." In this manner only will a man be able to find Hashem through his prayer.

MISSION OF THIS SEFER

The mission of this *sefer*, presented in a lesson-a-day format, is two-fold: to impart the concepts and underpinnings of *tefillah* — penetrating the external shell of the formal prayer — as well as to provide a solid understanding and appreciation of the practical aspects of *tefillah* and how it affects our lives.

In this vein, Rav Pam[3] cited a teaching from *Mishlei*:[4] "*Wealth gained by vanity* [i.e., dishonesty] *will diminish, but what one gathers by hand*

---

1. *She'arim B'Tefillah*, p. 8.
2. *The World of Prayer* by Rabbi Dr. Elie Munk (Feldheim Publ.), Vol. 1, Preface, p. 1.
3. *Rav Pam* by Rabbi Shimon Finkleman (ArtScroll/Mesorah), p. 102.
4. 13:11.

will increase. Our sages explain: If a person studies a great deal of new material at once, he will not retain his knowledge, but if one *gathers by hand,* meaning that he studies small quantities at a time, he will thereby increase his knowledge[5]

When Rav Pam wrote his *sefer, Atarah LaMelech,* he made one request:[6] "Do not read this *sefer* as one reads a newspaper, superficially and without a sense of purpose. The masters of *mussar* would say that one who seeks to be influenced and inspired by something he learns must review the subject matter again and again, and most importantly, he must ponder it well."

The purpose of our *sefer* is not to say "*vertlach*" (brief insights); rather, it is to inspire all of us toward profound prayer with an emphasis on the joy and pleasure which one can experience in praying.

POINTS TO PONDER

To encourage readers to "review the subject matter again and again, and most importantly … ponder it well," we have included "Points to Ponder" at the end of each day. These should be read in conjunction with the entire contents of the day. They are included to assist the reader in remembering the main concepts presented.

CALENDAR

Another feature of this book is the learning calendar displayed on the margin of each day's lesson. While keeping to this calendar can strengthen one's sense of purpose in undertaking this daily learning, the more important goal is to learn each day in sequence.

If one begins the *sefer* on a later date or misses a day of learning, he should resume with the next consecutive day rather than seek to stay with the calendar. In this way, the logical progression of the learning will be maintained.

CONCLUSION

Read one day at a time — or more if you choose — of the teachings of the Gemara and the great *Rishonim* and *Acharonim* from whose reservoirs of Torah wisdom we will learn. You are sure to find inspiration.

---

5. *Avodah Zarah* 19a.
6. *Rav Pam,* p. 110

Ultimately, however, the objective of this book will be realized through the desire it engenders in the reader to improve his *tefillah*.

In *Michtav MeEliyahu*,[7] Rav Eliyahu Dessler writes that a person who is inspired regarding an important task should know with certainty that it is incumbent upon him to fully accept the assignment. Hence, our role is merely that of one inspired from Heaven, who has gathered the wisdom of others and feels compelled to share these treasures with all who are interested.

May it be Hashem's will that our modest attempts to gather these meaningful teachings will inspire you, the reader, to more effective and satisfying prayer, and may our *tefillos* bring strength and comfort to *Klal Yisrael* in the time of crisis in which we live, and hasten the Redemption.

---

7. Vol. 1, Intro., p. 17.

ACKNOWLEDGMENTS

Many thanks are in order to those instrumental in allowing this book on prayer to be written and for bringing it to its successful conclusion. This book represents the culmination of many hours of toil and effort. However, it has been a labor of love. First, I thank *HaKadosh Baruch Hu* for providing me with the health, the means, the knowledge, the ideas and the time necessary to undertake this endeavor.

I thank **HaRav Matisyahu Salomon Shlit"a,** Mashgiach of the Lakewood Yeshivah, and **Rabbi Yisroel Reisman, Shlit"a,** Rav of Agudath Israel of Madison, for graciously taking the time to prepare a foreword for this book. Their profound wisdom and words on the topic of *tefillah* will IY"H continue to encourage those seeking to change the way they *daven.* I thank **Rabbi Yaakov Yosef Reinman** for adapting the Mashgiach's foreword from the Hebrew text.

Thanks to **Rabbi Meir Zlotowitz** and **Rabbi Nosson Scherman** of Artscroll, who have provided thousands the opportunity to learn about so many vital topics affecting their spirituality.

Thanks to **Avrohom Biderman** and **Mendy Herzberg** for coordinating all the aspects of the project at ArtScroll until its completion. Thanks to **Ms. Sury Reinhold,** assisted by **Ms. Sara Rivka Spira,** for their typesetting expertise. Thanks to **Rabbi Sheah Brander,** ArtScroll's master craftsman, whose indelible fingerprint is on every page. Thanks to **Ms. Chaya Perel Teichman,** for skillfully paginating the book and ensuring that each page is aesthetically pleasing.

Mrs. Mindy Stern's devoted attention to every word and nuance in this book has added immeasurably to its quality. A master of her craft, her contributions are highly valued and deeply appreciated.

Thanks to **Ben Gasner Studio** of Jerusalem for his expert design of the all-important book cover. Thanks to **Reb Michael Rothschild,** Director of the Chofetz Chaim Heritage Foundation (CCHF), for his assistance. Thanks to **Mrs. Shaindy Applebaum** of CCHF for helping to organize the calendar for this book, and to **Mrs. Leah Sekula** of CCHF for her assistance.

Much thanks go to **Mrs. Ethel Gottlieb, Rabbi Avrohom Marmorstien,** Rav of K'hal Minchas Chinuch of N.Y.C., and **Mrs. Elana Felder** for their involvement in the initial editing of this book.

Great thanks to **Mrs. Judi Dick** of ArtScroll who selflessly gave of her editing talents, experience, and dedication in bringing this work to its completion. The largesse of her dedication and selflessness is surpassed only by her heart. Thanks to her husband **Reb Nachum Dick** for welcoming me into their home to complete the editing with Mrs. Dick.

I offer a special note of thanks to the principal editor of the book, **Mrs. Chana Nestlebaum** — not just from myself, but on behalf of the readers of this book who will benefit most from her words of passion, expertise in editing, and ability to "keep it flowing." May Hashem shower her with great merit for all she has done.

I would also like to thank my dear son, **Rabbi Daniel Osher Kleinman** of the Brisker Kollel in Jerusalem, as well as **Rabbi Ezra Bloch** of Lakewood, N.J., for reviewing the manuscript and the many footnotes. I pray that the footnotes will enable the scholar to take a more enlightened approach to understanding this book. Thanks once more to **Rabbi Yisroel Reisman, Shlit"a,** who assisted with some of the most difficult halachic passages.

Thanks to **Melvin and Shirley H.** of Milwaukee for their inspiration. Thanks to **Reb Yermie Lehrman** who is always available to lend a helping hand. Thanks to **Reb Zev Saftlas,** author of "Motivation That Works," who gave guidance in finding the right title for the book. Thanks to **Reb Shaya Herskovich** for his constructive comments dealing with the *Bircas Avos* segment.

A special note of gratitude to **Moshe and Venezia Zakheim** for their encouragement, and for their dedication to the success of this book.

The Gemara[1] advises: "Go up a step to choose a confidant." Rashi[2] explains that it is advisable to attach oneself to people who are of greater distinction than himself so that he will come to emulate them.

---

1. *Yevamos* 63a.
2. Ibid.

I am truly blessed to have "attached myself" to **Rabbi Mordechai Gelber**. His *tzidkus* and compassion for the individual as well as for the *tzibbur* is well-known by all in Flatbush, Brooklyn, N.Y. **Rabbi Gelber** is co-founder of Hakhel, a not-for-profit volunteer organization formed in Flatbush in 5755 for the purpose of uniting our communities through the study of Torah, acts of *chesed*, and the proper performance of mitzvos. He is author of the "Hakhel Community Awareness Bulletins," and publishes the "Hakhel Master Gemach List." In the course of these and the many other community projects in which he is involved, he has enlightened many and enabled countless people to grow spiritually. All that he does is without fanfare and the recognition which he so justly deserves.

Chazal tell us, "Gedolim tzaddikim b'misasan." The *tzaddik* remains alive by the essence of his words which continue to influence others to live a true Torah life long after the *tzaddik* has physically left this world. Ever since I first opened the volumes of **HaRav HaGaon Rav Eliyahu Eliezer Dessler zt"l's** *Michtav MeEliyahu*, I was enthralled by his quantitative and qualitative depth of wisdom. His illuminating words are included throughout this *sefer*. I thank the publisher of *Michtav MeEliyahu*, who allowed me to cite the *sefer* many times.

Chazal teach that one's wife is called the "home." Special thanks to my wife Bruria, a true *aishes chayil*, for creating a home in which the learning and teaching of Torah and the doing of *chesed* is paramount. Because of her selfless support, I was able to disappear for hours on end in order to undertake the writing of this book. May Hashem bless her with great merit for all she does.

I apologize to anyone who assisted in this book in any way, whose name I have inadvertently omitted. To **all** who have assisted with **Praying With Fire**, may Hashem shower you with the great merit that accrues to those who enlighten and uplift the public.

Finally, I thank you, the reader, for your desire to help *Klal Yisrael* to bring the redemption by improving the way we all *daven*. I pray that each day of learning brings each of us a step closer to the day when the prayers, tears, and longings for the redemption uttered by Jews throughout the centuries will be answered by our loving Father.

PROLOGUE: THE JOURNEY

SURMOUNTING THE OBSTACLES

*C*hazal teach that *tefillah* stands at the highest point of the world.[1] However, the significance of *tefillah* lies not only in its Heavenly quality, but also in its very earthly place in the human heart. *Tefillah* emanates from man. It is the province of young and old, men and women, the wealthy and the poor, the healthy and the sick.

Despite the fact that there is not one person anywhere whose life is not profoundly affected by the quality of his prayers, many people do not fully understand prayer, even on the most practical level. They may pray without any coherent understanding of why they are doing so, what it is that they are saying, and what their prayers ultimately accomplish. They may not realize how very much the quality of their prayers really does matter.

On a deeper level, however, our souls do understand the workings of prayer. In moments of crisis, we are seized by a need to pour out our hearts to Hashem, both as individuals and as a community, on a national and international level. In times of crisis in Israel, special gatherings are held to pray and beseech Hashem for compassion. We assemble and pray when a tragedy occurs in our community *r"l*. Individuals with pressing needs, whether for livelihood, health, children, or concerns of a spiritual nature, likewise turn to *tefillah*.

---

1. See *Berachos* 6b with *Rashi*. Rav Bibi bar Abaye was asked, "What is the meaning of the phrase — *kerum zuluss to people*?" He answered: "These are things which stand at the pinnacle of the world but which people treat lightly." *Rashi* states: "An example is prayer, which rises up to Heaven."

Yet this passion is largely missing from our everyday prayers, which are often recited in haste and with a dearth of concentration. If we automatically resort to *tefillah* in times of crisis, why then do we find it so difficult to pray with focus and emotion on a daily basis?

The Gemara[2] speaks of four areas that need strengthening: Torah, good deeds, prayer, and one's worldly occupation. The *Malbim*[3] explains that the Evil Inclination fights against spiritual endeavors on two fronts: it discourages one from even starting, and then it impedes one's progress once he has embarked.

In terms of *tefillah*, the first altercation with the Evil Inclination occurs before prayer. This involves the struggle to find a *minyan*, daven on time, and overcome the distractions that take on such urgency just as we prepare to pray. The second challenge occurs during the *tefillah* itself, when the Evil Inclination continually attempts to interrupt our thoughts.

The distractions come in an unrelenting wave — acquaintances we feel we must acknowledge, conversations that suddenly seem riveting, problems that are impossible to ignore, and an agenda that demands the speediest possible conclusion of *tefillah* so that we can "get on with the day."

Why do so many obstacles stand in the way of our *tefillah*? The Vilna Gaon comments that just as a greater person has a greater Evil Inclination, so too does a greater mitzvah have a greater Evil Inclination standing in opposition to it. *Tefillah* is clearly such a mitzvah. The Evil Inclination, for one, evidently has no problem recognizing the true value of *tefillah* for the Jewish people.[4]

How do we begin to overcome these obstacles and improve the way we pray? In *Michtav M'Eliyahu*[5] Rav Dessler suggests that before improvements can be implemented, amends must be made for the past. Rejection of past habits, he explains, is the workman's tool for spiritual growth. Moreover, the degree of this rejection — which must be strong in order to endure — influences the degree of change. This step, which may at first appear to be an imposing obstacle, is necessary to achieve meaningful *tefillah*.

Rav Dessler[6] reassures us that when striving to reach a worthy goal, a person will willingly work hard to achieve it regardless of the obstacles

---

2. *Berachos* 32b.
3. *Yehoshua* 1:6.
4. Also see *She'eilos U'Teshuvos Teshuvos V'Hanhagos*, Vol. 4, *Orach Chaim, Siman 27*, where Rav Moshe Sternbuch comments that the fact that so many people have such great difficulty praying with *kavannah* is evidence of its importance.
5. Vol. 5, p. 241.
6. Ibid. Vol. 1, p. 20, s.v. *Hinei*.

that he may face. By gaining a greater understanding of the incomparable power we possess when we pray, we can see clearly that effective *tefillah* is a goal worthy of our greatest effort.

SPIRITUAL APTITUDE

There is yet another tactic the Evil Inclination employs in preventing us from improving the quality of our *tefillah*. It is perhaps the most damaging tactic of all, for it prevents us from even approaching the starting line. How does the Evil Inclination accomplish this? By confirming our own suspicion that we are just ordinary people, and that our desire for a greater closeness with Hashem is a goal not befitting our stature. To believe in our ability to achieve, we must have an accurate concept of the true spiritual potential that resides within every Jew.

> The Gemara[7] says that an angel teaches the entire Torah to the fetus in its mother's womb. Before the baby is born, the angel taps it on the upper lip and all the learned Torah is forgotten.

Rav Dessler asks:[8] Since the baby forgets everything he was taught, what was the purpose of learning all of Torah in the first place? His remarkable answer helps us appreciate our potential for spiritual excellence: The Torah is so completely spiritual that, had we not learned it prior to birth, it would be impossible to comprehend it in this material world. *Chazal* inform us of this in order to make us aware that we do have the ability, albeit dormant, to recognize and understand the truth of Torah in its full intensity and clarity.

Spiritual greatness is inborn within each of us, and therefore, the goal of bringing it to the surface is within our grasp. Rav Dessler[9] quotes the *Tanna d'Vei Eliyahu Rabbah*, which states that every Jew should feel obligated to ask, "When can my deeds match those of our ancestors, Avraham, Yitzchak, and Yaakov?" In this light, we can see how mistaken we are to doubt our spiritual capabilities and think to ourselves, "Who am I to aspire to higher spiritual levels?" When one aspires to the deeds of our Forefathers, he finds himself propelled along the path of spiritual growth because the opportunity truly does exist to reach the loftiest level.

Why, then, do so many people doubt their own potential? Rav Dessler explains that these individuals have never encouraged or strengthened themselves properly. Were they only to push through the barriers con-

---

7. *Niddah* 30b.
8. *Michtav MeEliyahu*, Vol. 5, pp. 242-243.
9. Ibid.

straining them, their eyes would open to remarkable opportunities. They would then see clearly that the Gates are open and Hashem is reaching out to them with unlimited Divine assistance.

PASSING THE TEST

An individual becomes inspired to bring his tefillah to a higher level. His children are approaching marriageable age, his business is teetering, and his elderly parents are prone to various health problems. There is much he needs from Hashem, and he resolves that the time has come to serve Him with more desire and devotion. He recognizes that opportunities have been wasted and decides to start immediately — the very next day — by making sure to get to shul on time. The next morning, he leaps out of bed, gets dressed, settles behind the steering wheel of his car, and turns the key. The car moans and sputters, but doesn't start. He tries again and again, but soon the moaning gives way to a faint buzzing sound. The battery is dead. And so, he thinks, is his resolution.

"Why," he wonders, "when I'm all set to really try to serve Hashem properly, does He place an obstacle right at the beginning of my path? Why does this have to be such a hassle?"

Life brings many obstacles — some minor and some far more difficult — to challenge our best intentions. Rav Dessler[10] reassures us that these challenges are not a rejection of our efforts. He explains that each person has a unique mission in life, which is accomplished through a set of tests and challenges especially tailored for him. Therefore, a person dealing with difficulties should not be disheartened. The obstacles are, in reality, an expression of Hashem's kindness, for they provide opportunities to overcome the Evil Inclination and to bond with Hashem.

The Manchester Rosh Yeshivah, Rav Yehudah Zev Halevi Segal,[11] writes that we must recognize that every situation that transpires, and indeed all of life, is a test. One who triumphs in this constant battle with the Evil Inclination will merit entry to the Garden of Eden.

Emerging victorious from a fray that is constant and ongoing might seem impossible to many people. They reason that eventually, a person runs out of energy with which to fight. There is, however, a simple, winning strategy. Rav Segal[12] advises that each person simply do whatever is before him to do and forge ahead step by step. He must pro-

---

10. Ibid. Vol. 5, p. 275.
11. *Yirah V'Daas*, Vol. 1, p. 26.
12. Ibid. p. 91.

ceed slowly and not allow thoughts of weakness and doubt to enter his mind. This approach will ultimately endow a person with the strength to succeed.

What does one do if he feels that even this process of gradual growth seems impossible to implement in the area of *tefillah*? Hashem in His compassion stands ready to help this person find his way. He need only plead: "Hashem, I truly feel lost, and I sincerely regret being in this situation."[13] Hashem will then set him on the path that leads to closeness with Him.

It is on this aspect of Hashem's compassion that the Gemara[14] states, "There are those who acquire eternity in one moment." This refers to a person who has simply turned to Hashem, asking that He take over and set him on a path of growth and self-improvement.

A CHANGE OF HEART

Once a person feels a commitment to improve his grasp of *tefillah*, he still has to choose a path toward his goal. Is the best path through the mind — in pursuit of knowledge, or through the heart — in pursuit of inspiration? *Chazal* answer this question in a discussion of another area of spiritual growth — that of the *teshuvah* needed to bring the Final Redemption.

Chazal depict two great individuals who will emerge in those times. Mashiach ben Yosef will appear first, and will inspire us with the emotional arousal necessary to do *teshuvah*. He will be followed by Mashiach ben David, who will present the intellectual component of *teshuvah*, the clarification of the truth. Mashiach ben Yosef alone is not capable of bringing the Final Redemption; Mashiach ben David is needed as well.[15]

Similarly, spiritual growth requires more than an initial sense of excitement to launch the person onto the right path. Excitement and inspiration cannot single-handedly sustain long-term success.

This is equally true regarding prayer; the first awakening and enthusiasm alone will not suffice to achieve an enduring positive change. Movement requires not just fire, but fuel. In addition to the fire of inspiration, we need to constantly supply the fuel of knowledge and understanding. By learning about *tefillah*, we provide the substance upon which our steady, forward progress depends.

---

13. *Michtav MeEliyahu*, Vol. 1, p. 26.
14. *Avodah Zarah* 10b, 17a, and 18a. Also see *Michtav MeEliyahu*, Vol. 1, p. 29.
15. *Michtav MeEliyahu*, Vol. 4, p. 143.

There is a final ingredient necessary in order to achieve long-lasting success in any spiritual endeavor — the sincere wish to change. It is not enough merely to be inspired to change the way we pray and to have a better and clearer understanding of *tefillah*; one must also desire change with all one's heart.

A verse in *Mishlei*[16] states: *Bring your heart to discipline, and your ears to words of knowledge.* The Vilna Gaon[17] explains that that which a person truly craves with all his heart, and considers vitally important, will endure. He continues: "Therefore, I say to you, bring your heart (to discipline) so that the words will remain in your heart for many days. And bend your ears (to words of knowledge) so that you should desire to run always to hear words of knowledge."

Rav Dessler[18] explains that it is not enough to "understand" with one's head, since actions are based on the level of our *heart's* understanding. What we refer to as *binah* —understanding — is clearly based in a person's heart; it is the result of the intellect's processing of an idea, which is then internalized by the person. *Binah* is the information that the person retains in his heart — that which becomes part of his reality and impels him to act upon the idea without the need for any further inspiration.

Furthermore, our actions are a reflection of the level of our heart's understanding. That which a person understands only as abstract knowledge, which is not absorbed into the heart, does not become a part of him and, ultimately, will not last.[19]

In reality, a person's spiritual level is a complex amalgam of many factors of his upbringing. Parents and family, friends, environment, and mentors, along with everything one has read, heard, and seen, all influence an individual's spiritual profile.

Ultimately, a person's genuine spirituality is visible in those actions which emanate from the heart — the essence of the inner self — since that is where one battles with his specific Evil Inclination. Actions performed by force of habit are not an accurate reflection of one's spirituality. By striving and aspiring with all one's heart to attain a deep inner understanding of the mitzvos one performs,[20] especially *tefillah* which

---

16. 23:12.
17. Ibid.
18. *Michtav MeEliyahu*, Vol. 5, p. 196.
19. Ibid. p. 220.
20. Ibid. Vol. 3, p. 131.

Chazal call "a labor of the heart,"[21] one will merit true spiritual growth and success.

---

21. *Taanis* 2a. The Gemara explains, "*And to serve with all your heart*: Which service is with all your heart? This is prayer."

CHAPTER 1:

THE IMMEASURABLE POWER OF PRAYER

A SWORD,
A SHIELD,
A WELLSPRING

1
Tishrei

1
Teves

1
Nissan

1
Tammuz

As the century of horrific world war has ended, an era of heartless terrorism has begun. Alongside the tragedies playing themselves out on the public stage are myriad personal tragedies — young children mourning parents, parents mourning a child, marriages dissolving in turmoil, young people wandering from the path of Torah, and breadwinners struggling against formidable financial strain. Our sense of security is eroded daily with each new headline, each tragic loss, and each report of the dangers that seem to lurk everywhere. How should we, who strive to react to world events with *emunah*, respond in troubled times?

The *Midrash Rabbah*,[1] in discussing the verse,[2] "Va'eschanan el Hashem ba'eis hahee leimor," *I exhorted Hashem at that time saying*, explains that the word *leimor* means: "say" to the generations that during troubled times they should pray.

The Rambam[3] rules, "It is a mitzvah from the Torah to cry out to Hashem for help … whenever trouble and persecution strike the community."[4]

When we pray during troubled times, besides performing a mitzvah from the Torah to pray to Hashem, we confirm our belief that only Hashem can help us. In this light, the *Sefer HaIkrim*[5] comments: "It is fitting and obligatory for every believer in Hashem's overseeing of [our day-to-

---

1. *Devarim* 2:6.
2. Ibid. 3:23.
3. *Taanis* 1:1.
4. According to the Ramban, however, our daily *tefillah* is a Rabbinical mitzvah (see Day 15); nonetheless, he agrees that *tefillah* in troubled times is a mitzvah from the Torah.
5. *Maamar* 4, Ch. 16.

day] existence to believe that prayer is effective and can save him from an evil fate.[6] Someone who does not pray in his hour of need must either be lacking faith that Hashem is watching, or lacking faith that Hashem is all-powerful, and both of these are utter heresy."

The *Sefer HaChinuch*[7] adds: "And someone who is in difficult circumstances and does not call out to Hashem to save him has violated this mitzvah of prayer … for it is as if he has removed himself from the overseeing of Hashem."

Sometimes, however, a person does not refrain from praying because he lacks confidence in Hashem's power, but because he lacks confidence in his own worthiness. From a true perspective, however, Hashem is available to every person whether he is worthy or not.[8] As the *Sefer Ha'Ikrim*[9] explains, everything Hashem provides each day is not due to man's righteousness but rather to Hashem's benevolence and compassion. As the *pasuk*[10] says: *Turn Your ear, Hashem, and listen; open Your eyes and see our desolations, and the city upon which Your Name is proclaimed. For not because of our righteousness do we pour out our supplications before You, but because of Your great compassion.*

We need not be perfect, or even close to it, to beseech Hashem in prayer. We simply need to reach for the lifeline He is extending to us, and to grasp it gratefully, confident that at the other end is the One Power Who can save us.

Points to Ponder

▸ The Torah teaches that one should pray during troubled times.

▸ Failing to pray for Hashem's help reflects a lack of belief in His supervision and His power.

▸ One should not feel that it is futile for him to pray because he lacks merit. Hashem answers prayers out of His kindness, not the petitioner's worthiness.

---

6. See Ch. 7: "Finding Answers to Unanswered Prayers."
7. Mitzvah 433 (at end), according to the Ramban.
8. See *Orach Chaim, Siman* 98, *Se'if* 5.
9. *Maamar* 4, Ch. 16.
10. *Daniel* 9:18.

DAY 2

AROUSING THE HEART

2
Tishrei

2
Teves

2
Nissan

2
Tammuz

*S*he had everything for which to be thankful — good friends, wonderful parents, an interesting job, and excellent prospects for finding a marriage partner. When she opened her siddur each morning, she came to Hashem with a somewhat complacent heart. As time passed and no prospect of marriage seemed imminent, the young woman was beset by fears. "What if I never get married? What if I have to spend my life alone?" Now when she prayed, there was no trace of complacency. Her prayers rose up from deep within her and she reached out to Hashem with all her might. She needed to feel Hashem's closeness. In her troubles, she found the key to her solution.

According to Rav Tzadok HaKohen,[1] every problem is structured in such a way that *tefillah* can overcome it: "Anything that Hashem desires to bring to the world or to an individual … can also have opposite effects, Heaven forbid … and when the person feels an appropriate fear and prays, the result is that good occurs."

Elaborating on this crucial point, Rav Yeruchem Levovitz,[2] Mashgiach of the Mirrer Yeshivah in Europe, says that it is our feelings of fear that cause us to pray, which in turn enable good to occur. Our usual way of thinking is that when trouble occurs, we must pray to Hashem; we would prefer, however, that the difficulty not arise in the first place.

Rav Yeruchem explains that this perspective indicates a lack of understanding as to what is actually taking place.

---

1. *Tzidkas HaTzaddik*, Os 170.
2. *Daas Chochmah U'Mussar*, Vol. 1, Maamar 4; Vol. 2, Maamar 72.

In reality, the purpose of the trouble or pain is to rouse us to pray and to pour out our hearts to Hashem, and for Him to then respond with the salvation. He conveyed this point with an analogy: Before a tree can bear fruit, the ground must be plowed and the sapling planted. Similarly, the afflictions that we must endure in life represent the plowing and sowing that compel us to pray to Hashem so that we can then reap the fruit of His salvation.

Thus, misfortune must be recognized as a necessary component of Hashem's deliverance, to the point that perhaps it should be referred to as "a part of our salvation."

> When the Chazon Ish, the leader of his generation, was told of bad news or faced a troubling situation, he would often comment, "Nu, Hashem must be eager for us to daven!"[3]

If we can see the troubles in our world and in our own lives in this light, the anxiety we endure will serve its purpose. Instead of draining us, it will energize and activate us, bringing us to call out to Hashem with all our might, which in turn will bring us the salvation for which we are so fervently longing.

Points to Ponder

▸ Difficulties are designed to spur us to pray.

▸ Hashem wants us to pray so that He can answer our prayers with good.

---

3. Cited in *Kovetz Sichos Maamar Mordechai*, Vol. 1, p. 123.

THE PRIMAL FORCE

3 Tishrei

3 Teves

3 Nissan

3 Tammuz

*T*he Gemara[1] tells of a demonic spirit that frequented the beis midrash where Abaye taught. It was so brazen that it did not wait for the cover of night or seek out solitary individuals to attack. Even two people entering the beis midrash together in broad daylight were injured by this spirit. When Abaye heard that Rav Yaakov, the son of Rav Acha ben Yaakov, was coming to visit, he ordered, "Let no one provide him lodging (thereby compelling him to lodge in the beis midrash). Perhaps a miracle will happen" [the merit of Rav Yaakov's prayer would permanently banish the demon]. Rav Yaakov spent the night in the beis midrash, where the demon appeared to him as a seven-headed serpent. Each time Rav Yaakov bowed his head in prayer, one of the heads fell off.*

The Maharsha[2] questions how Abaye could place Rav Yaakov in danger by forcing him to remain overnight in the *beis midrash*. Why was he so sure that Rav Yaakov would merit this miracle? Furthermore, even if the miracle did occur, would it not diminish Rav Yaakov's merits in this world?

He explains that any benefit derived from *tefillah*, no matter how incredible it appears, can be considered natural, since prayer has been an innate part of existence since the time of Creation. Furthermore, such benefit, since it is not considered a miracle, does not diminish a person's merits.

Chazal teach that *tefillah* was woven into the very fabric of Creation and designed by Hashem to be a fundamental

1. *Kiddushin* 29b.
2. Ibid.

element of life. The Torah states,[3] *And all the plants of the field were not yet on the earth and all the herbs had not yet sprouted, for Hashem had not brought rain upon the earth and there was no man to work the soil.*

Rashi explains that the plants could not grow because rain had not yet fallen; and without man, there could be no rain. When Adam HaRishon was placed on the scene, there a being who had both the capacity to understand that the soil needed water in order for the vegetation to sprout, and the ability to call upon Hashem to provide the rain. His prayers were answered, and the world became lush and green.

The entire Creation, everything on earth, was complete; all was in readiness. Yet the world remained barren and dry, awaiting Adam's prayers for the rain that would allow the natural world to spring to life and begin to function. Such is the paradoxical nature of prayer; nothing is more basic, and nothing is more powerful.

Points to Ponder

▸ *Prayer is an innate part of Creation whose function is to draw Hashem's goodness into this world.*

▸ *Every answered prayer is a "natural" phenomenon rather than a miracle.*

▸ *The world was in a barren state of preparedness until Adam prayed for rain.*

---

3. *Bereishis* 2:5.

THE ULTIMATE WEAPON

*T*he soldiers face a heavily armed enemy. The battle is a crucial one that they cannot afford to lose. Which weapon does the general choose for his forces to employ? The one that is most powerful, that hits its target most precisely, and that has proven itself time and time again.

For the Jewish people, *tefillah* is that weapon. It is what our leaders turn to during our nation's times of utmost challenge, because they know that it is the most precise and powerful weapon we have. The extent of its power, however, is greatly underestimated.

The Gemara[1] says that prayer stands at the very heights of the world, yet it is "looked down upon and degraded by man." Rav Yechezkel Levenstein[2] — the Mashgiach of the Mirrer Yeshivah in Europe and Shanghai and later of Ponevezh Yeshivah in Israel — ascribes this lack of respect to an inadequate appreciation of *tefillah's* true value.

Elsewhere, the Gemara[3] describes Torah learning as the key to eternal life and *tefillah* as the key to our temporal life; just as Torah study can bring a person to enjoy eternal happiness in the World to Come, prayer can provide all the necessities of this world, such as good health, a livelihood, peace of mind, and spiritual growth.

Hashem so treasures *tefillah* that he made the Jewish people's very existence contingent upon it. The Gemara[4] explains that our Patriarchs were infertile because Hashem desires the prayers of the righteous. Had our Patriarchs not turned to prayer in their moment of need, they would

---

1. *Berachos* 6b with *Rashi*. See note 1 in "The Journey — Surmounting the Obstacles."
2. *Ohr Yechezkel, Inyanei Emunah.*
3. *Shabbos* 10a.
4. *Yevamos* 64a.

not have been blessed with children and there would not have been a Jewish nation. Only when they reached into the depths of their souls and cried to Hashem were they blessed with offspring.

Yaakov, too, turned to *tefillah* to fight the battle of his life. When he left Lavan and traveled homeward for an encounter with his brother Esav, Yaakov prayed:[5] *Rescue me, please, from the hand of my brother, from the hand of Esav, for I fear him lest he come and strike me down, mother and children.* Hashem answered his prayer, as reflected in the verse:[6] *Yaakov came intact* (with his entire family) *to the city of Shechem.*

When the Jewish people could no longer bear the oppression of Egypt, they followed the example of the Patriarchs, delving within themselves to find their most potent weapon. The Torah says:[7] *The Jewish nation was groaning because of their subjugation and they cried out and their cries went up to Hashem because of the work.*

Their voices rose again when they faced what seemed like certain doom at the Reed Sea. The verse states:[8] *They became very frightened and Bnei Yisrael cried out to Hashem.*

When the Jews committed the sin of the Golden Calf, Moshe knew that the only means he could depend upon to bring them forgiveness was prayer:[9] *Hashem, why unleash Your wrath against Your people whom You brought out of Egypt with great power and a show of force.* The Torah relates that Moshe's plea was answered:[10] *Hashem reconsidered regarding the evil that He declared He would do to His people.*

Moshe's power of prayer was called upon again to save the Jewish people when the men who were sent to spy on the Land of Israel prior to the Jews' entry came back with a slanderous report. Hashem warned Moshe:[11] *I will smite*

---

5. *Bereishis* 32:12.
6. Ibid. 33:18.
7. *Shemos* 2:23.
8. Ibid. 14:10.
9. Ibid. 32:11.
10. Ibid. v. 14.
11. *Bamidbar* 14:12.

Points to Ponder

‣ Prayer is recognized throughout Jewish history as the most potent means to overcome adversity.

‣ Our Patriarchs prayed for help when faced with the prospect of not having children.

‣ Moshe turned to prayer to bring forgiveness for the grave sin of the Golden Calf and for the sin committed by the spies.

‣ Although tefillah is just one of many mitzvos, it is unparalleled in its power to bring goodness and salvation.

them with the plague and annihilate them ... Moshe set to work to avert this dire decree:[12] *Moses said to Hashem ... Forgive now the iniquity of this people according to the greatness of Your kindness and as You have forgiven this people from Egypt until now.* His plea was answered with the words that have stirred Jewish souls every Yom Kippur since: *And Hashem said, "Salachti kidvarecha," I have forgiven in accordance with your words."*[13]

Moshe so deeply understood the power of prayer that even though he knew Hashem had decreed otherwise, he prayed to be allowed to enter the Land of Israel. He did not rely on the boundless merit of his righteous life. He prayed![14]

Ramban[15] observes that all the miracles performed by the prophets were a result of their prayers. When Joshua stopped the sun and Elijah and Elisha resurrected the dead, it was not because they were endowed with mysterious supernatural powers. Rather, their prophetic spirit brought them closer to G-d so that they could pray with greater intensity.[16]

Tefillah is one mitzvah of the many the Torah has given us to bring us close to our Creator. The *Sefer Halkrim*,[17] however, urges us not to make the mistake of viewing it in the same light as other mitzvos. In its unique capacity to arouse Hashem's mercy, save us from afflictions, and bring us forgiveness and blessing, prayer is a mitzvah like no other.

---

12. Ibid. vs. 13-19.
13. Ibid. v. 20.
14. *Berachos* 32b.
15. *Devarim* 34:11.
16. *A Letter for the Ages* by Rabbi Avrohom Chaim Feuer (ArtScroll/Mesorah Publ.), p. 121.
17. *Maamar* 4, Ch. 20.

OPENING HEAVEN'S GATES

I n accessing the treasures stored for us in Heaven, *tefillah* is the key. Even though the treasures are there, and they are being held in store for each of us, they do not automatically flow into our lives. They remain locked in Heaven until we pray.

5 Tishrei

5 Teves

5 Nissan

5 Tammuz

> *A person lives in unbearable poverty his entire life. He never has enough food. He can't pay his bills. He cannot help others in need. Everyone tells him that there is a treasure buried under the floorboards of his house, but he doesn't believe it. He gives the floor a half-hearted kick every so often, thinking maybe he'll hear the jingle of coins, but he only hears the thunk of his heel against the wood. Then, on the last day of this man's life, someone walks in, lifts up a plank and reveals an iron chest filled with gems and gold. All the wealth the dying man could ever have needed is in that chest. His whole lifetime of miserable struggle plays out before his dimming eyes; the stab of what could have been is the last sensation he ever feels.*

That piercing remorse is the lot of one who does not believe in and utilize the power of prayer. The *Nefesh HaChaim* expounds this through the verse:[1] *He recounts to a person what were his deeds.* This, he explains, refers to the revelation people will experience in the World to Come regarding the gifts that would have been theirs had they only believed in the power of prayer and used it.

Rav Pam explains: "These people will be shown how their prayers could have made a difference had they been said with heartfelt concentration. The sick person *could* have been healed; the childless couple *could* have been

---

1. *Amos* 4:13.

answered, the person looking for a spouse *could* have found one. "[2]

This principle is dramatically illustrated by the Jewish nation's redemption from Egypt, as we are told:[3] *Hashem heard their moaning, and Hashem remembered His covenant with Avraham, with Yitzchak, and with Yaakov. Hashem saw the Children of Israel and Hashem knew.*

The Ramban[4] asks why the Torah mentions the numerous factors that caused Hashem to redeem the Jewish nation; after all, their exile was predestined to end after 430 years, as the Torah states:[5] *It was at the end of four hundred and thirty years, and it was on this very day that all the legions of Hashem left the land of Egypt.*

Rashi[6] cites a *Mechilta* that explains the phrase, *it was at the end of four hundred and thirty years.* It tells us that once the preordained end of the exile arrived, Hashem did not delay the Jews from leaving for even the "blink of an eye."[7] But the arrival of the preordained time was not enough by itself to set the redemption in motion, the Ramban explains. It was when "Hashem heard their moaning" that He remembered His covenant. "They were not … redeemed, except for the fact that their prayers were accepted with pity and mercy."

Tefillah, along with repentance, will be the catalyst that sets in motion the Final Redemption as well. The *She'arim B'Tefillah*[8] notes that even if everything is prepared and ready for the Redemption, if the Gates of *Tefillah* are not opened, nothing will be accomplished. This is the meaning of the verse,[9] *With weeping will they come, and with*

---

2. *The Pleasant Way* by Rabbi Sholom Smith (Israel Bookshop Publ.), p. 54.
3. *Shemos* 2:24-25.
4. Ibid. v. 25.
5. *Shemos* 12:41.
6. Ibid.
7. See Rashi ibid. who writes that on the 15th of Nissan the angels came to Avraham to inform him that Yitzchak would be born on that date the following year; on the 15th day of Nissan Yitzchak was born, and on that day 30 years earlier the decree of the *Bris Bein HaBesarim* had been proclaimed.
8. P. 10.
9. *Yirmiyahu* 31: 8.

50 / PRAYING WITH FIRE

supplications will I lead them.[10] As the *Darchai Noam*[11] comments, "One must be very careful with his *tefillos*, certainly in the time when the arrival of Mashiach is at hand … for it is on them — those very *tefillos* — that the coming of Mashiach depends." Rav Yaakov Emden[12] writes that if the Jewish people would pray even one *tefillah* properly in all aspects, they would be instantly redeemed.

Prayer is the natural cause of every effect in this world; just as rain causes flowers to grow, so does prayer cause Hashem to grant us His blessings. It is the key to all worldly good fortune.[13] Incredibly, Hashem has entrusted us with the key to His storehouse; He waits only for us to use it.

Points to Ponder

▸ *Even rewards destined for us will not come to us unless we pray for them.*

▸ *Just as the redemption from Egypt was predicated upon the Jews' prayers, so is the Final Redemption.*

▸ *In giving us the ability to pray, Hashem has given us the key to His storehouse of blessings.*

---

10. *Chazal* [see *Rashi* there] interpret that the "weeping" refers to prayer and repentance. According to *Metzudas David*, the Redemption will come about through repentance and prayer.
11. P. 79a.
12. *Siddur Yaavetz*, Introduction, p. 51.
13. Since prayer opens all doors, it is difficult to understand the concept of *tzaddik v'ra lo* — that a righteous person suffers and that a person may be punished for reasons unknown to us. See *Michtav MeEliyahu*, Vol. 1, pp. 19-23 for an in-depth explanation of this concept.

OUTSHINING
THE STARS

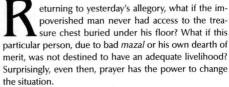

6
Tishrei

6
Teves

6
Nissan

6
Tammuz

Returning to yesterday's allegory, what if the impoverished man never had access to the treasure chest buried under his floor? What if this particular person, due to bad *mazal* or his own dearth of merit, was not destined to have an adequate livelihood? Surprisingly, even then, prayer has the power to change the situation.

Throughout the Torah, however, reward appears to be completely dependent on merit:[1] *If you will listen diligently to the voice of Hashem, and you will do what is just in His eyes, and you will listen to His commandments and observe all His statutes — then any of the diseases that I placed upon Egypt, I will not place upon you, for I am Hashem your healer.'*[2]

The second paragraph of *Shema*[3] also tells us: *And it will be that if you will listen to My commandments that I command you today, to love Hashem, your G-d, and to serve Him with all your heart and with all your soul …*

Then, we are told, the benefits and rewards will be:[4] *And I shall provide the rain of your land in its time, the early rain and the late rain; and you shall bring in your*

---

1. However, see *Kiddushin* 39b, which states that according to R' Yaakov there is no reward for fulfilling mitzvos in this world. See *Rambam, Hilchos Teshuvah* 9:1 for an elucidation of these verses according to R' Yaakov. For a similar explanation, see *HaEmunah VeHaBitachon HaMeyuchas LeHaRamban*, Ch. 7. See also *Maharsha* to *Sotah* 14a s.v. *V'amar lei HaKadosh Baruch Hu; Nefesh HaChaim Maarachah "Shin," Os* 74; *Sefer Chassidim, Siman* 210 and *Bnei Yissaschar, Sivan, Maamar* 5, *Os* 27, who provide similar answers. Finally, see *Maharsha* to *Kiddushin* 39b, s.v. *Sechar mitzvah b'hai alma* for a different approach.
2. *Shemos* 15:26.
3. *Devarim* 11:13.
4. Ibid. vs. 14-15.

grain, your wine, and your oil. And I shall provide grass in your field for your cattle and you will eat and you will be satisfied."[5] [Hashem says:] Once you do what is incumbent upon you, I too will do what is incumbent upon Me. In view of these verses, the average person might come to believe that if he performs the mitzvos, blessing will come to him, even if he does not pray.

The Torah also pays heed to another powerful influence on a person's destiny — his *mazal*, the celestial signs that are dominant at the moment of a person's birth. In the Gemara,[6] Rava says that a person's children, life, and livelihood do not depend on the merit of mitzvos but rather on *mazal*. The Ramban[7] explains that the influence of *mazal*, for good or bad, is integral to Hashem's Creation. If *mazal* holds this G-d-given authority over our lives, it would seem that prayer would be powerless to affect our destiny.

The Ritva reconciles these difficulties. He explains that neither the merit of one's mitzvos nor the influence of one's *mazal* has the power to fully determine a person's fate. *Mazal* is a mighty ruler, but it must contend for influence with other forces that can, under the right circumstances, overthrow it: "Heaven forbid that [our fate] should be dependent on *mazal* entirely, [first] because it is established that *mazal* does not control Israel,[8] and [second] because otherwise you would invalidate all the blessings and curses of the Torah ... Rather ... [our fate] is not entirely dependent on meritorious deeds [doing

---

5. Ibid. v. 14.
6. *Moed Katan* 28a.
7. *Devarim* 18:9.
8. The Gemara in *Shabbos* 156a relates a disagreement as to the effect of *mazal* on the nation of Israel: "R' Chanina says that the celestial sign of one's birth ... controls even [the nation of] Israel. Rabbi Yochanan says the celestial sign of one's birth does not control Israel."

The *Maharsha* comments that this dispute is only relevant to the fortunes of an individual, but not to the well-being of the community as a whole. A similar distinction is brought by the *Rashba* in *She'eilos U'Teshuvos HaRashba*, Vol. 1, *Siman* 148. See also *Rabbeinu Bachya* to *Devarim* 31:14.

mitzvos], as *mazal* also holds sway, except that a great merit can abolish [bad] *mazal*."[9]

What is that great merit?

Tosafos Yom Tov reveals: "*Tefillah* is needed, since a merit by itself … cannot always change [bad] *mazal*."[10] In the same vein, Rabbeinu Bachya comments,[11] "This is why our Sages mentioned that children, life, and livelihood are affected by *mazal*, in order that we realize how necessary *tefillah* is for these blessings … with *tefillah*, *mazal* can be reversed and overcome."[12]

> *Rav Bunim of P'shis'che was a successful business-man in the years prior to his appointment as Rebbe. During that time, he once traveled to visit the Chozeh of Lublin. He had hoped to have the opportunity to learn with this holy man, and to receive a blessing from him.*
>
> *The Chozeh, however, was not able to tell Rav Bunim what he wanted to hear. Instead, he foresaw financial disaster in Rav Bunim's future. "You are des-tined to lose all your money this year," the Chozeh told him.*
>
> *The year progressed, and the Chozeh's prediction failed to materialize. At the end of the year, Rav Bun-im returned to the Chozeh to report that he had not suffered a loss.*
>
> *"What did you do to thwart the evil decree?" the Chozeh asked.*
>
> *"I cried to Hashem the entire year," he answered.*
>
> *"My words that you would lose your money were without [your] tears," the Chozeh explained. "How-ever, when you prayed, everything changed."[13]*

---

9. *Ritva* on *Mo'ed Katan* 28a. Also, see *Tosafos, Shabbos* 156a, s.v. *Ein mazal.*
10. *Mishnayos Kiddushin*, Ch. 4, Mishnah 14.
11. *Devarim* 31:14.
12. See *Rabbeinu Bachya* to *Devarim* 11:13, where he writes that prayer can change nature and cancel any harsh decree. Also see *Ran*, cited in *Sifsei Chaim, Pirkei Emunah V'Hashgachah*, Vol. 1, p. 263, where it states that it is possible to change one's *mazal* through the great merit of prayer.
13. *Tiferes Avos*, p. 46.

Our destiny does not reside in the stars alone, or in our merit alone. Prayer can pluck us out of the mire in which we feel stuck, and open each person's life to blessings that are far beyond his due.

Points to Ponder

▸ *The blessings of Heaven are not dependent upon good deeds alone or on mazal alone.*

▸ *Mazal has a powerful influence on one's life. However, through prayer, one's mazal can be changed.*

HASHEM ALONE

When one knows with all his heart that the solution for his desperate situation resides with
one particular person, he will call, write, or
bang down the door, if necessary, to solicit help for his
plight. The ardent nature of his entreaties reflects his belief that this is his only avenue of salvation.

The Torah tells of numerous individuals whose deep
faith that Hashem was their only Source of help brought
them to "bang down the door" of Heaven. Their prayers,
fueled by this total trust, are a template for our own *tefillah*.

> The Midrash[1] tells us that Chanah and Elkanah were
> childless for nineteen years, throughout which time
> Chanah prayed for children to no avail. It was only
> when her husband exclaimed, "Why do you weep,
> Chanah? Am I not better to you than ten sons?" that
> she realized he no longer had any hope of her having
> a child.
>
> Alone, she then poured out her heart to Hashem,
> convinced that only a miracle would enable her to
> have a child. This time her prayers were answered,
> and Chanah gave birth to a child who grew up to
> be one of the greatest leaders of the Jewish nation,
> Shmuel HaNavi.

Rav Moshe Ahron Stern, Mashgiach of the Kaminetzer
Yeshivah, probed further into this episode.[2] Why, he
asked, did Chanah receive so much more than she asked
for? Her request was to be blessed with an ordinary child;
nonetheless, her son became a unique leader who was

---

1. *Pesikta Rabbasi, Parashah* 43.
2. Cited in *Siddur Shaarei Tefillah*, p. 10.

instrumental in the establishment of the monarchy — he was the one who anointed David HaMelech whose dynasty will reign for all eternity.[3]

Rav Stern explains that Chanah did not merely ask Hashem for help — she placed all her hope and trust in Him, knowing that only a miracle would produce results.

The remarkable potential with which her child, Shmuel HaNavi, was blessed, arose from the power of his mother's tearful entreaties.

> Rabbi Chaim Shmulevitz was praying at the kever of Rachel Imeinu on her yahrtzeit, the eleventh of Cheshvan, when he heard a woman praying on the other side of the partition.
>
> "Mama Rachel, you know what it means not to have children. You know the hardship of living many years without children. Can't you help me?"[4] These were the only words he heard.
>
> Rabbi Shmulevitz subsequently sent a talmid to the woman's home with the following message: "Your prayers have been accepted in Heaven. You will have a boy next year and I wish to be sandek at the bris." And so it was.

In telling this story,[5] Dayan Aharon Dunner of England explained why her prayers were answered. "This woman was not a saint, but merely a simple person who felt that she needed something, that only Hashem could help her, and that she had absolutely no control over her life. Her prayer was relevant to her — she prayed with all her heart and soul and that truly made a difference."

The Torah not only instructs us to pray — it shows us by example how to make our prayers a true instrument of salvation.

Points to Ponder

▸ Hashem has brought miraculous help to people who have turned to Him in times of need.

▸ Effective prayer is predicated on the belief that Hashem is one's only Source of help.

▸ Even an ordinary person can pray with complete faith and thereby arouse Hashem's mercy.

---

3. Shmuel HaNavi also anointed the first king, Shaul. However, Shmuel's greatness lies in the fact that he was the one chosen by Hashem to anoint the eternal House of David.

4. In the depth of her anguish, the woman expressed herself this way. Her intention was that Rachel Imeinu go before the *Kisei HaKavod* and with the *zechus* of our *Avos* intervene on her behalf. See also Day 55, note 2.

5. Keynote Session, 5758 Convention of Agudath Israel of America.

When we tell Hashem, "You and You alone can help me," we turn wishes and hopes into answered prayers.

THE MEASURE OF A PRAYER

DAY 8

Adam prayed for the first rain; our Patriarchs pleaded for children; Moshe supplicated for his people; and other Torah giants throughout the ages have prayed for the needs of their fellow Jews. Prayer is indeed a powerful force in the hands of these men — but can such a force be harnessed by an ordinary person?

The answer is a resounding "yes." Our prayers have the potential to do as much for us as the prayers of our great ancestors did for them.

David HaMelech taught us an everlasting lesson when he wrote in *Tehillim:*[1] *Hashem is close to all who call upon Him, to all who call upon Him sincerely.* A prayer imbued with respect, dignity, and sincerity is a prayer that is filled with power. It is a prayer that Hashem will answer.

As previously mentioned, the Gemara states that Hashem desires the prayers of the righteous. This refers not to the person himself, but to the manner in which he prays.[2] A sincere and dignified prayer is a prayer of the righteous.

The verse from *Tehillim* teaches us that our ability to draw close to Hashem in prayer, and thus make ourselves heard, depends upon the authentic quality of the prayer. This is true for "all who call upon Him."

The *Talmud Yerushalmi*[3] relates a story illustrating the capacity of a sincere prayer to find acceptance in Heaven:

> A ship was sailing the sea when suddenly a storm began to rage. The many non-Jewish passengers cried out for help, but the storm's fury was unabated. They turned to the sole Jewish child on board saying, "Rise

8 Tishrei

8 Teves

8 Nissan

8 Tammuz

---

1. 145:18.
2. See *The Pleasant Way* by Rabbi Sholom Smith (Israel Bookshop Publ.), p. 54.
3. *Berachos* 9:1.

my son, call out to your G-d, because we heard that your G-d answers you when you cry out to Him, and He is mighty." The child immediately cried out to Hashem with all his heart, and the sea fell silent.

Upon reaching dry land, all the passengers except the Jewish child went to shop. When asked, "Isn't there anything you need to buy?" the child responded, "Why do you care what a worthless and forsaken guest needs?" They exclaimed, "We are worthless and forsaken! We are here and our idols are in Babylonia. However, wherever you go, your G-d is with you."

Even the idol worshipers recognized that Hashem is always with us, and that we are never forsaken. As long as we pray with sincerity and respect — as did the Jewish child — our prayers are accepted. Wherever we go, Hashem is with us.

Despite a person's doubts that his own prayers are worthy of Hashem's response, the following Midrash[4] reassures us that no sincere prayer is wasted: Hashem said to Israel, "Be careful and prudent in your prayers, because there is no other measure more beautiful than this. And it [prayer] is greater and mightier than the animal offerings [in the Holy Temple]. And even if one is not worthy to be answered with his or her prayers, and for benevolence and favor to be done for the person, because the person prays and pleads many times, I [Hashem] will be benevolent with that person."

Sincerity turns an ordinary person's prayer into a prayer of greatness, and sincerity is a quality anyone can develop. It arises naturally from the recognition that Hashem alone has the power to help us, and that our words of prayer are our only means of setting this power in motion.[5]

---

4. *Midrash Tanchuma, Parashas Vayeira, Siman* 1.
5. See *Toldos Yaakov Yosef, Parashas Eikev.*

DAILY MIRACLES

Tefillah, the invincible force that set in motion the Exodus from Egypt and the splitting of the Reed Sea, plays another, less dramatic but far more pervasive role as well: it keeps one's heart beating, one's paycheck coming, one's children growing and learning. Tefillah is not just the ultimate weapon in times of great need; it is the essential tool of daily living.

There are times when the need for Hashem's mercy is obvious, and prayer is the natural response. For instance, if a person is sick and in dire need of healing, the solution is tefillah. Many people do not, however, associate that same need for Heaven's mercy with the mundane details of life. As long as they are functioning smoothly, those aspects of life seem to require no Divine maintenance. This is an outright misconception.

The word adam, man, consists of the same Hebrew letters as the word me'od, much. The nature of man is that he needs "much." As Chazal tell us, a man who has one hundred desires two hundred.[1] Clearly, it is only with Hashem's help that a person can achieve his goals. If every person requires Hashem's compassion in order to fulfill his desires, then every person is dependent upon tefillah — the most effective means for soliciting Heaven's mercy.

One such basic desire is a livelihood, or for some, a life of affluence. The Gemara[2] advises those who seek financial success to pray for mercy from Hashem, the source of all riches. Even someone who conducts himself honestly in business must pray for mercy from Hashem in order to succeed.

9	Tishrei
9	Teves
9	Nissan
9	Tammuz

---

1. *Koheles Rabbah* 1:13.
2. *Niddah* 70b.

> One of the Chofetz Chaim's students asked him for a
> blessing for livelihood. The Chofetz Chaim answered,
> "It leads to an absurdity, that one poor man turns to
> a second poor man for help, at a time when both of
> them can turn to a rich Father. It is He Who proclaims
> and says, 'Mine is the silver, Mine is the gold,'[3] and
> 'Salvation is from Hashem.'"[4]

Another basic request is for the intelligence and understanding necessary to achieve success in life. The Gemara[5]
advises one who wants wisdom to pray for mercy from
Hashem, the Source of all wisdom. "Engaging a lot in study
... without (prayer) does not suffice."

> This concept was close to the heart of the Chazon
> Ish, who proved by his deeds that he knew well the
> source of his Torah wisdom. His older brother, Rav
> Meir Karelitz, credited the Chazon Ish's great stature
> as a renowned scholar, whom thousands sought for
> advice, to two sources: his diligent study of Torah,
> which he undertook with no motive other than ser-
> vice of Hashem, and the emphasis he placed on the
> berachah for wisdom in the Shemoneh Esrei (Atah
> Chonein).[6]
>
> This was not just a theoretical recognition of
> Hashem's essential role in endowing man with in-
> telligence. Whenever the Chazon Ish or his brother
> encountered difficulty in their learning, they would
> close their books and turn to Hashem to pray for
> understanding.[7]

The Chazon Ish knew on the deepest level that Hashem
was not only behind the epic historic event of the giving
of the Torah on Mount Sinai, but also that He was behind
the daily struggles of two men seeking clarification of the
Torah's wisdom. In turning to Hashem for clarity in learning, success in a job — even pleasant weather on vacation

---

3. *Chaggai* 2:8.
4. *Tehillim* 3:9.
5. *Niddah* 70b.
6. Cited in *Kovetz Sichos Maamar Mordechai*, Vol. 1, p. 128.
7. *Ibid.* p. 129.

— a person expresses his belief in Hashem's pervasive Presence and affirms his deepest faith that He is in charge of it all.

Points to Ponder

‣ *Tefillah's efficacy is not confined to historic dramas or personal crises. It is equally relevant to one's daily activities.*

‣ *Wealth and wisdom depend on Hashem's mercy, for which one must pray.*

PARENTS' PRAYERS

10 Tishrei

10 Teves

10 Nissan

10 Tammuz

ore than money, more than wisdom, a person's deepest desire is for his children's welfare. How can a person realize his fervent desire to have children, and to help them thrive and grow into good, productive, Torah-observant Jews? Continuing the previously quoted formula, the Gemara answers,[1] "Let him pray for mercy from Hashem, Who controls the birth of children."

The young kollel couple's happy anticipation of their first child quickly turned to fear, and then piercing pain. The little boy, born prematurely, lived for only 11 hours. Bewildered and heartbroken by their loss, they arrived at the home of the great Torah leader Rav Chaim Kanievsky to request a berachah. Beyond that, they wanted advice: What mitzvah could they take on, what practice could they adopt, that would serve as a great merit to help the next pregnancy proceed normally?

As they waited for the husband to be admitted into the Rav's presence, they discussed their readiness to take on whatever he would suggest. Even though money was tight, they would be willing to give more charity. Even though the young man learned Torah all day, he would add more learning somehow. Whatever it took, they agreed, they would do.

Finally, the husband was asked to come in to meet with Rav Chaim. "My wife and I want to accept upon ourselves something special, something especially unique as a segulah for our situation," the young man said. "We are willing to accept anything the Rav suggests."

---

1. *Niddah* 70b.

Rav Chaim unhesitatingly responded with just two words "Zeit mispallel! (Pray!)"

Thinking that Rav Chaim had misunderstood their willingness to go "above and beyond," he asked again, and again he received the same answer: "Zeit mispallel."

"But is there anything exceptional we can do," the young man asked again. After all, he already prayed. In fact, since the tragedy, he had prayed every day at sunrise (Vasikin) at the Kosel, which was in itself a special segulah.

This time, Rav Chaim answered, "Bracha VeHatzlacha (blessings and success)," and sent the young couple back out into the evening, confident that they were doing the one and only thing that Rav Chaim felt could truly help them bring a healthy child into the world.

Many great rabbis have stressed the importance of tefillah in successful child rearing.

Rav Avraham Pam, Rosh Yeshivah of Yeshivah Torah Vodaath, spoke of two ingredients that bring success in raising children: tefillah and positive role models provided by the parents. The Chofetz Chaim often commented, "Success with children is 100 percent based on Hashem's help."[2] Rav Chaim Kanievsky expressed in his advice to the young couple in the above true story his own firm belief in the singular power of prayer. He once stated, "One must pray a lot to succeed with children and no other advice is helpful."[3]

The Chasam Sofer was asked the secret of his success in raising a child such as his son, the K'sav Sofer. He responded, "Do you know how many tears went into davening for my son?" Similarly, when speaking of raising his son, the Brisker Rav said, "Success

---

2. Tehillim Treasury by Rabbi Avrohom Chaim Feuer (ArtScroll/Mesorah Publ.), p. 231.
3. Derech Sichah, p. 71.
4. Toras Chaim p. 110.

▸ *A person
who wants
children and
success in
raising them
must pray
for Hashem's
mercy.*

▸ *Tefillah is
essential
for success
with one's
children,
even once
they are
grown.*

▸ *Small
changes in
one's prayer
habits can
make large
changes in
one's life.*

*with raising children comes only with Tehillim and
tears."* [4]

*A man asked the Steipler Gaon, for a blessing in
bringing up his child. The Steipler replied, "You must
pray! What do you think? Until this day I still pray for
my son's (Rav Chaim Kanievsky's) success." This episode occurred when the Steipler's son was 52 years
old.* [5]

Rabbi Yeruchem Levovitz, Mashgiach of the Mirrer Yeshivah in Europe, frequently described *sincere* prayer as
"the *only* activity that can generate tremendous profit and
yet does not consume any free time, as the person is praying anyway." [6] With a nominal addition of feeling, a person
can transform rote prayer into meaningful prayer, and in
doing so, draw Hashem's mercy into the daily tasks and
labors of love that fill his days.

---

5. Ibid.
6. *Daas Chochmah U'Mussar*, Vol. 2, Intro., *Os Gimel, Eisek
HaTefillah.*

GOING FOR THE GOLD

DAY 11

A person who is told that there may be gold buried in his backyard will dig and dig, but if he finds nothing, he eventually begins to doubt that the gold is there. He will then work a little less assiduously, and finally, he concludes that the rumor is false. He puts away his shovel, reseeds the lawn and puts his effort elsewhere.

In contrast, a person who knows for certain that there is gold buried somewhere in his backyard never stops trying. He digs up every inch of soil, and if that does not yield the treasure, he digs deeper and deeper. He feels that his unwavering effort is worthwhile, because he knows he will eventually succeed, and his payoff will be extraordinary wealth.

11 Tishrei

11 Teves

11 Nissan

11 Tammuz

One who attempts to improve the quality of his *tefillah* — and thus, his entire life — is searching for the purest gold, and *Chazal* testify that it certainly exists. As he embarks on his search, he must realize that at times he may fail. If he begins to doubt that the potential is there within him, he will abandon the effort. One who knows for certain that he has the capacity to reach that higher level, however, will keep striving. He will delve within himself until he finds the treasure.

The Gemara[1] teaches us that every person can be certain of finding the treasure. It is within each of us, without exception. There is never a true justification for the self-doubt that can cause us to lose sight of our goal.

The Gemara tells of Elazar ben Dordia, who is said to have visited every woman of ill repute in the world. Upon hearing of one in a distant city across the ocean,

---

1. *Avodah Zarah* 17a.

he took a purse of gold coins and crossed seven rivers until he reached her ... She [then] expelled a breath and said, "As this breath will never return to its place, so will you (Elazar ben Dordia) never be received in teshuvah."

Elazar ben Dordia then sat between two mountains and requested that they ask for mercy on his behalf. They replied, "How can we plead for your mercy when we ourselves are in need of mercy?" He then asked the heavens and earth, the sun, the moon and the stars to plead for him, but they all replied with an identical negative response.

Finally, Elazar ben Dordia exclaimed, "The matter of teshuvah depends on me alone!" and cried aloud until his soul departed. A Bas Kol, Heavenly Voice, then declared, "R' Elazar ben Dordia is destined for life in the World to Come ..." Upon hearing this, Rebbi (R' Yehudah HaNasi) wept and said, "One may acquire eternal life in many years, and another may acquire eternal life in one moment."

Elazar ben Dordia's actions raise several questions: Did he expect the mountains and valleys, the stars and constellations, etc. to pray for him with no effort on his part? Furthermore, why would he proclaim, "It depends upon me alone," when it is obvious that *teshuvah* and self-improvement depend on the person who did wrong?

Rav Yonasan Eibeshutz[2] explains that people who err have the tendency to blame other factors such as environment or inborn tendencies, and will not accept responsibility for their own actions. Elazar ben Dordia followed this pattern by first claiming that the environment caused his downfall and asking the mountains and valleys, and the heavens and earth to pray for him. He next turned to the sun and the moon, the stars and constellations — forces that influence human nature — and blamed them. Ultimately, Elazar ben Dordia accepted the truth and understood that *teshuvah* depended on him alone.

---

2. *Yaaros Devash*, Vol. 2, *Derush* 10.

This is a powerful message for one who wishes to re-shape his approach to spirituality, especially *tefillah*. Many people claim that they cannot pray properly or do not gain fulfillment from praying because it was never taught to them well. Some believe that the atmosphere in which they pray is not conducive to proper concentration. Others believe that their habits are too deeply ingrained — that it is not within their nature to change their ways and improve their *tefillah*.

Rav Chaim Shmulevitz[3] explains that the weeping of Rebbi sprang from his recognition that while each and every person has been given the ability to change for the better, this precious gift often languishes unopened. In daily life, people often overlook the opportunities that are placed before them.

Each of us must understand that the capacity to improve is indeed within us. Motivated by the certainty that, ultimately, we will find what we are seeking, we must continue to delve and explore until we unearth our full capacity to beseech the Heavens with sincere, powerful prayer.

3. *Sichos Mussar*, 5731, *Maamar* 31.

Points to Ponder

▸ Every person has within himself the power to change and improve, and with consistent effort, this potential will be uncovered.

▸ Change is only possible when one accepts responsibility for one's actions.

▸ Improving one's *tefillah* operates on the same principles as all other areas of spiritual self-improvement.

CHAPTER 2:

ACHIEVING PERSONAL GROWTH THROUGH PRAYER

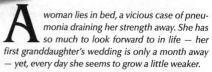

THE NEW YOU

A woman lies in bed, a vicious case of pneumonia draining her strength away. She has so much to look forward to in life — her first granddaughter's wedding is only a month away — yet, every day she seems to grow a little weaker.

12
Tishrei

12
Teves

12
Nissan

12
Tammuz

"Everything is for the good." This is a bedrock belief of the Jewish faith. We believe that our troubles serve a greater purpose. Sometimes we are able to perceive the purpose; sometimes it remains hidden until we reach the World of Truth.

In this light, what should the bedridden woman do? If this affliction is Hashem's decree, it is, by definition, "for the good." Should she use the power of prayer to try to reverse an affliction that is for her own benefit? Even if the answer is "yes," how would her prayer suffice to change all the factors that have gone into Hashem's decision to bring about the illness?

The *Sefer Halkrim*[1] addresses this question, asking how prayer, can accomplish its function of changing *mazal* and altering harsh decrees if all that occurs in life is ordained by Hashem. The Maharal poses a similar paradox:[2] Why aren't a worthy person's requests granted even without prayer, and conversely, why is an unworthy person able to use pleading and prayer to gain undeserved benefits?

Rav Chaim Volozhin[3] examines the dilemma further, posing the question presented in the story of the bedridden woman. If a person's illness provides atonement for his sins, why would he pray that Hashem heal him? Wouldn't this be akin to asking a doctor to halt a painful treatment, even though it is the sole cure for his disease?

---

1. *Maamar* 4, Ch. 18.
2. *Nesivos Olam, Nesiv HaAvodah*, Ch. 2.
3. *Nefesh HaChaim, Shaar* 2, Ch. 11.

72 / PRAYING WITH FIRE

Perhaps the individual should simply accept the affliction, trusting that Hashem knows what is best.

A common theme emerges from these questions: We are incapable of changing Hashem's righteous judgment — nor would we wish to — as only He knows what is best. Therefore, *tefillah's* primary purpose could not be to serve as the courier for our personal wish list. What then is the purpose of prayer?

Rav Yosef Albo[4] explains that prayer neither changes a harsh decree nor alters the negative *mazal* itself. Rather, it is the *person* who is changed through *tefillah*. As he reaches a higher spiritual level, he develops a higher capacity for receiving Hashem's blessings — blessings that he now indeed deserves.

Rav Albo explains that Hashem issues decrees, whether good or bad, according to a person's current spiritual level. Just as a person on a lower intellectual level may not be able to receive and absorb the beauty of a higher level of wisdom, so a person on a lower spiritual level may not have the capacity to receive a higher level of blessing.

> It was once decreed that a certain farmer be granted a successful crop. However, he neither plowed nor planted his fields. Even with a perfect balance of rain and sunshine, this farmer could not enjoy an abundant harvest.

When a person elevates his spiritual status through prayer, he lays the groundwork for receiving Hashem's blessings. He recreates himself as a "new being" who, Rav Albo concludes, "can receive an abundance of goodness or abolish … the harmful decree." Prayer doesn't change Hashem's mind; it changes us, and that changes everything.

Points to Ponder

▸ If everything Hashem does is for the good, why do we pray to reverse a Divine decree?

▸ Sincere prayer has the power to change a person's spiritual level and, in effect, change the person.

▸ The "new person" who emerges from spiritual growth is deserving of a new level of Divine blessing.

---

4. *Sefer Halkrim*, Maamar 4, Ch. 18.

LETTING IN THE LIGHT

*T*he brilliant morning sun beat against the window. A great day awaited — a day full of friendship, growth, and all the delights the world had to offer. The slumberer, however, had blackout shades drawn down tightly. Nothing of the day's wonders would be his.

This is the fate, the Ramchal tells us, of those who fail to awaken.

The Ramchal[1] defines *tefillah* as an instrument devised by the Supreme Wisdom to arouse His creations to draw near to Him, so that they can receive His abundant blessings. This abundance is "pulled" toward a person according to the measure of closeness he achieves. For one who cannot even be aroused to strive toward spiritual growth, however, the blessings and goodness remain hidden. In the words of the Ramchal: "With the 'light' of Hashem there is no change ... the changes are only [dependent on] us ... when we 'clean our windows' the 'light' will shine for us."

Shlomo HaMelech[2] also reinforces the intrinsic link between prayer and spiritual elevation: *He who turns his ear away from hearing the Torah, even his prayer is an abomination.* A person who turns away from Torah cuts himself off from the very root of his soul. Thus, his prayers are like flowers cut off from their roots — dead and destined for decay, no matter how lovely they may look at first. Yet, if prayer were merely a wish list — rather than a vehicle to elevate one's spiritual status — the rejection of Torah would have no effect on the value of one's prayers.

---

1. *Derech Hashem* 4:5.
2. *Mishlei* 28:9.

If the true purpose of prayer is to serve as a vehicle of spiritual elevation, why do we use it as a means to beseech Hashem for worldly needs such as health, sustenance, and success in raising our children? One way to understand this concept is to think of the relationship between a mother and young child. The child turns to his mother for all his needs. Were he to turn to the next-door neighbor instead, his mother would surely feel estranged from him. His reliance upon her builds his closeness with her, and his closeness builds his sense of reliance. Prayer reflects this cycle: we make requests, Hashem responds; we thank Him and thereby come closer to Him.[3]

Inspired by this perspective, we can find spiritual elevation in each request we make of Hashem. We need only adjust our vision to see ourselves standing before Him — beloved children seeking the blessings of our Father.

Points to Ponder

▶ Prayer was created by Hashem to bring us closer to Him so that we can receive His blessings.

▶ Prayer of one who turns away from Torah is repulsive to Hashem.

▶ The material requests we make in prayer are an avenue for spiritual elevation, not a contradiction to prayer's real purpose.

---

3. See *Nefesh Shimshon*, p. 344.

THE INNER WORKINGS

14
Tishrei

14
Teves

14
Nissan

14
Tammuz

*T*o some people, using a computer means pressing the "on" button and clicking the right icons. Others understand the workings of the memory, the various drives, the programs, and the settings. Those who understand how a computer works can use it to its full capacity; those who don't are confined to a few simple applications. And so it is with prayer. One must understand what makes prayer work in order to tap its boundless potential.

The Maharal[1] offers the following insight: When praying with sincerity, a person relinquishes his very being to Hashem by humbly recognizing his own inadequacy and affirming his trust in Hashem's all-encompassing power. This humility and trust ultimately complete all that is lacking in the person.

This process brings a person to the highest possible level of closeness to Hashem, thus achieving the core purpose of prayer. At the spiritual heights newly attained through *tefillah*, a person may no longer need to suffer affliction. This is what gives *tefillah* the ability to eliminate sickness and suffering.[2]

Rav Dessler explains[3] that through the spiritual elevation effected by *tefillah*, one becomes worthy of receiving the various tools one needs in order to live a life in accordance with the Torah. He concludes that this is the meaning of the *Tosafos*,[4] "By means of a great merit or virtue [*tefillah*] *mazal* can be changed."[5]

1. *Nesivos Olam, Nesiv HaAvodah*, Ch. 2.
2. Ibid. However, see Ch. 7, "Finding Answers to Unanswered Prayers."
3. *Michtav MeEliyahu*, Vol. 4, p. 99.
4. *Shabbos* 156a, s.v. *Ein Mazal*.
5. See also *Nefesh HaChaim, Shaar* 2, Ch. 14.

Rav Yechezkel Levenstein[6] explains that *tefillah* is not merely the utterance of words; rather, it is a vehicle created to transport a person on an upward progression from one spiritual level to the next.

On a practical level, how can we achieve this closeness with Hashem in our daily prayers?

We can strive to internalize prayer's limitless power so that we can approach it with the awe that it justly deserves. We can inject into our recitation of the morning blessings our sincere appreciation for the rejuvenation of body and soul. We can make ourselves mindful of our debt to Hashem, Who has given us the glories of nature, as we offer thanks in the *Pesukei D'Zimrah*. We can focus on our desire to succeed in our life's service to Hashem, accepting the yoke of Heaven and mentioning *Yetzias Mitzraim* in *Krias Shema*.

Shemoneh Esrei presents a unique opportunity to connect with Hashem. Our praises of Hashem in the first three blessings awaken us to Hashem's attributes of greatness. In *Modim*, we have the opportunity to focus upon the unbounded goodness Hashem gives us every day, and to arouse a sense of gratitude in our hearts.

The Rambam[7] advises one who wants to forge a stronger bond with Hashem to start by reciting the first *berachah* of *Shemoneh Esrei* with *kavannah*.[8] He continues: "When you will become accustomed to this and maintain it for many years ... then you will be able to continue and attune yourself to becoming closer and closer with Hashem all the time."

Rav Shimshon David Pincus[9] explains that *Shemoneh Esrei* influences us and infuses us with the realization that we need only rely on Hashem for everything we require in life.

---

6. *Ohr Yechezkel, Darchei HaAvodah.*
7. *Moreh Nevuchim* 3:51.
8. See Day 27, "Right From the Start," where it is explained that an essential *kavannah* for *Shemoneh Esrei* involves the *peirush ha'milim*, understanding the meaning of the words, which is required, at a minimum, during the first *berachah*.
9. *Nefesh Shimshon*, p. 349.

▸ *Tefillah is
a vehicle
for upward
spiritual
progression.*

▸ *Understand-
ing tefillah's
inner
workings
helps us to
approach
it with the
dignity it
deserves,
which in
turn makes
it more
effective on
our behalf.*

▸ *With proper
perspective,
each aspect
of tefillah
can provide
an avenue
of spiritual
growth.*

According to the *Rivash*,[10] when one prays the silent *Shemoneh Esrei*, the merit of reciting this prayer elevates him and attaches him to Hashem even when he is not praying.

Praying can be an exhilarating experience through which we capture an exalted sense of closeness with Hashem as a regular feature of our daily lives. It imbues our lives with a sense of security — the knowledge that we are never alone. Our Father in Heaven's loving care is always there for us; we need only reach out to Him. Unleashing this surge of spirituality into daily life can transform the experience of those who spend most of their day at work or at home caring for children.

One of the most precious aspects of the gift of prayer is that it is given to us in perfect form. We do not have to contrive a formula of our own in order to connect with Hashem. *Tefillah* is a built-in, daily opportunity to grow spiritually and to mature in our understanding of the true essence of life.

Exploring the inner workings of *tefillah*, one discovers a mechanism of exquisite engineering, a true "miracle machine" capable of accomplishing anything and everything. With this understanding, we will naturally approach *tefillah* with the respect and caring that it deserves. In doing so, we guarantee that its awesome power will never fail us.

---

10. *Tzavaas HaRivash*, p. 4

MORE THAN A MITZVAH

Given *tefillah's* immense importance, one would expect it to be conveyed to the Jewish people in an unequivocal decree of the Torah, "You shall pray three times a day." Yet, such a clear commandment does not exist. In fact, although *tefillah* is unquestionably a mitzvah, the Rambam and the Ramban differ as to whether it is a mitzvah from the Torah or one of Rabbinic origin. According to the Rambam[1] it is a mitzvah from the Torah, derived from the verse,[2] *and to serve Hashem with all your heart* (referring to *tefillah*). He also writes:

"The responsibility of this mitzvah (*tefillah*) is such that a person should beseech and pray each day, and express praise of Hashem, and afterward … ask for his needs in supplication and prayer, and then give praise and thanks to Hashem for the favor, kindness, and good which Hashem showers upon us."

The Ramban[3] disagrees and says that the connection between our daily *tefillah* and the verse, *and to serve Hashem with all your heart,* is of Rabbinic origin, and, therefore, the mitzvah of *tefillah* is itself Rabbinic. Most authorities[4] agree with the Ramban's opinion that *tefillah* is a Rabbinic mitzvah.[5]

This provokes a question: Can there be such tremendous power in a mitzvah of Rabbinic origin? Moreover,

---

1. *Hilchos Tefillah* 1:1 and 1:2.
2. *Devarim* 11:13.
3. *Hasagos HaRamban, Sefer HaMitzvos, Mitzvas Asei, Siman* 5. The Ramban agrees, however, that *tefillah* in troubled times is a mitzvah from the Torah.
4. See *Magen Avraham, Siman* 106, *Se'if Katan* 2; *Mishnah Berurah* ibid. *Se'if Katan* 4.
5. See *Emek Berachah* and *Chidushei Rabbeinu Chaim HaLevi* on the Rambam, *Hilchos Tefillah,* Ch. 4, *Halachah* 1.

▸ *Tefillah's
importance
does not
stem from
its status as
a mitzvah,
but rather
from its
ability to
bring a
person to
a higher
spiritual
level.*

▸ *Tefillah's
elevating
power
comes from
a person's
acknow-
ledgment
that
everything
depends on
Hashem's
mercy.*

▸ *Women are
required to
engage in
the time-
related
mitzvah
of prayer
because
they, too,
require
Hashem's
mercy.*

how can the *Sefer Halkrim* conclude that the mitzvah of *tefillah* is greater than all the other mitzvos?[6]

The answer to these questions lies in the established precept that *tefillah's* tremendous power stems from its ability to transport the person who is praying to a higher spiritual plane. It is *tefillah's* elevating effect, not its status as a mitzvah, that invests it with so much power. This transformation occurs when we turn to Hashem in prayer, acknowledging that everything comes from Him, and that we need His mercy to succeed in any aspect of life.

The Gemara in several places[7] describes *tefillah* as "a request for Hashem's compassion." In this light, one can see clearly that prayer is essential to every human being. That is why women are required to recite *Shacharis* in the morning and *Minchah* in the afternoon even though they are exempt from performing time-based mitzvos.[8] Women, no less than men, need Hashem's mercy. Therefore, they must pray.

The Alter of Kelm explains: "The masses think that *tefillah* is a mitzvah comparable to any other mitzvah ... (however) *tefillah* exists as the method to merit to revere Hashem and to be able to feel and perceive the goodness of Hashem."

This is the concept we must understand in both our minds and our hearts. Through it, we can see *tefillah* as it really exists — an awesome force that is constantly present and available to us, every day of our lives.

---

6. See *Sefer Halkrim, Maamar 4*, Ch. 20.
7. I.e., *Berachos* 12b, 26a; 60a; *Shabbos* 32a and 67a, and elsewhere.
8. *Mishnah Berurah, Siman 106, Se'if Katan* 4. Many *poskim* rule that women must *daven* the morning and afternoon prayers. However, see *Halichos Bas Yisrael*, Ch. 2, *Se'if Katan* 2, and *Ishei Yisrael*, Ch. 7, fn. 19, which states that a woman who is unable to *daven* in the morning because she is busy with the household and small children should at least say a short prayer praising Hashem, making a request, and giving thanks to Him. She should still recite the afternoon prayer.

FILLED WITH DUST

If prayer is the "key" that opens Hashem's storehouse of blessing, one might wonder why there are people who acquire wealth and success without ever having to use the key. How does one account for those who have no relationship with Hashem, yet have everything money can buy?

> A man once asked the Rebbe, Rav Bunim of P'shis'che, the following question: "How can a person who does not wear tefillin, desecrates the Shabbos, and does not uphold the laws and customs of an upstanding Jew, be wealthy and generally successful?"[1]
>
> Rav Bunim answered with the verse:[2] "And Hashem, G-d, said to the serpent, 'Because you have done this [that you caused the woman to eat from the fruit] you are more cursed than all the cattle and beasts of the field; on your stomach you shall go, and you shall eat dust all the days of your life.'"

While dust would not be considered a tasty diet, it is certainly plentiful and always accessible. Hashem seems to have "blessed" the snake with a promise that he would never go hungry. Rav Bunim explains that, in actuality, this was the ultimate curse.

The curse Hashem pronounced upon man, *By the sweat of your brow shall you eat bread*,[3] guarantees that when a person finds himself short of food he will pour out his heart in prayer to *HaKadosh Baruch Hu*. Similarly, since woman was cursed, *In pain shall you bear children*,[4] she

16
Tishrei

16
Teves

16
Nissan

16
Tammuz

---

1. *Kol Mevaseir*, Vol. 1, *Bereishis* 3:14. See *Matzmiach Yeshuos*, p. 27.
2. *Bereishis*, 3:14.
3. Ibid. v. 19
4. Ibid. v. 16.

▸ The serpent
  in the
  Garden of
  Eden is the
  paradigm
  for those
  who have
  plenty and
  therefore do
  not pray or
  otherwise
  build a
  relationship
  with
  Hashem.

▸ Man's curse
  of working
  the soil and
  woman's
  curse of
  painful
  childbirth
  provide the
  motivation
  to pray and
  come close
  to Hashem.

will ultimately pray to Hashem for His compassion when giving birth. Both of these "curses" are a means to assure that man will always have the motivation to forge a bond with Hashem by coming before Him in prayer.

The serpent, on the other hand, was provided with all its needs. As a result, the serpent would never have reason to ask Hashem for anything and thus would never forge a connection with Him. This is the ultimate curse.

In the same way, Hashem sometimes grants health and wealth to a person who does not pray. With all his physical needs satiated, the person sees no reason to come before Hashem in prayer; this, obviously, cannot be considered a blessing. As in the case of the serpent, his blessing of material plenty is in reality a curse. His sense of satiation leaves him no spiritual appetite — no room for the longing that would spur him to seek Hashem.

Of all the benefits one can ask for in prayer, there is no greater benefit than the ability, the desire, and the need to pray. Through prayer, our needs and wants become the source of our greatest blessing — closeness to Hashem.

MORE PRECIOUS
THAN LIFE

K ing Chizkiyahu lay upon his sickbed, feeling with certainty the approach of death. The Gemara[1] tells us that in pleading with Hashem to let him live, he presented what he saw as an irrefutable merit: He had hidden the Book of Cures, which contained the cure for every disease. Rashi[2] explains that Chizkiyahu hid this book so that sick people would not be tempted to place their faith in it and would instead feel the need to pray to Hashem.

Rav Mordechai Gifter[3] posed the following question: If nothing is more sacred than human life, and one may even desecrate the Shabbos to save one individual, how could King Chizkiyahu have endangered so many people who may have been cured had the book still been accessible?

Rav Gifter answers that this episode teaches us the incomparable value of *tefillah* — even the potential loss of life did not outweigh it. Had the book been available to all, there would have been no compelling reason to pray to Hashem. This, more than loss of life, would have been the ultimate loss. It was preferable to hide the Book of Cures at the risk of human suffering and death rather than risk snuffing out man's desire to pray.

Similarly, the verse,[4] *For Your kindness is better than life; my lips will praise You,* is explained by the Malbim[5] to mean that the fact that our lips can praise You [Hashem] is better than life itself. Rav Shimshon David Pincus[6] elucidates this idea with an allegory:

17
Tishrei

17
Teves

17
Nissan

17
Tammuz

---

1. *Berachos* 10b.
2. Ibid.
3. Cited by Rabbi Avrohom C. Feuer in *Tehillim Treasury* (Artscroll/ Mesorah Publ.), p. 96.
4. *Tehillim* 63:4.
5. Ibid.
6. *She'arim B'Tefillah*, p. 137.

▸ Chazal demonstrate that it is a major loss for one to lose his desire to pray.

▸ The real benefit of prayer is the closeness with Hashem that it affords us.

▸ Although one asks for material benefits, the primary objective of prayer is to achieve its spiritual benefits.

A person diagnosed with a serious illness hopes to find the ideal doctor — an expert in his field who also has a wonderful bedside manner to reassure and encourage his patients. The patient will not only be cured, but will be fortunate enough to form a relationship with a special individual who will care for his every need.

People who receive the blessings of this world without sincere prayer bypass the essential purpose of life: the opportunity to grow spiritually and connect with Hashem. As Rav Yechezkel Levenstein explains,[7] a primary goal of man's creation is to draw near to Hashem by breaking the barriers that separate us from Him. The goal is not, as people may think, merely to enjoy the benefits of this world.

Thus, when beseeching Hashem for health, a livelihood, the best for our children, and all our other needs, our primary objective is to connect with Him. The spiritual growth and closeness to Hashem that we achieve through prayer is far more valuable than anything we receive in return. In truth, it is more precious than life itself.

---

7. *Ohr Yechezkel*, Vol. 1, p. 222.

BEING HUMAN

A car transports. A scissor cuts. A computer computes. What does man do? What is his essential function — the purpose the Inventor had in mind when He made this highly complex creation?

That question is answered in *Bereishis*[1] with the appearance of the "prototype" of mankind. Adam enters the world and prays. His prayer brings to fruition all the latent blessings in creation, as we have seen in Day 3, "The Primal Force." Subsequently, Adam and Chavah are cursed; however, it is in a manner that assures that mankind will forever need and want to draw closer to Hashem through prayer.

The desire to seek Hashem is the very definition of man. The Mishnah[2] lists four categories that cause property damage and refers to one category as *mav'eh*, an unusual term defined by Rav as referring to "man." The *Gemara*[3] explains that this definition is derived from the verse:[4] *The watchman said, Morning comes and also night; if you shall seek it, seek (be'ayu).* In this context, the word *be'ayu* (from the same root as *mav'eh*) represents mankind, for it is a person's ultimate mission to continuously seek Hashem through prayer and Torah.

The Torah[5] describes the creation of the first human being with the words, *and man became a living soul.* Rashi[6] explains that this phrase refers to man's power of reason-

18
Tishrei

18
Teves

18
Nissan

18
Tammuz

---

1. 2:5.
2. *Bava Kamma* 2a.
3. Ibid. 3b.
4. *Yeshayahu* 21:12.
5. *Bereishis* 2:7.
6. Ibid.

▸ *Prayer is
built into
the nature
of mankind,
as illustrated
by the fact
that Adam's
first act was
to pray.*

▸ *A person's
ultimate
mission is to
continuously
seek
Hashem.*

▸ *Man's "living
soul" is
defined as
his desire
to connect
to Hashem
through
prayer
and Torah
learning.*

ing and speech — this is the essence of his soul, the element that gives him spiritual life in the physical world. It is the defining characteristic of man's existence.[7]

Targum Onkelos[8] defines a *living soul* as a speaking soul. The *Zohar*[9] adds that man's goal is to connect to Hashem through speech, expressed in prayer and Torah study. One who does not pray, then, is effectively muzzling his "speaking soul."

Through prayer, we remove the muzzle. We allow our Divine Essence to emerge into the physical world, doing precisely what Hashem equipped man to do when He blew into us the breath of life.

---

7. *Rabbeinu Bachya, Introduction to Parashas Vayigash.*
8. *Bereishis 2:7.*
9. *Parashas Tazria.*

"LET HIM SLEEP"

A normally hard-working student drifted off in class. The teacher knew that the child would want to hear what was being taught, so he shook the child's shoulder and called his name, waking him up. The next day, another child drifted off in class. This child, however, was continuously disruptive and obviously not interested in learning. The teacher looked at the sleeping child and thought to himself, "There's no point in waking him. I'll just let him sleep."

19 Tishrei

19 Teves

19 Nissan

19 Tammuz

Sometimes, a person seems to amass great fortune without exerting the slightest effort in spirituality. When this happens, it is the worst fortune of all, because it indicates that Hashem has given up hope that arousing the person will spur him into self-improvement. He is the student about whom the teacher says, "Let him sleep."

As Rav Dessler[1] elucidates: "Although we see that material benefits are sometimes given even to wrongdoers, it is not really a blessing, since there is no Heavenly help in them; they lack a spiritual source. In addition, these successes bring no satisfaction to them ... they accomplish nothing."[2]

Rav Dessler[3] further explains that, while every person pursues material well-being to some extent, there are five different spiritual levels on which one can operate. The lowest of these belongs to the person who achieves wealth and success but never recognizes Hashem's hand in his

---

1. *Michtav MeEliyahu*, Vol. 1, pp. 18, 203.
2. Ibid., Vol. 5, p. 270. Also see *Sifsei Chaim, Pirkei Emunah V'Hashgachah*.
3. *Michtav MeEliyahu*, Vol. 1, p. 197.

**Points
to
Ponder**

▸ *Material
benefits
may not be
a blessing
when they
lack a
spiritual
source.*

▸ *One who
achieves
success
without
prayer
becomes a
tool of the
yetzer hara.*

▸ *Only
through
prayer does
one fulfill
his purpose
and have
assurance
that his
successes
are real
blessings.*

achievement. Why, one might wonder, does Hashem grant such a person success? It would seem that Hashem would afflict this person in a way that would cause him to recognize and seek his Creator.

Rav Dessler's answer conveys a very important lesson.[4] There are individuals who are in such complete denial of Hashem's supervision that they become unworthy of being awakened by Him. The Evil Inclination acquires the power to draw these people even further along their own foolish path, allowing them to believe that their very success proves the validity of their approach to life.

Such unwarranted success may plant a seed of doubt in the minds of others regarding Hashem's role as the sole provider. This transforms the recipient of the riches, sadly, into a tool of the *yetzer hara*. His ostensibly *good* fortune is thus the ultimate misfortune.

Rav Dessler concludes with a powerful final warning: "How low is the spiritual level of these individuals! They are troops of the *yetzer hara* … all the abundance and largesse they enjoy in this world emanates from the depths of impurity and defilement, and they will be lost in the end."[5]

No one, however, need remain in this degraded state. Every person has the ability to utilize *tefillah* to release himself from the grasp of the *yetzer hara*. Ultimately, drawing closer to Hashem in prayer is the true expression of our humanity. The successes that flow from this source are achievements we can identify, with full confidence, as the blessings of Heaven.

---

4. Ibid. p. 203.
5. Also see ibid., Vol. 5, p. 238.

CHAPTER 3:
GAINING A PROPER UNDERSTANDING OF KAVANNAH

KAVANNAH: THE SOUL OF PRAYER

I n 1950 in London, the students of Rav Dessler read these startling words in a letter from their rebbi:[1]

We are accustomed to saying that we pray; however, that is totally untrue. Indeed, we have not yet even arrived at tefillah, and accordingly have not yet prayed. And the truth is we should be forbidden to pray entirely ... with difficulty (we were) allowed (to pray) so that the whole idea of tefillah should not be entirely forgotten. Can the babbling of words be called tefillah? This is a terrible and appalling deterioration in the conception (of tefillah) that will cause the Heavenly doors to be closed to the power of tefillah.

Rav Dessler's stark rebuke echoes that of Rabbeinu Bachya,[2] who warned that a person who prays with his lips while his heart is focused upon his business and financial affairs is considered a sinner.[3] "... Because if one prays and does this he estranges himself in his thoughts from the King, Hashem, and to a human king he would not do this (to speak to him while thinking of his business affairs)."

The *Seder HaYom*[4] likewise comments: "Prayer without *kavannah* does not help at all ... to the contrary, it causes the declaration of one's sins in Heaven."

Attention to the purpose and meaning of prayer is an essential component, just as it was an essential part of the animal offerings in the Holy Temple. In the Temple's absence, prayer fills the role of "service"[5] to Hashem. The

---

1. *Michtav MeEliyahu*, Vol. 4, end of p. 361.
2. Introduction to *Parashas Terumah*.
3. Also see *Mishnas Rav Aharon*, Vol. 1, p. 102, which states that one who treats prayer frivolously commits a severe sin since he disgraces Hashem's honor.
4. P. 35. Also see *Ohr Zarua*, *Siman* 102.

Shulchan Aruch [6] rules that just as certain foreign thoughts can invalidate the sacred offerings, certain foreign thoughts can invalidate our prayers. [7]

The Gemara [8] teaches, "One who prays must concentrate his heart (in all the prayers)." In fact, *tefillah* is called a labor of the heart, as the Gemara [9] explains, "*And to serve with all your heart*: Which service is with all your heart? This is prayer."

The *Smak* [10] classifies prayer as a mitzvah of the heart: "What is the service of the heart? Prayer with concentration ... that one should think about the meaning of every word." This concept is embedded in the word *tefillah* itself, which comes from the word "*pi'lail*," which means thought, [11] because *tefillah* requires *kavannah*. [12]

These teachings leave no doubt that *kavannah* is a requirement of *halachah*, [13] not merely a stringency. If one is not speaking from the heart, and not speaking with an awareness of Hashem, one is not fulfilling the basic requirements of prayer.

Even if a person knows every *halachah* relevant to *tefillah* and every word of prayer and its meaning, only when he opens his heart does he truly know how to pray.

Points to Ponder

▸ *Prayer without kavannah is not considered a proper prayer.*

▸ *Prayer can be invalidated if recited while distracted by certain foreign thoughts.*

▸ *Kavannah is a halachic requirement of prayer.*

---

5. *Sifri, Parashas Eikev:* "Inasmuch as the work of the Altar (sacrificing animals in the Holy Temple) is called *avodah*, service, so too, prayer is called service." See *Berachos* 26b and *Magen Avraham, Siman* 1, *Se'if Katan* 12, with *Machtzis HaShekel*, ibid., which states that the daily prayers are a substitute for the morning and evening *temidim* offerings.
6. *Siman* 98, *Se'if* 4.
7. Continuing the comparison to a *korban*, the *Shemoneh Esrei*, unlike other mitzvos, must be said while standing, just as the Kohen was required to stand when bringing an offering.
8. *Berachos* 34b.
9. *Taanis* 2a.
10. Ch. 11.
11. See *Rashi, Bereishis* 48:11.
12. *Sifrei Maharal, Be'er HaGolah, Be'er HaRevi'i*, p. 52.
13. See *Aruch HaShulchan, Siman* 93, *Se'if* 4.

DAY
21

KAVANNAH: THE SOUL OF PRAYER, PART II

21
Tishrei

21
Teves

21
Nissan

21
Tammuz

A man once approached a great rabbi with a question: "Is it not true, Rabbi, that if a person refrains from speaking idle words for forty days, he merits the revelation of Eliyahu HaNavi?"

The rabbi confirmed that this was indeed so.

"Well, then," the man continued, "I would like to know why, after I have done this for the past forty days, I have not merited a revelation."

"Have you prayed during these last forty days?" the rabbi asked.

"Yes, I have," the man replied.

"If you have done so without kavannah," said the rabbi, "then you have spoken many idle words."[1]

Kavannah has been called the neshamah, the soul and spirit of prayer.[2] Without it, prayer is considered merely a guf, the lifeless body of tefillah.[3] The root of the word "kavannah" indicates "direction," and it is indeed the element that gives our tefillos their Heavenward direction.[4]

Just as an arrow's power and distance depend on the pressure exerted by the archer on the bow, the effective-

---

1. B'Mechitzas Rabbeinu [Hagaon Rav Yaakov Kamenetsky] (Feldheim Publ.), p. 61.
2. See Chovos HaLevovos, Shaar Cheshbon HaNefesh 3:9, which states that the words of prayer are like the peel of a fruit and the thoughts behind the words are like the heart of the fruit. Thus, words of prayer without kavannah are like a peel without the fruit inside.
3. See Nefesh Shimshon, p. 242. He cites Keser Rosh, Os 25, in the name of Rav Chaim Volozhiner that tefillah without kavannah is similar to a korban minchah. This offering, brought from flour, had no soul, in contradistinction to an animal offering that had a neshamah.
4. A Letter for the Ages by Rabbi Avrohom Chaim Feuer (ArtScroll/Mesorah Publ.), p. 105.

92 / PRAYING WITH FIRE

ness of prayer depends on the power of the supplicant's thought behind his prayers.[5]

The *Abudraham* notes that the numerical equivalent of the words "*tefillah*" and "*b'kavanas halev*" (with concentration of the heart) is the same — 515 — indicating that "according to the level of *kavannah* will prayer be accepted."[6]

The word *lev*, heart, in all its variations, appears in the Torah a total of 113 times; this is also the total number of words found in the final sentences of all the *berachos* of *Shemoneh Esrei* (e.g., "*Baruch Atah Hashem Magen Avraham*" is five words). From this connection we learn that the concentration of our *lev* (*kavannah*) is what draws into our lives the many aspects of Hashem's goodness expressed by the *berachos* of *Shemoneh Esrei*.[7]

The words of *Tehillim*[8] hold out the promise of a true, deep connection to Hashem for those who pray with their hearts: *Hashem is close to all who call upon Him, to all who call upon Him sincerely.* The *Radak*[9] says that this verse refers to those whose prayers are a unified harmony of mind, heart, and words. Fueled by *kavannah*, these are the prayers with the power to reach their destination.

Points to Ponder

▸ *Kavannah is the soul of prayer.*

▸ *The root of the word kavannah indicates that this is the element that sends prayer in the right direction.*

▸ *Prayer fueled with kavannah always reaches its destination.*

---

5. See *Bereishis* 48:22 with *Rashi*. Also see *Gur Aryeh* ibid.
6. *Abudraham HaSheim* (Revised and Expanded Edition, Jerusalem 1963) pp. 92-93, s.v. *Ezras Avoseinu*.
7. *Baal HaTurim*, *Shemos* 40:21.
8. 145:18.
9. Ibid.

UNLOCKING THE GATES

"From the day the (Second) *Beis HaMikdash* was destroyed, the Gates of Prayer are locked," says the Gemara.[1] The Satmar Rebbe[2] posed two questions: First, why do we pray if the Gates of Prayer are locked? Furthermore, *Chazal*[3] tell us that our prayers rise to "the pinnacle of the heavens." What purpose do they serve there if they cannot pass through the gates?

The Satmar Rebbe returns to the Gemara,[4] to offer a beautiful answer: "Even though the Gates of Prayer are locked, the Gates of *Dim'ah*, tears, are not locked." A person's *tefillos*, standing at the "pinnacle of the heavens," cannot penetrate the locked Gates of Prayer until he weeps with emotion during prayer. At that moment, the Gates of Tears open. All the *tefillos* standing in wait, including those previously said without tears, can then be swept through to the Throne of *HaKadosh Baruch Hu*.

This inspiring thought has one drawback: It is highly unlikely that the average person would be able to command this intensity of emotion in the absence of any real emotional upheaval. How, then, does this concept equip us on a practical level to open Heaven's gates to our daily prayers?

Rav Yonasan Eibeshutz[4] offers an astounding insight that resolves the problem. The numerical equivalent of the word *b'chi*, crying (which can be substituted for *dim'ah*, tears), is 32, the same as the word *lev*, heart. This teaches

---

1. *Berachos* 32b.
2. *Divrei Yoel, Parashas Eikev*, p. 67.
3. *Berachos* 6b with *Rashi*; see above, "The Journey — Surmounting the Obstacles," fn. 1.
4. *Yaaros Devash*, Vol. 2, *Derush* 11.

that the *tefillos* of the one who prays with *kavannah*, intent of the heart, enter Heaven through the ever-open Gates.

Kavannah transforms our daily prayers into heartfelt supplications able to reach the Throne of *HaKadosh Baruch Hu*. It not only propels our present *tefillos*, but reaches back in time to "repackage" the distracted, rushed, and mumbled prayers of our past and send them Heavenward with renewed power.

SPEAKING TO
THE SOUL

composer hears a beautiful melody in his
head. He sits down at the piano and works
out the precise notes that bring his melody
to life. The harmonies and counterpoints, the phras-
ing and timing all come together to make the song
into a force that has the power to uplift the hearts
and touch the souls of others.

As beautiful and powerful as his masterpiece is,
however, it accomplishes little until it is played out
loud. And so it is with prayer. The words on the page,
composed with fine-tuned perfection by our Sages,
possess only a minute fraction of their transforming
power until they are actually verbalized.

23
Tishrei

23
Teves

23
Nissan

23
Tammuz

The *Shulchan Aruch* states,[1] "One must not pray in his
heart alone, rather, he must say the words with his lips so
they can be heard." One who merely thinks of the words
without pronouncing them has not fulfilled the requirement to pray, even *bedi'eved*, after the fact.[2]

Why is enunciation of the words so integral to prayer? If
kavannah is the essential element, why can't a sincere, silent *tefillah* fulfill the requirement to pray? Why does one
need to verbalize his prayers when Hashem is well aware
of every thought in a person's mind?

One of the reasons[3] is related to a challenge that is
specific to any kind of internal, spiritual activity. Human

1. *Siman* 101, *Se'if* 2. See *Siman* 206, *Se'if* 3; *Siman* 185, *Se'if* 2; *Siman*
62, *Se'if* 3, and *Mishnah Berurah*, *Siman* 101, *Se'if Katan* 5, where it
is stated that as long as one actually uttered the words he is considered to have prayed properly even if he did not hear himself
say them.
2. *Mishnah Berurah*, *Siman* 206, *Se'if Katan* 13; ibid. *Siman* 185, *Se'if
Katan* 2; ibid. *Siman* 62, *Se'if Katan* 6; *Beur Halachah*, *Siman* 101,
Se'if 2.
3. See *Likkutei Shaish on Avos* 2:13, which cites *Tiferes Yehoshua* who
lists five additional reasons why prayer requires speech.

nature is such that until a thought or feeling is concretized into an action, it remains ephemeral, prone to dissipate into thin air. The Rambam deals with this challenge in the realm of *teshuvah*, repentance. He states:[4] "When one repents … from sin, he must confess before Hashem … that is, confession with words." Like *teshuvah*, *tefillah* is an internal, spiritual experience. Without the concrete action of speaking, neither process can effect a change upon the soul; they remain nothing more than thoughts in one's mind.[5]

Prayer's true purpose is to bring a person closer to Hashem.[6] This is a vital quest, central to a person's entire purpose in life. Obviously, a goal so crucial cannot be accomplished completely with the ephemeral entity of thought (*kavannah*) alone. To assure that the thoughts become integrated into one's personal reality — into one's soul — they must be spoken.

In general, *Chazal*[7] tell us that one can acquire *shleimus*, a state of completeness, by performing an abundance of positive actions. For *tefillah*, uttering the words of the prayers is the requisite action that allows us to acquire *shleimus*.[8]

Yet, prayer is called a labor of the heart, not a labor of the mouth. Although speech plays a crucial role in *tefillah*, its true essence, its *neshamah*, is *kavannah*.

Points to Ponder

▸ *The halachah requires that words of prayer be spoken.*

▸ *Speaking the words of prayer enables them to effect spiritual growth.*

▸ *Even spoken tefillah, if it lacks kavannah, is missing its essence.*

---

4. *Hilchos Teshuvah* 1:1.
5. See *Michtav MeEliyahu*, Vol. 5, p. 260.
6. See Ch. 2, "Achieving Personal Growth Through Prayer." Also see *Mishnas Rav Aharon*, Vol. 1, p. 92, where Rav Aharon Kotler teaches that the purpose of prayer is to bring a person closer to Hashem, and thereby, to enable him to understand that everything comes from Him.
7. See *Pirkei Avos* 3:15.
8. See *Beis Elokim, Shaar HaTefillah*, Ch. 3.

24
Tishrei

24
Teves

24
Nissan

24
Tammuz

I f kavannah is so vital to prayer, it would seem almost nonsensical for anyone to invest time each day into praying without it. The quest for kavannah, however, comes with a price; it takes time, and few people have enough time. The person who arrives at a 7 a.m. minyan knowing he must catch an 8 o'clock train to work does not have the luxury of slowing down and concentrating on every word. Simply finding the time to say the words — in any manner whatsoever — seems enough of an achievement.

With the guidance of a rabbi, under certain limited circumstances, one may be permitted for a specified duration to sacrifice the quantity of certain prayers in order to increase the quality (kavannah) of tefillah. "It is better [to say] fewer supplications with kavannah than more without kavannah."[1] A person who, due to unavoidable circumstances, recites a shorter tefillah in order to have kavannah, is considered by Hashem to have uttered the longer supplication.[2]

For example, the Shulchan Aruch[3] urges us to recite Pesukei D'Zimrah carefully, in an unrushed manner. Initially a person may feel that saying the entire Pesukei D'Zimrah with kavannah is an overwhelming task. For this

---

1. Shulchan Aruch, Siman 1, Se'if 4. See Aruch HaShulchan, Siman 51, Se'if 9, which states that if the congregants are reciting Pesukei D'Zimrah speedily and he desires to say Shemoneh Esrei together with the minyan, it is better to skip parts of Pesukei D'Zimrah than to say them quickly with the minyan. On this it is said, "It is better [to say] fewer supplications with kavannah than more without kavannah." Also see Rav Schwab on Prayer (ArtScroll/Mesorah Publ.), p. 120.

2. Mishnah Berurah, Siman 1, Se'if Katan 12: "One who [says] more and one who [says] less [are the same] provided their intentions are [directed] toward Heaven."

3. Siman 51, Se'if 8.

person, reciting a smaller portion with proper *kavannah* is preferable to rushing through the complete text.

This does not mean that skipping sections of *tefillah* is a permanent solution. It is a beginning step in a plan that allows a person to target one segment of prayer at a time. A person might start by focusing on the meaning and pronunciation of a specific paragraph of *Pesukei D'Zimrah*, until the *kavannah* becomes an integral part of the *tefillah* itself, and saying those particular words naturally evokes the appropriate feeling. At that point, the person can focus on a new segment, and paragraph by paragraph, he can actually entwine his soul with every word of the *Pesukei D'Zimrah*, or another part of the daily prayers. In this systematic way, he can transform his *tefillah* in a relatively short time, gaining benefits that will endure forever.

A similar strategy can vastly enhance the merit of reciting *Tehillim*. To truly tap into the merit inherent in saying *Tehillim*, one can follow the plan outlined above, tackling one chapter at a time until its meaning and emotional content are ingrained in his heart. In this way, chapter by chapter, one can master these *tefillos* and evoke the full weight of their merit when one recites them in a time of need.[4]

The principle that "it is better (to say) fewer supplications with *kavannah* than more without *kavannah*" guided Rav Shlomo Zalman Auerbach[5] in answering an oft-asked question:

> Two Shacharis minyanim began at 7 a.m.; one proceeded slowly, allowing for more kavannah, while the other progressed much faster, making kavannah nearly impossible. An individual who had to catch a bus to work at 7:45 asked whether he should pray with the faster minyan and remain until after the last Kaddish, or pray with the slower minyan where he

---

4. See *Yaaros Devash*, Vol. 1, *Derush 8*, p. 163, which states that rather than completing the entire *Tehillim* every day without *kavannah*, it is more acceptable to recite fewer chapters of *Tehillim* with *kavannah* each time.
5. See *Halichos Shlomo* (tefillah), Ch. 1, *Siman* 2. Also cited in *Tefillah K'Hilchasah*, Ch. 2, fn. 28.

▸ It is possible
that a
person may
be permitted
(preferably
under the
guidance
of a Rav) to
minimize
the amount
of prayer
recited in
order to
maximize
the
kavannah in
the prayers
he says.

▸ After
kavannah
becomes
ingrained
in one's
recitation of
a segment
of prayer, he
should begin
working on
another part
of prayer.

*could have greater kavannah but would be forced to
leave before the end.*

*Rav Auerbach answered: "It appears that it is pref-
erable to pray a tefillah with kavannah even if one
must, as a result, depart before the conclusion, because it is better [to pray] less with concentration
than more without concentration." He noted, however, that the person should make known the reason
for his early departure so as to avoid a possible chillul
Hashem.*[6]

Our Torah sages can see beyond the horizon, to the
destination our *tefillos* are intended to take us. They tell
us that we will get there only by slowing down, finding the
right direction, and proceeding with a sense of purpose.
Otherwise, we are running in frantic circles.

---

6. See *Mishnah Berurah*, *Siman* 90, *Se'if Katan* 33, which states that a
chillul Hashem may occur if the individual in question is a *talmid
chacham* — i.e., one whom others look up to.

PURITY OF THE HEART

raining a child — to form his letters, ride his bike or master any task — succeeds through persistent repetition. The more frequently he repeats the task, the better he becomes at it.

Hashem, it seems, trains the human heart in the same manner, urging us to do as many mitzvos as possible, as frequently as possible, as the means to refine our souls. The Mishnah states,[1] "… ve'hakol lefi rov hamaaseh" — *and everything is according to the abundance of [a person's] actions*. The Rambam[2] explains this phrase to mean that a person grows mainly through the abundance (quantity) of his mitzvos, rather than their magnitude (quality).

With regard to *tefillah*, however, quality is clearly more desirable than quantity. This sets it apart from all other areas of spirituality. Why does *tefillah* operate differently?

According to the Maharal,[3] prayer is nothing less than the outright relinquishment of one's entire being to Hashem. Sincere prayer is a humble admission of our own inadequacy and an affirmation of our belief in Hashem's power to make all things occur.

It is in this spirit, says the Maharal,[4] that a person would bring an offering to the Holy Temple. He would be considered to be delivering himself to Hashem, like a servant whose every possession belonged to his master. The offering, like *tefillah*, conveys the belief that everything belongs to Hashem and that there is no one besides Him.

25
Tishrei

25
Teves

25
Nissan

25
Tammuz

---

1. *Avos*, 3:15.
2. Ibid.
3. *Nesivos Olam*, Vol. 2, *Nesiv HaAvodah*, Ch. 2. Also see Ch. 2, "Achieving Personal Growth Through Prayer."
4. *Nesivos Olam*, Vol. 1, *Nesiv HaAvodah*, Ch. 1.

Rav Dessler[5] states further that, in order for a person to actually accomplish the task of delivering himself to Hashem, the offering must be a choice one, unlike that of Kayin,[6] whose inferior offering was not accepted. He concludes, "The main acknowledgment of [Hashem's] Oneness is with the purity of the heart of the one bringing the offering; that is the aspect of quality. On the contrary, an abundance of quantity in this matter is likely to be a detriment."

Like a diamond, a prayer's value is far more dependent on its internal purity than its mass. The small, flawless diamond is worth far more than the larger, imperfect one. Its purity not only defines its value, but it also expresses the purity of devotion with which it is being tendered.

These concepts converge into one sharp point: The objective of prayer — like that of bringing an offering in the Holy Temple — is to declare the Oneness of Hashem and to come closer to Him. This can be accomplished only with a heart whose intent is pure.

Kavannah provides the life-force of *tefillah*, and one must strive to understand how to activate this "vital organ" of our souls. We will begin by exploring the inner power of our most eloquent tool for beseeching Hashem — the *Shemoneh Esrei*.

---

5. *Michtav MeEliyahu*, Vol. 4, p. 15.
6. *Bereishis* 4:3-5.

CHAPTER 4:
KAVANNAH IN SHEMONEH ESREI: THE PINNACLE OF PRAYER

SACRED WORDS

26
Tishrei

26
Teves

26
Nissan

26
Tammuz

*O*ne hundred and twenty of the greatest computer scientists in the world are brought together and given unlimited access to the most advanced technology available. They are joined by visionaries able to discern every possible requirement of future generations of computer users. Their mission is to write a program for a supercomputer designed to remain state-of-the-art for all time.

Imagine — were such a development even possible — the infinite power of this remarkable device! This portrayal is but a glimpse in contemporary terms of the extraordinary process which culminated in the sacred and ever-powerful words of *Shemoneh Esrei*.

The text of *Shemoneh Esrei* was composed through Divine inspiration by the one hundred and twenty elders who comprised the Men of the Great Assembly — among them, many prophets — at the beginning of the era of the Second *Beis HaMikdash*. Four hundred years later, after the *Beis HaMikdash* was destroyed, the text was rearranged into our current format under the direction of Rabban Gamliel, as the original sequence had been forgotten.[1]

From their soaring spiritual heights, the Men of the Great Assembly grasped the inner powers hidden within each word of each blessing. They understood the sweeping cosmic effects of each letter and word combination, grant-

---

1. See *Megillah* 17b-18a; also see *Shitah Mekubetzes* on *Berachos* 28b, s.v. *Tanu Rabbanan*, which states that the Divinely inspired text of *Shemoneh Esrei* was not changed; rather, the original sequence that had been forgotten was later rearranged to its current format. Also see *Beis Elokim L'HaMabit, She'ar HaYesodos*, Ch. 61, s.v. *U'ma sheshanah b'Megillah*.

ing them the ability to formulate each prayer into a mighty force whose impact could shake the very heavens.[2]

Even with these Divine origins, the *Anshei Knesses HaGedolah* composed the *Shemoneh Esrei* using straightforward, relatively easy-to-understand language.[3] They devised the order of *Shemoneh Esrei* — the first three *berachos* of praise, the middle twelve *berachos* of requests for our daily needs, and the last three *berachos* of thanks — leading the supplicant's heart toward *kavannah*.

Kavannah is so vital to the integrity of *Shemoneh Esrei* that a person who does not understand the meaning of its holy words may, according to some opinions, pray in another established[4] language.[5] This, however, can only be done if he is careful to have *kavannah* when praying in that language[6] and until he becomes acquainted with the Hebrew text.[7]

---

2. *Beur Halachah, Siman 101, Se'if 4, s.v. Yachol l'hispallel.*

3. *Rabbeinu Bachya, Devarim 11:13.*

4. *Beur Halachah, Siman 62, Se'if 2, s.v. Yachol likrosa.* See *Igros Moshe, Orach Chaim, Vol. 4, Siman 70 (4)*, which states that one should not translate the Hebrew text according to his own understanding. Also see *She'eilos U'Teshuvos Teshuvos V'Hanhagos, Vol. 1, Siman 355*, which states that Hashem's Name should not be translated into, for example, "L-rd." Rather, one should say Hashem's Name in Hebrew.

5. See *Mishnah Berurah, Siman 101, Se'if Katan 13*, which states that according to the *She'eilos U'Teshuvos Chasam Sofer, Orach Chaim, Simanim 84 and 86*, this is permitted only for individuals. An entire congregation may not pray in another language. The *chazzan*, who leads the prayer, *must* pray in Hebrew. However, see *Mishnah Berurah, Siman 55, Se'if Katan 1.*

   See *Mishnah Berurah, Siman 62, Se'if Katan 3*, which states that nowadays one should avoid reading *Krias Shema* in any language other than Hebrew because there are several words that cannot be properly translated.

6. *Mishnah Berurah, Siman 62, Se'if Katan 3*. This also applies to *Bircas HaMazon, Kiddush, birchos ha'mitzvos, birchos ha'peiros* and *Hallel*. Also see *Shulchan Aruch HaRav, Siman 62, Se'if 2*. However, see *Aruch HaShulchan, Siman 101, Se'if 9*, which states that the permission to pray in another language does not refer to *Shemoneh Esrei*, only to *Selichos* and other similar prayers. Additionally, see ibid. *Siman 62, Se'if 4*, which states that it also does not apply to *Krias Shema* and other *berachos*.

7. See *She'eilos U'Teshuvos Teshuvos V'Hanhagos, Vol. 1, Siman 355*, where Rav Moshe Sternbuch allows one who is just starting to read Hebrew to say *Shemoneh Esrei* in English if he otherwise would not pray at all. However, the first *pasuk* of *Krias Shema* should be said in Hebrew.

‣ *The words
of the
Shemoneh
Esrei were
established
with Divine
inspiration.*

‣ *The Divinely
inspired
words are
replete with
potential to
impact in
Heaven.*

‣ *The order of
Shemoneh
Esrei's
blessings
facilitates
kavannah.*

Needless to say, however, praying from the original text is preferred. [8]

In giving us the language with which to address Hashem, the Men of the Great Assembly provided us with an envelope — addressed, stamped, and ready for delivery directly to Hashem's Throne of Glory. But the envelope will arrive with something essential missing, unless we, through *kavannah*, fill it with the contents of our hearts.

---

8. See *Mishnah Berurah, Siman 62, Se'if Katan 3*, which states: "The most preferred way of performing the mitzvah is to use Hebrew exclusively." Also see ibid. *Siman 101, Se'if Katan 13*. Additionally, see *Beur Halachah* ibid. s.v. *Yachol*, and the *Shulchan Aruch HaRav, Siman 101, Se'if 5*, who cites the *Sefer Chassidim, Siman 588*.

RIGHT FROM
THE START

*T*he scene would almost be comical: One of several thousand employees of a giant corporation is invited to meet with the venerable company president to ask for whatever he needs to better perform his mailroom job. The employee barges in five minutes late, stops to catch up on office news with a colleague, rushes through the door checking his watch, and begins reciting some laudatory words that he had memorized for the occasion.

The employee has mail to sort, so he quickly rattles off the memorized words and checks his watch once more to see how much time this meeting has wasted. The company president sits and stares in astonishment, thinking, "Who does this man think he is?"

27
Tishrei

27
Teves

27
Nissan

27
Tammuz

How a person approaches someone is an immediate indicator of their relationship. In approaching Hashem in *Shemoneh Esrei*, the *kavannah* can make or break the effectiveness of the entire *tefillah*. Either it tells Hashem that He is our King and we are standing humbly before Him, or it tells Him that we have no awareness of the gravity of the occasion.

Kavannah[1] is one of five essential prerequisites of *tefillah*. The Rambam states that one who does not have *kavannah* in *Shemoneh Esrei* must repeat it. In his first mention of this rule, he applies it to the entire prayer. He later concludes, however, "… if one concentrated and had the proper intentions during the first *berachah* (of *Shemoneh Esrei*) it is unnecessary to repeat it," indicating that *kavannah* during the first *berachah* is sufficient.[2]

---

1. *Rambam, Hilchos Tefillah* 4:1. The other four requirements are: clean hands, covering of nakedness, a clean place to *daven*, and [an absence of] distracting things.
2. Ibid. 10:1. See also note 10 below.

Rav Chaim Brisker[3] elucidates the Rambam's two statements by explaining that there are two forms of *kavannah* necessary in *Shemoneh Esrei*. The first *kavannah*, as defined by the Rambam, obligates a person to view himself as standing before the Master of the Universe. This *kavannah* is required during the entire *Shemoneh Esrei*, and is based on the Gemara:[4] "One who prays must view himself as if Hashem's Divine Presence is opposite him as it says,[5] *I have set Hashem before me always.*" Thus, one's thoughts and intentions when reciting *Shemoneh Esrei* must reflect a steadfast awareness that one is directly beseeching Hashem. (Note: There is disagreement as to whether a lack of this *kavannah* would invalidate the *tefillah*.)[6]

The other essential *kavannah* involves the *peirush ha'milim*, understanding the meaning of the words, which is required, at a minimum, during the first *berachah* of *Shemoneh Esrei*.[7]

---

3. *Chidushei Rabbeinu Chaim HaLevi, Hilchos Tefillah*, Ch. 4.
4. *Sanhedrin* 22a.
5. *Tehillim* 16:8.
6. See *Avi Ezri* (HaRav Shach), Ch. 4 *Hilchos Tefillah*; the *Hasagos of the Chazon Ish* on the *Chidushei HaGrach on the Rambam*; and the *She'eilos U'Teshuvos Yabia Omer, Orach Chaim* 3, *Siman* 8, which state that having the *kavannah* that one is standing before the *Shechinah*, Hashem's Divine Presence, is not required during the entire *Shemoneh Esrei*.
7. If one did not fulfill this *kavannah* requirement during the first *berachah* of *Shemoneh Esrei*, one of the following alternatives may be used:
 • See *Mishnah Berurah, Siman* 101, *Se'if Katan* 4, which states that if one realizes that he did not have *kavannah* before he recites *"Baruch Atah Hashem"* at the end of the first *berachah*, he should return to *"Elokei Avraham"* and repeat the *berachah*.
 • In *She'eilos U'Teshuvos Teshuvos V'Hanhagos*, Vol. 4, *Siman* 28, Rav Moshe Sternbuch cites from Rav Chaim Kanievsky in the name of the Chazon Ish that even if one did not have *kavannah* for the meaning of the words of the first *berachah*, one is considered to have recited a proper *Shemoneh Esrei* provided he thinks of the meaning of the words of the first *berachah* before he begins saying the next *berachah*, *"Atah Gibor."*
 • According to the *She'eilos U'Teshuvos Eretz Tzvi (Siman* 22), if one had *kavannah* at the end of the *berachah* he satisfies the *kavannah* requirement.
 • Alternatively, see *Beur Halachah, Orach Chaim, Siman* 101, s.v. *V'ha'idnah*, which states that one may wait quietly until *chazaras hashatz* and then have in mind to satisfy his requirement to have

According to the *Shulchan Aruch*,[8] "One who prays must concentrate in his heart regarding the explanation of the words (that come) from one's mouth." However,[9] "... if one cannot concentrate (on the meaning of the words) in all the *berachos*, at a minimum (he must have proper *kavannah*) during (the first *berachah* called) *Avos*."[10]

> *Rav Shlomo Zalman Auerbach was once asked what resolutions he made for Rosh Hashanah and Yom Kippur. He replied, "To recite the first blessing of Shemoneh Esrei with kavannah."*[11]

Our obligation in approaching Hashem is to know Whom we are approaching. However, we can only pay sincere tribute to the "G-d of our Fathers," if we understand what we are saying. The subject matter of the next three days will focus on the first *berachah* of *Shemoneh Esrei* called *Bircas Avos*.

Points to Ponder

▶ One aspect of *kavannah* is, at a minimum, to understand the meaning of the words during *Bircas Avos*.

▶ A lack of *kavannah* in *Bircas Avos* can compromise the entire *Shemoneh Esrei*.

▶ During *Shemoneh Esrei* another aspect of *kavannah* is to be aware that we are standing before Hashem.

---

kavannah in the first *berachah* by listening to the *shaliach tzibbur* saying the *berachah*. Also see *She'eilos U'Teshuvos Yabia Omer, Orach Chaim*, Vol. 3, *Siman* 9; and *She'eilos U'Teshuvos Az Nidberu*, Vol. 2, *Siman* 59.

• See *Halichos Shlomo* (*Tefillah*) (Rav Shlomo Zalman Auerbach) Ch. 8, *Siman* 9, fn. 32, which states that (according to one of the *Rishonim*) even if one did not have the proper *kavannah* for the words of *Bircas Avos*, as long as he had even fleeting *kavannah* during the duration of the *berachah* that he is saying *Bircas Avos*, then he is considered to have *davened* the first *berachah* properly.

• Finally, according to the *Roke'ach* (cited in *Kehillos Yaakov, Berachos*, *Siman* 26) and *Sefer Chassidim, Siman* 158, if one did not have the proper *kavannah* during the first *berachah* of *Shemoneh Esrei* he should have *kavannah* when reciting *Modim* in *Shemoneh Esrei*.

8. *Siman* 98, *Se'if* 1. Also see *Siman* 5, *Se'if* 1.

9. *Siman* 101, *Se'if* 1.

10. If one did not concentrate in *Avos*, even though he did during the rest (of *Shemoneh Esrei*), essentially he must return to repeat the *Shemoneh Esrei*. However, the *Rama* in *Siman* 101, *Se'if* 1 rules that nowadays one should not repeat *Shemoneh Esrei* since he cannot be assured of proper *kavannah* even the second time.

11. *The Man of Truth and Peace* by Rabbi Yoel Schwartz (Feldheim Publ.), p. 127.

28
Tishrei

28
Teves

28
Nissan

28
Tammuz

L
ike the preset numbers of a combination lock, the established combination of words that comprise *Bircas Avos* opens the door to all of the essential, life-sustaining blessings that *Shemoneh Esrei* holds for us. Clearly, one must learn and understand these words well.[1] With this goal in mind, we will search for greater insight into their profound meaning (Days 28-30).[2]

The first *berachah* is called *Bircas Avos* because it elucidates that we are praying to the same "Being" as did the *Avos* — Avraham, Yitzchak, and Yaakov. It reflects on the magnificence of these great individuals, each of whom recognized the Master of the Universe in his own unique way. It is in their merit that Hashem will help each new generation, all the way until the days of Mashiach.

Let us now focus word by word on this vital *berachah*:

▶ *Baruch* — Blessed[3]

We acknowledge that Hashem is blessed, meaning that He is perfect and complete. We recognize that Hashem is the Source of all blessing,[4] and offer thanks for all that He bestows upon us.

---

1. Preferably, one must concentrate on the meaning of the words of the entire *Shemoneh Esrei*. However, at the very least one should do his utmost to have *kavannah* during (in descending order): (1) the first *berachah* of *Shemoneh Esrei*, *Modim*, and the ending of each *berachah* (see *Mishnah Berurah, Siman* 101, *Se'if Katan* 1 and 2); (2) the first *berachah* and *Modim* (*Mishnah Berurah, Siman* 101, *Se'if Katan* 3; *Daas Torah, Siman* 101, *Se'if Katan* 1; also, see *Beis Yosef, Siman* 101); (3) the first *berachah* (*Mishnah Berurah, Siman* 101, *Se'if Katan* 1); or (4) *Modim* (*Roke'ach*, cited in *Kehillos Yaakov, Berachos, Siman* 26; *Sefer Chassidim, Siman* 158).
2. See *Michtav MeEliyahu*, Vol. 3, p. 81 for a complete explanation of *Bircas Avos*.
3. See *Derech Sichah*, p. 540.
4. *Sefer HaChinuch* 430. See *Mishnah Berurah, Siman* 124, *Se'if Katan* 24, who cites the *Chayei Adam, Siman* 6, which states that "for example,

▶ *Atah* — You

We beseech Hashem directly.[5] The Tzlach[6] explains: When a person says *'Atah'* in his *tefillah* ... he is speaking with the King of kings 'face to face,' *kaviyachol*, as it were."[7] The Chofetz Chaim points out that *"Atah"* — You [Hashem], refers to the fact that one beseeches Hashem *directly* in prayer.[8]

▶ *Hashem*[9] —
Master of All, Who always was, is, and will be[10]

When one mentions the Divine Name, he should have in mind the meaning of the Name as it is *read*,[11] referring to His Mastery and that He is the Master of all creation.[12]

---

when the *chazzan* says *Baruch Atah Hashem Magen Avraham*, You are Blessed, L-rd, Shield of Avraham, a person who responds 'Amen' should have in mind, 'It is true, the Name of the L-rd, Who was the Shield of Avraham, *should be blessed*. One should have an equivalent intention for all *berachos*." Also see *Pachad Yitzchak, Iggaros U'Kesavim*, letter 52, p. 86.

For further elucidation on the meaning of "*Baruch*," see *Nefesh HaChaim, Shaar* 2, Chs. 2-4. Also see *She'eilos U'Teshuvos HaRashba*, Vol. 5, *Siman* 51, who writes that *Baruch* [*Atah*] means, [You are] the Source of Blessing. The word "*baruch*" is derived from "*bereichah*" — a pool or spring of flowing water. For an analysis of the meaning of "*Baruch*," see *Pathway to Prayer* by Rabbi Mayer Birnbaum (ArtScroll/Mesorah Publ.), Appendix, p. 75.

5. *She'eilos U'Teshuvos HaRashba*, Vol. 5, *Siman* 52; *Yesod V'Shoresh HaAvodah*; also cited in *Halichos Shlomo (Tefillah)*, p. 362, s.v. *Yeish davar m'yuchad*.

6. *Berachos* 30b, s.v. *Ein omdin l'hispalleil*.

7. Likewise, in all the requests in the blessings [of *Shemoneh Esrei*] and with similar *berachos*, they are said as if Hashem's Presence is directly in front of him; [for example], "*Atah chonein l'adam daas*," You graciously endow man with knowledge.

8. Cited in *Halichos Shlomo (Tefillah)*, p. 362, s.v. *Yeish davar*. "*Atah*" is recited a total of 33 times in *Shemoneh Esrei*.

9. The word in *Shemoneh Esrei* is actually *written* with the letters *yud, hei, vav* and *hei*. It is *pronounced* as if the letters are *aleph, dalet, nun* and *yud*.

10. *Siman* 5, *Se'if* 1. Cf. *Halichos Shlomo (Tefillah)*, p. 2, *Dvar Halachah* 4.

11. See *Mishnah Berurah, Siman* 5, *Se'if Katan* 2, which states that one should also have in mind the meaning of the Name as if it is *written* with the letters *aleph* (with a *chataf pasach*, but not with a *pasach* alone or with a *sheva* alone), the letter *dalet* (with a *cholam*) and the letter *nun* (with a *kamatz*). (See *She'eilos U'Teshuvos Har Tzvi, Orach Chaim, Siman* 4.) One must also stress the letter *yud* so that it is clearly noticeable.

12. *Siman* 5, *Se'if* 1.

▸ The words of Bircas Avos link us with the merit of our Forefathers and acknowledge our complete reliance upon Hashem.

▸ The merit of the Avos still sustains us today.

▸ Our desire is to serve Hashem with the devotion of the Avos.

> ▸ *Elokeinu* — Our G-d

Our G-d is Omnipotent and Almighty,[13] a powerful Master Who monitors and oversees each and every one of us on a personal basis.[14]

> ▸ *Vailokei Avoseinu* — And the G-d of Our Patriarchs

After declaring that we are ready to serve and connect with Hashem at our own level, we then express our desire to serve Him with the intensity of our Forefathers — with equal dedication and zeal.[15] We reach back to our spiritual roots and draw from them the nourishment with which to nurture our love and awe of Hashem.

---

13. Ibid.
14. *Aderes Eliyahu, Vilna Gaon on Devarim* 1:6; *Nefesh HaChaim* 3:11; *Alei Shur*, Vol. 2, p. 375. See *Michtav MeEliyahu*, Vol. 4, p. 63, which states that we accept upon ourselves Hashem's dominion and render ourselves as insignificant before Him. We announce that we are ready to serve and connect with Hashem (according to our individual capabilities).
15. Ibid.

THE MERIT OF OUR FATHERS, PART II

Reinforcing the bond with our Forefathers through this prayer not only calls upon their merit, it also calls upon us to identify our own path to spiritual greatness. As we recite their names, we are reminded that each served Hashem in his distinct way.

▸ *Elokei Avraham, Elokei Yitzchak, Vailokei Yaakov* — The G-d Of Avraham, the G-d of Yitzchak, and the G-d of Yaakov

The *chesed* of Avraham Avinu — the benevolence that he displayed to others — was his core characteristic, through which he emulated the *chesed* of Hashem. Because he perceived Hashem's existence through the magnificent gift of Creation and Hashem's continual benevolence, he followed this path to bring Hashem's light into the world.[1]

Gevurah v'yirah, mightiness and fear, characterized Yitzchak Avinu. By calling upon his inner strength and fear of Heaven, he exemplified the power of Hashem, for the world to see.

The primary character trait of Yaakov Avinu was *emes v'tiferes*, truth and perfect harmony. His personality combined the seemingly contradictory traits of Avraham's benevolence and Yitzchak's mightiness and fear.[2]

As we recite the names of the *Avos*, we strive to awaken their traits within ourselves. In doing so, we will arrive at our own individual source of strength, with which to perform our own unique service of Hashem.

▸ *HaKeil* — The Almighty

Hashem's powers are unlimited.

---

1. See *Michtav MeEliyahu*, Vol. 2, pp. 162-163.
2. See ibid. Vol. 5, pp. 51 (end) and 215 for the meaning of *tiferes*.

▸ HaGadol, HaGibor, VeHaNora —
The Great, the Mighty, and the Awesome

Gadol refers to Hashem's attribute of *chesed*; He proclaims His presence in this world by performing acts of benevolence.

The attribute of *Gibor*, strength, refers to mightiness in judgment, for Hashem proclaims His presence in this world by meting out perfect justice.

Finally, Hashem is *Nora*, Awesome, in that He proclaims His presence through truth and beauty. [3]

▸ Keil Elyon — The Supreme G-d

Hashem is supreme and every one of His attributes is all-encompassing. Just as water rushes with force from a high position to a lower point, so too does Hashem's goodness flow with constant force from the Heavens above to the world we inhabit. [4]

▸ Gomeil chasadim tovim —
Who bestows beneficial kindnesses

Although Hashem is supreme and exalted, He nevertheless bestows never-ending kindnesses to even the smallest creatures in the world. The kindness of Hashem, Who can foresee the future, is completely beneficial and greater than that of any human being. [5]

▸ V'konei hakol — And possessing everything

The entire world is Hashem's by virtue of His creating and maintaining it with kindness. Everything in this world testifies that Hashem created it, and has the ability to teach us His benevolence, charity, and favor. [6]

▸ V'zocheir chasdei Avos —
And (Hashem) Who remembers the great deeds
of our Patriarchs

Hashem recalls the charity and benevolence performed by our *Avos* as if they were being performed today. They

---

3. Ibid., Vol. 4, p. 64.
4. Ibid.
5. *Abudraham HaSaleim* (Revised and Expanded Edition, Jerusalem 1963), p. 94.
6. *Michtav MeEliyahu*, Vol. 4, p. 64.

are a merit in our Heavenly account, available to us when we identify ourselves to Hashem, claiming with full understanding of our words, that "These are our Forefathers!"

Points to Ponder

▸ Each of the Avos represents a primary trait through which one can serve Hashem.

▸ One awakens these traits by paying attention to the meaning of this part of the berachah.

▸ Hashem views the deeds of the Avos as if they were being performed today.

KING, HELPER, SAVIOR, AND SHIELD

The fears and troubles we face in life are a means to an end — a dramatic and triumphant end that will unfold with the coming of Mashiach. The merit of the Forefathers is integral to this final chapter, for it is out of love for them that Hashem promises redemption to their children.

▸ *U'meivee Goel* —
And He (Hashem) brings the Redeemer (Mashiach)

In this light, we can see that our difficulties serve a purpose. They are all part of the preparation for the Final Redemption.

▸ *Livnei v'neihem* — **To their children's children**

At the end of all generations, even if the merit of our Patriarchs has been totally depleted, Hashem will eventually bring Mashiach.[1]

▸ *Lemaan Shemo* — **For His Name's sake**

For the sake of Hashem's Name, He will reveal His honor and glory to the nations of the world; this is the purpose and objective of Creation.

▸ *B'ahavah* — **With love**

Everything Hashem does is with love, and is for the purpose of bringing the Final Redemption. Even the current Diaspora, with all its torment, is part of a plan that we will eventually comprehend with the coming of Mashiach.

▸ *Melech Ozeir u'Moshia u'Magen* —
King, Helper, Savior, and Shield

There are four levels of *Siyata D'Shmaya*, Heavenly help:[2]

---

1. *Baruch She'amar* (Am Olam Publ., Israel 1970), p. 116.
2. *Jewish Meditation* by Aryeh Kaplan (Schocken Books), p. 117.

Melech, a King, Who remains in His palace providing help from afar; *Ozeir*, a Helper, Who can be readily approached for assistance — an initial acknowledgment of our close relationship with Hashem; *Moshia*, a Savior, always close enough to rescue us, even at a moment's notice (as when a drowning person is plucked from a raging river); and *Magen*, a Shield, Who protects us from harm when there is not even a moment available for a savior's assistance.[3]

▸ **Baruch Atah Hashem —
See Day 28, The Merit of Our Fathers.**

▸ **Magen Avraham — Shield of Avraham**

Hashem granted Avraham the special protection of a shield, so that even if his enemies would shoot arrows at him he would remain unscathed. "Anochi magen loch, secharcha harbei me'od." *I am your shield; your reward* (spiritual and material) *is exceedingly great*, said Hashem.[4] As Hashem told Avraham, *al tira*, do not fear, for you are completely shielded and nothing can penetrate your armor.[5]

When we call upon Hashem, the Shield of Avraham, we place ourselves under His sole protection. No matter what we face as we travel the difficult road toward the Final Redemption, we need not fear.

Points to Ponder

▸ *Difficulties serve the purpose of paving the way for the arrival of Mashiach.*

▸ *Hashem promises redemption in the merit of the Patriarchs.*

▸ *Even if their merit is depleted, Hashem promises redemption.*

▸ *Hashem helps, rescues, and shields us as we face life's difficulties.*

---

3. As discussed in Day 78, "Behind the Scenes," according to *Michtav MeEliyahu*, Vol. 4, p. 65, there are *three* levels of *Siyata D'Shmaya*: *Ozeir*, a Helper, Who thwarts an *existing immediate* danger from overpowering a person; *Moshia*, a Savior, Who cancels a danger that is *threatening* to overpower a person; and *Magen*, a Shield, Who prevents trouble from *approaching* the person in the first place.

4. *Bereishis* 15:1.

5. *Michtav MeEliyahu*, Vol. 3, p. 84; Vol. 4, p. 65.

ADDRESSING THE KING

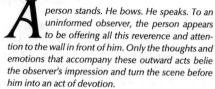

A *person stands. He bows. He speaks. To an uninformed observer, the person appears to be offering all this reverence and attention to the wall in front of him. Only the thoughts and emotions that accompany these outward acts belie the observer's impression and turn the scene before him into an act of devotion.*

Knowing the meaning of the words one says is essential, but knowing and feeling that these words are being addressed to an exalted and holy King are more essential still. Otherwise, one performs a recitation, not a prayer.

The *Shulchan Aruch*[1] defines the correct state of mind: "(One) should regard it as if the *Shechinah* (Divine Presence) is before him ... for if he were speaking before a human king, he would arrange his words and concentrate on them so that he would not stumble or fail. How much more so, before the King of kings Who examines all thoughts and intentions."

> *Rav Moshe Feinstein would stand motionless and erect when reciting Shemoneh Esrei.[2] When asked why, he related that he was once brought in for interrogation by the Communist authorities in the city of Luban, Russia, and forced to stand at attention during the entire ordeal. Rav Moshe resolved that from that time on, he would do the same when reciting Shemoneh Esrei. After all, he reasoned, standing at attention in Luban was a display of submissiveness to the*

---

1. *Siman* 98, *Se'if* 1.
2. Cited in *Five Great Lives* (ArtScroll/Mesorah Publ.), p. 174. However, see *Mishnah Berurah*, *Siman* 48, *Se'if Katan* 5, which states that whether one sways back and forth during *Shemoneh Esrei* depends on individual preference.

1 Cheshvan

2 Shevat

1 Iyar

2 Av

> *Russian authorities; surely Hashem, Melech malchei ha'melachim, the King of all kings, deserved no less.*
>
> *In davening, Rav Dessler stood completely motionless like a stick. At the same time, the veins on his head literally bulged out from the intense concentration that he brought to every tefillah.*[3]

The *Me'iri*[4] states that "a person must concentrate on his *tefillah* (and) not divert his heart to anything other than *tefillah* ... (and must) remember before Whom he is standing."

Rav Yaakov Kamenetsky illustrated how this concept came to life in the following incident involving his rebbi, the Alter of Slobodka:

> *One day during World War I, the Alter was reciting Minchah and in the middle of Shemoneh Esrei, bombs began to fall. Instinctively, everyone in the room threw themselves to the floor, with the exception of the Alter, who stood erect until the completion of Shemoneh Esrei. He then looked around and asked in all innocence, "What happened here?"*[5]

The *Chazon Ish*[6] offers the following guidelines for achieving the correct *kavannah*: "The task of a person during *tefillah* is to visualize that Hashem is listening to every word of the prayers that are uttered by human lips and scrutinizing the thoughts of those who pray to Him."

A person saying *Shemoneh Esrei* should literally feel transported to his personal audience with Hashem.[7]

> *Rav Shimon Schwab related that when the Mirrer Mashgiach, Rav Yeruchem Levovitz, prayed, he spoke to Hashem as if he were talking to a much revered friend. Similarly, Rav Mendel Zaks testified to the fact that his father-in-law, the Chofetz Chaim, would often converse with Hashem during tefillah in a very*

3. *Rav Dessler* by Yonoson Rosenblum (Artscroll/Mesorah Publ.), p. 221.
4. *Beis HaBechirah, Berachos* 30b.
5. Cited in *Kovetz Sichos Maamar Mordechai*, Vol. 1, p. 127.
6. Ibid. p. 126.
7. See *Nefesh Shimshon*, p. 310.

personal way. He once overheard him saying, "Ribbono Shel Olam, You have heard my prayers many times in the past. Please accept them today as well." [8]

These personal conversations with Hashem are not the privilege of the great luminaries alone. We, too, have been granted this same opportunity each and every day.

A prominent rabbi was once asked, "How long should it take to *daven Shemoneh Esrei*?" He replied, "As long as it takes to present your requests to the King!"

A person stands to pray and he thinks about the Majesty of the One before Whom he stands. He bows, and thinks about the reverence he owes his Master and Creator. Then he is ready to speak, and Hashem is ready to listen.

---

8. Cited in *Kovetz Sichos Maamar Mordechai*, Vol. 1, p. 126.

THE PALACE RULES

What does it mean to a modern citizen of a democratic country to "stand before a king"? Most people today could not imagine treating a fellow human being with such utter deference, worrying over every detail of their comportment lest they inadvertently offend the all-powerful ruler.

In generations ruled by kings, a person had a real basis upon which to grasp the grandeur conveyed by the title "King of kings." In our day, we must search for ways to imbue ourselves with the unfamiliar emotions of awe and reverence that are an essential *kavannah* of *Shemoneh Esrei*. *Halachah* provides us with the means to do this, mandating that we, like subjects coming before the throne, follow certain rules that convey our recognition of the King's majesty.

Before we even begin saying the words of *Shemoneh Esrei*, after walking forward three steps,[1] we recite a verse that reminds us how completely incapable we would be of beseeching Hashem on our own power. We are able to pray only because Hashem, in His love for us, stands us upon our feet, opens our mouths, and gives us the intelligence and courage to speak before Him and request our needs. Therefore, before we even begin to pray *Shemoneh Esrei*, we recite a verse acknowledging that our ability to pray is completely dependent upon Hashem's grace: *Hashem, open my lips ...*[2] This sets the tone for the *Shemoneh Esrei* to follow.[3]

2 Cheshvan

3 Shevat

2 Iyar

3 Av

---

1. *Tefillah K'Hilchasah* 12:21.
2. *Tehillim* 51:17.
3. *Berachos* 9b. See also the *Levush, Siman* 111. Although we may not interrupt between *Geulah* and *Shemoneh Esrei* (in the morning *tefillah*), this *pasuk* is not considered an interruption. Rather, since it is a crucial plea for concentration, it is called an extension of *Shemoneh*

As we close our private conversation with Hashem we dare not finish abruptly and rush off to the next activity. The *halachah* requires us to take three steps back when completing *Shemoneh Esrei*, replicating the slow, respectful departure of[4] a servant taking leave of his master.[5]

Because the communication with Hashem is a real, albeit invisible event, those in proximity to a person who is praying *Shemoneh Esrei* must pay heed to the Presence that is there. They may not stand, sit, or pass within four *amos*, cubits (approximately 6.3 — 7.6 feet)[6] in front of an individual who is in the midst of reciting *Shemoneh Esrei*.[7] It appears from the *Chayei Adam*[8] that this applies even if the person who is praying has closed his eyes and his concentration would therefore not be broken. Others may not interpose themselves between two parties engaged

---

Esrei. Thus, even when the *chazzan* starts reciting *Shemoneh Esrei* aloud, he must again say this verse. See *Siman* 111, *Se'if* 2. According to *Mishnah Berurah* ibid. *Se'if Katan* 10, it is desirable to say it quietly. However, according to the Arizal cited by *Kaf HaChaim* ibid., one should recite the verse aloud.

4. *Mishnah Berurah, Siman 123, Se'if Katan* 1.

5. See *Mishnah Berurah* ibid. *Se'if Katan* 2 and *Beis Yosef, Siman* 123, who cite additional reasons for taking three steps back at the conclusion of *Shemoneh Esrei*.

6. There is disagreement concerning the measurement of four *amos*. According to the *gaon Rav Avraham Chaim No'eh* (as cited in *Shemiras Shabbos K'Hilchasah*, Vol. 1, p. 11), four cubits equal 6.3 feet, as follows: There are 6 *tefachim* in each cubit. A *tefach* equals 3.1496 inches. Therefore, one cubit equals 18.8976 inches (6 x 3.1496 inches = 18.8976 inches). Four cubits equal 75.5904 inches, which when divided by 12 = 6.3 feet (rounded).

According to *Igros Moshe, Orach Chaim*, Vol. 1, *Siman* 136 and *Yoreh De'ah*, Vol. 3, *Siman* 66, four cubits equal 7.083 feet, as follows: A *tefach* equals 3.5416 inches. Therefore, one cubit equals 21.25 inches (6 x 3.5416 inches = 21.25 inches). Four cubits equal 85 inches, which when divided by 12 = 7.083 feet.

According to the Chazon Ish (as cited in *Shemiras Shabbos K'Hilchasah*, Vol. 1, p. 11), four cubits equal 7.6 feet, as follows: A *tefach* equals 3.77952 inches. Therefore, one cubit equals 22.67712 inches (6 x 3.77952 inches = 22.67712 inches). Four cubits equal 90.70848 inches, which when divided by 12 = 7.6 feet (rounded).

7. *Siman* 102, *Se'ifim* 1 and 2. See *Mishnah Berurah, Siman* 102, *Se'if Katan* 2 and *Kaf HaChaim, Siman* 102, *Se'if Katan* 5, which discuss cases where there is a partition in front of the person *davening Shemoneh Esrei*.

8. *Klal* 26. Also see *Beur Halachah, Siman* 102, and *She'eilos U'Teshuvos Teshuvos V'Hanhagos*, Vol. 1, *Orach Chaim, Siman* 75.

in conversation, and this is especially so when one of the parties is the Eternal King.

Finally, the *Magen Avraham*[9] rules that a person may not interrupt his *tefillah* in the middle of *Shemoneh Esrei* even if he may then lose his money, unless he is faced with a life-threatening danger.

The *Kaf HaChaim*[10] raises the following question: We know that no more than a fifth of one's income may be spent for the sake of a mitzvah. Why, then, would one not be permitted to interrupt *Shemoneh Esrei* if he is in danger of losing a great deal of money?

His answer underscores an awesome reality: We literally stand before Hashem's Divine Presence — the *Shechinah* — during *Shemoneh Esrei*. The gravity of interrupting a conversation with the King of kings overrides any other concerns.

The Gemara teaches:[11]

> When Rav Eliezer became ill, his students came to visit him and said, "Our teacher, show us the way of life that we may merit the World to Come (eternity)." Said Rav Eliezer, "When you pray, know before Whom you are standing (in prayer). And because of this you will merit a life in the World to Come."

By mindfully following the *halachos*, each of us has the opportunity to feel the overwhelming reality of standing before a King of infinite majesty. The Gemara promises that by fulfilling our role as Hashem's reverent subjects in this world, we earn a place as the King's beloved servants in the World to Come.

---

9. *Siman* 104, *Se'if* 1, *Magen Avraham, Se'if Katan* 1.
10. *Orach Chaim, Siman* 104, *Se'if Katan* 6.
11. *Berachos* 28b.

CHAPTER 5: FEELING THE SHECHINAH'S PRESENCE

THE RADIANCE OF THE SHECHINAH

*Y*ou arrive in a strange town. It's time for Shacharis, so you find the local shul. You open the door and look inside, and your eyes scan the faces within. Sitting at one table, you see the unmistakable countenance of Rav Moshe Feinstein. Next to him, radiant with holiness, sits the saintly Chofetz Chaim himself. The Steipler Gaon and the Baal Shem Tov sit right behind them, next to Rav Dessler and Rav Shach.

The room is vibrant with holiness and purity as you weave your way among the tables to find a seat, and you pray with an intensity and clarity you never thought possible. You actually feel Hashem's Presence right there in the room, listening to your every word.

One who can vividly imagine this experience can understand what it means to feel the *Shechinah's* Presence as he prays. For most people, however, this is difficult, for to them the *Shechinah* remains an enigma. The efficacy of our prayers may depend on our willingness to look more deeply into the nature of this unseen Presence, and gain an understanding of how It manifests Itself in our world.

The Gemara¹ teaches that the *Shechinah* resides in places of holiness: the Holy Temple, Jerusalem, and in a shul when ten men pray together. The *Shechinah* is also present when three judges sit in judgment, and when even one person studies Torah.

A fundamental question arises: If Hashem is Omnipresent, why do we single out the *Shechinah's* Presence in certain holy places such as a shul during *tefillah*? What is the

---

1. *Berachos* 6a.

significance of the *Shechinah's* Presence in these sacred places if Hashem is everywhere and anywhere?

Rav Chaim Friedlander, Mashgiach of the Ponevezh Yeshivah, citing the Ramchal, explains that "*Shechinah*" — from the phraseology "*that which resides in your midst*" — represents *our* relationship with Hashem.[2] Although Hashem is indeed Omnipresent, *our* ties to His Presence are stronger when we are inspired by an occasion or a place of holiness. To the extent that we seek the *Shechinah*, we find It.

The *Aruch LaNer* [3] explains the significance of the *Shechinah's* Presence as follows: The Torah calls the *Shechinah* "the Glory of Hashem," and specifies locations in the earthly sphere where the *Shechinah's* Presence is apparent: *And the Glory of Hashem dwelled on Mount Sinai* and *the Glory of Hashem filled the Mishkan.*[4]

In reality, the *Glory of Hashem* refers both (1) to the origin of sanctity and holiness — a place which is concealed in Heaven, and (2) to the aura of holiness that emanates from It and inspires a sense of sanctity here on earth.

The *Aruch LaNer* explains the difference between these two facets of the *Shechinah* with an analogy to the sun, and the light and heat that emanate from it. When we remark, "The sun is out," we do not mean that it is actually before us — after all, the sun is situated 93 million miles away from earth. Yet, despite this great distance, we can see the sun's light and feel its heat.

The same idea applies to the *Shechinah*; the Glory of Hashem resides in the distant Heavens, while the *Shechinah's* Presence on earth — for example, in the place where a person is reciting *Shemoneh Esrei* — refers to the force of holiness and sacredness that emanates from the Glory of Hashem so far away.

---

2. *Sifsei Chaim, Pirkei Emunah V'Hashgachah*, Vol. 1, p. 170. See *She'eilos U'Teshuvos Noda B'Yehudah, Mahadura Tinyana, Orach Chaim*, Siman 107, s.v. *U'mitchilah*, which states that "*Shechinah*" refers to "*hasmadas hashgachah*" — the continuous supervision — the "*Hashgachah Pratis*" that Hashem exercises over *Klal Yisrael*.

3. *She'eilos U'Teshuvos Binyan Tzion*, Siman 3.

4. *Shemos* 24:16; 40:34.

▸ *Although
Hashem
is Omni-
present, the
Shechinah's
Presence
is felt in
certain
places and
in specific
circum-
stances.*

▸ *The
Shechinah
is defined
by our
relationship
with
Hashem.*

▸ *Feeling the
Shechinah's
Presence
enhances
our
recitation of
Shemoneh
Esrei.*

This analogy explains how different degrees of *Shechinah* rest in diverse holy places; the *Ohr HaChaim HaKadosh*[5] writes that the levels of *kedushah* emanating from the *Shechinah* are many, i.e., where ten men study Torah together, and to a lesser degree, where two, or even one, learn. Just as the strength of the sun's rays varies from place to place, the force of the sacred "rays" of the *Shechinah* also varies according to the particular holy place or occurrence.[6]

Our task as we pray is to expose our souls to the "rays" of the *Shechinah* — to shed the layers of distraction and habituation — and to feel Its radiant Presence all around us.

---

5. *Bereishis* 46:4
6. See *Ben Yehoyada, Yoma* 21b, s.v. *Nimtza Bayis Rishon*; and *She'eilos U'Teshuvos Yabia Omer, Orach Chaim* 1, *Siman* 35.

UNDEREXPOSURE

*I*magine that after decades of research, medical science develops a miracle cure for heart disease. It's a light — a purple light whose waves are absorbed through the skin and into the blood, where they instantly unblock arteries and restore the patient to perfect health. One patient, however, insists upon undergoing the treatment wearing a heavy winter coat, thick woolen pants, a cap, and a scarf. When his symptoms fail to improve, he insists that the treatment is a hoax. "It doesn't do a thing for me," he complains.

A person can be in the presence of an overwhelming spiritual force and notice nothing. He can be standing right in front of the *Shechinah* and sense only the man standing next to him. This happens, not because, as the patient in the story believes, the benefits are not there for him. It is because the person has entered into an environment of holiness and awe, but is insulated from head to toe against its effects.

Continuing the *Aruch LaNer's*[1] comparison of the *Shechinah* to the sun, when obstacles are placed in the way of the sun's rays, its warmth and light are limited. In the same way, when we place obstacles in the path of the holy "rays" of the *Shechinah*, we limit Its profound impact.

Rav Dessler in the name of the Ramchal[2] explains why some people do not feel the *Shechinah*: "The limitation is with the receiver, since the windows of his heart are polluted ... the more one cleans them, the more light will enter."

4
Cheshvan

5
Shevat

4
Iyar

5
Av

---

1. *She'eilos U'Teshuvos Binyan Tzion*, Siman 3.
2. *Michtav MeEliyahu*, Vol. 3, p. 66.

The *Shechinah* dwells wherever ten men gather for prayer, removing from themselves the concerns of this world that prevent the "rays" of Holiness from being felt. In fact, the *Shechinah* radiates an intense spiritual power during *tefillah* — but we perceive it only if we place no obstacles in Its path. Furthermore, just as the light of the sun is brighter when it is focused directly on an object, the *Shechinah's* intensity increases in the presence of a person reciting *Shemoneh Esrei*.

Thus, when a person is receptive to the "rays" of the *Shechinah*, especially when praying, then Its "light" will shine on his heart and soul. He will experience the aura of holiness, and the power of his prayers will be immeasurably strengthened.

The Gemara[3] teaches that the *Shechinah* rests above the head of a sick person. The question arises: What special merit does the sick person possess that the *Shechinah* should rest above him? The Maharal[4] explains that a sick person is removed from the usual realm of nature (where good health prevails) and therefore, Hashem maintains a special guard over him.

When a person is healthy and enjoying life, he tends to forget Hashem, as the Torah says:[5] *And your heart will be haughty and you will forget Hashem, your God, Who took you out of Egypt from the house of slavery.* However, a sick person is in a situation not of his choosing. He is forced to recognize that he is not in control and therefore, he is more likely to turn to Hashem.[6]

As the *Me'iri*[7] states, "The sick person reflects in his heart on repentance and prays [to Hashem] with his whole heart." It is for this reason [his strong bond with Hashem] that he merits having the *Shechinah* rest above him as he desires to connect with Hashem.

---

3. *Shabbos* 12b.
4. *Netzach Yisrael*, Ch. 10 (cited in *Sifsei Chaim, Mo'adim*, Vol. 3, p. 376).
5. *Devarim* 8:14.
6. See *Sifsei Chaim, Mo'adim*, Vol. 3, p. 382, who explains the comparison between the *Shechinah* with *Klal Yisrael* and the *Shechinah* with a person who is ill.
7. *Beis HaBechirah, Shabbos* 12b.

We need not be lying in bed feeling downtrodden and vulnerable in order to bring the *Shechinah's* Presence into our hearts. We can bask in the rays of this Holy Light, standing upright and in good health, every time we say *Shemoneh Esrei*. There's nothing in the way but ourselves.

Points to Ponder

▸ *Even though the Shechinah is present during prayer, one may not feel Its Presence.*

▸ *One often creates obstacles that block out the Shechinah's "rays" of holiness.*

▸ *The Shechinah rests at the head of a person who is ill because he acknowledges his total dependence upon Hashem.*

SEEKING AND FINDING

DAY 35

5 Cheshvan

6 Shevat

5 Iyar

6 Av

A young woman arrives in Israel with a tour group. The very next morning, her group is shepherded to the Kosel, the Western Wall. She draws close enough to almost touch the stones and recalls the literally millions of tears that have been shed at this site for over 2,000 years, by those yearning for the rebuilding of our Holy Temple. Her eyes fill with tears and she begins to weep. Meanwhile, the other twenty-nine people on the tour glance around with mild interest as the guide discusses the Western Wall's history and the number of tourists who visit it each year.

If a person enters a holy place without any desire to seek out the *Shechinah,* he will indeed find and feel nothing, even if the room is saturated with His Presence. The Ramchal[1] teaches that although the *Shechinah*'s influence manifests Itself in certain holy places, It is only there for those who seek to connect to Hashem: "... Even though [Hashem's] Honor is everywhere, surely, It is revealed in one place more than in another place, and that [where It is revealed] is Its special place, where those who want can attach themselves to Him. And that is the subject [of the *pasuk*], *Rather, only at the place that Hashem, your G-d, will choose ... shall you seek Hashem's Presence and come there.*"[2]

The Torah[3] tells us that when Yaakov traveled from Be'er Sheva to Haran, he passed Beis El, which was the location of Har HaMoriah, the mountain upon which Avraham's in-

---

1. *Daas Tevunos, Siman* 160, p. 176, s.v. *V'teid'ee.*
2. *Devarim* 12:5.
3. *Bereishis* 28:11.

tended sacrifice of Yitzchak took place, and the future site of the Holy Temple. However, Yaakov did not stop to pray there. After arriving in Haran, Yaakov wondered, "Is it possible that I have passed the place where my fathers prayed and I did not pray there?"[4]

Yaakov immediately decided to return to Beis El, and a miracle occurred. In an instant, the distance to Har HaMoriah contracted, greatly shortening his journey.[5]

Yaakov merited this miracle only after acknowledging the sanctity that his forebears imprinted upon that location through their *tefillos*, and expressing the desire to connect with that holiness.[6] The Torah describes Yaakov's experience: *And he became frightened and said, "How awesome is this place. This is none other than the Home of G-d and this is the Gate of the Heavens."*[7]

Rav Yeruchem Levovitz, the Mirrer Mashgiach, explains[8] that clearly Yaakov's eagerness to connect with the *Shechinah* at that location was a key factor in earning *Klal Yisrael* the merit to build both the First and Second Beis HaMikdash there. In fact, to this day, our prayers are more easily received and accepted at that site.

If we travel to shul in the spirit in which Yaakov traveled to Har HaMoriah, longing to deliver our *tefillos* in a place imbued with holiness, then we too can hope to internalize the awesome recognition that "This is none other than the Home of Hashem."

Points to Ponder

▸ Even though the Shechinah's Presence is more intense in certain places, one must seek It to find It.

▸ Har HaMoriah was a place of intense holiness because Avraham and Yitzchak had prayed there.

▸ Yaakov felt Hashem's Presence at Har HaMoriah only when he felt the desire to seek It.

---

4. *Rashi, Bereishis* 28:17.
5. *Chullin* 91b.
6. See *Michtav MeEliyahu*, Vol. 3, p. 129.
7. *Bereishis* 28:17.
8. *Daas Chochmah U'Mussar*, Vol. 1, *Maamar* 99.

A SENSE OF PLACE

DAY 36

6
Cheshvan

7
Shevat

6
Iyar

7
Av

*O*ne shul has soaring, 20-foot-high ceilings, stunning stained-glass windows, and a massive ark of carved mahogany. The congregants, having long ago grown accustomed to their beautiful surroundings, produce a steady undercurrent of chatter that bounces off the acoustically perfect walls.

Another shul is located on the avenue, one flight above a large kosher grocery store. The ceiling tiles are water-stained and the floor is of ancient linoleum. The congregants, accustomed to the clank of the old pipes and the traffic noise outside, do their utmost to focus on their prayers.

Surprisingly, the "Glory of Hashem," the *Shechinah*, is far more apparent in the less glorious surroundings. That is because those entering the little shul upstairs enter for the sole purpose of finding the *Shechinah* there. They thereby supply that which no architect can.

Chazal[1] tell us that because we no longer merit having the Holy Temple, our shuls serve as a *Mikdash Me'at*, a small Sanctuary, and our prayers substitute for the offerings. So holy are these way stations of exile scattered throughout the world that, according to *Chazal*,[2] they will be transported to Jerusalem when Mashiach arrives.

The *Mishnah Berurah*[3] explains that since a shul is called *Mikdash Me'at*, the exhortation, *and My Sanctuary shall you revere,*[4] applies to every synagogue, each of which

---

1. See *Mishnah Berurah, Siman* 151, *Se'if Katan* 1 who cites the verse in *Yechezkel* 11:16: *And I will be to them a minor Beis HaMikdash.*
2. *Megillah* 29a.
3. *Siman* 151, *Se'if Katan* 1.
4. *Vayikra* 19:30.

has the halachic status of *kedushah*.[5] There are several *halachos* that help to preserve this status. For instance, a person is not permitted to conduct himself with levity in shul and in a house of learning[6] by acting in a foolish way or even engaging in idle talk.[7]

The building itself must be approached with the recognition of its exalted status. A person may not enter a shul to take shelter from inclement weather if there are other buildings available.[8] He may not use a shul as a shortcut or enter it for no purpose.[9] If someone is searching for a friend in shul, he should recite a *pasuk* or a *halachah* when inside, so that it does not appear that he is there merely for a mundane purpose.[10]

These are just a few of the *halachos* that help maintain the sanctity of the *Mikdash Me'at*. By preserving the shul as an environment of holiness in our midst, we demonstrate to Hashem our desire to maintain a place where we will be able to encounter and connect with the holy *Shechinah* in prayer.[11]

This demonstration of our desire to come close to Hashem has a powerful effect on any spiritual undertaking. *Chazal* teach us:[12] "Because of our efforts we merit to be helped by Hashem (as Hashem says): 'Open for Me an opening the size of the point of a needle and I will open for you an opening through which even wagons and trolleys can enter.'"

> *Giving the shul the reverence due a holy place causes us to immediately shift gears upon entering. Our*

---

5. See *Chayei Adam, Klal 17, Se'if 6; Pri Megadim, Mishbetzos Zahav, Siman 151, Se'if Katan 1; Sdei Chemed, K'lalim, Maareches Beis, Siman 43; She'eilos U'Teshuvos Maharsham*, Vol. 1, *Siman 10*, and *She'eilos U'Teshuvos Yabia Omer, Orach Chaim 7, Siman 24*, for a discussion of whether the *kedushah* is Biblical or Rabbinic.

6. *Siman 151, Se'if 1.*

7. For a further discussion regarding talking idle talk in a shul, see Ch. 8, "The Spoken Word: Our Downfall, Our Salvation."

8. *Siman 151, Se'if 1; Mishnah Berurah, Se'if Katan 4.*

9. *Siman 151, Se'if 5.*

10. Ibid. *Se'if 1.*

11. See *Sifsei Chaim, Mo'adim*, Vol. 3, p. 394.

12. *Shir HaShirim Rabbah 5:2.* Also see *Michtav MeEliyahu*, Vol. 3, p. 67.

‣ Nowadays a shul is called a "Mikdash Me'at" because it serves in place of the Holy Temple. Therefore, one must act with reverence there.

‣ Our prayers are in place of the offerings.

‣ Respect for the shul enables us to connect to Hashem.

frame of mind, our mood, and our thoughts become receptive to the Shechinah's Presence. At that point, we have shown Hashem a sincere effort. We have opened a small opening in our hearts, and Hashem will help us do the rest.

OUT OF HIDING

*I*t is difficult to conceive of any Jew in the days of the First Temple having difficulty perceiving the Shechinah's Presence. It manifested Itself in countless daily miracles that everyone could clearly see. Today, however, it is difficult to conceive of the Shechinah Itself; it seems to have gone into hiding.

The Rambam[1] teaches, " In the *Beis HaMikdash* and Jerusalem the original holiness remains forever ... because ... of the *Shechinah* which never ceases." Yet, in *Shemoneh Esrei* we pray for the return of the *Shechinah* with the words, "hamachzir Shechinaso le'Tzion" — *(Hashem) will return His Shechinah to Zion.* Based on the Rambam's teaching, this prayer would seem to be superfluous.

Aruch LaNer[2] resolves this difficulty by explaining that the Second *Bais HaMikdash* lacked five aspects that were present in the First *Beis HaMikdash*;[3] one of these was the *Shechinah.* However, this was not a total absence; rather, the absolute awareness of the *Shechinah* felt in the First *Beis HaMikdash* was replaced by a lesser manifestation in the Second. We pray daily for Hashem to restore the *Shechinah* to Its previous peak of glory with the coming of Mashiach.

In our times, the *Shechinah* is even less apparent; as the Gemara[4] states, the *Shechinah* is in exile with the Jewish nation. These are times of *hester panim*, meaning that Hashem's face is "hidden." Under this circumstance, recognizing His Presence (e.g., His overseeing of our daily lives) becomes a far greater challenge. Our difficulty in connecting with the *Shechinah*, even as we stand in a holy place speaking words of prayer, is one more painful aspect of exile.

7 Cheshvan

8 Shevat

7 Iyar

8 Av

---

1. *Hilchos Beis HaBechirah* 6:16.
2. *She'eilos U'Teshuvos Binyan Tzion, Siman* 3.
3. *Yoma* 21b.
4. *Megillah* 29a.

▸ *Difficulty in
connecting
to the
Shechinah,
even in holy
places during
prayer, is a
facet of exile.*

▸ *Hashem's
constant
Presence is
apparent
in His
protection of
the Jewish
people
throughout
history's
persecutions.*

▸ *Perceiving
Hashem in
our daily
lives is a
means by
which we
can come to
know before
Whom we
stand in
prayer.*

In reality, history provides ample testimony of Hashem's constant supervision. Throughout the ages, we have suffered at the hands of enemies who detest us, and even today, the world lends support to those who seek to destroy us, Heaven forbid. Thus, the survival of the Jewish people is itself ample proof that we benefit from Hashem's special protection. As *Chazal*[5] say, "Hashem loves *Klal Yisrael* simply because they are *Klal Yisrael*; even though [we] sinned, [we are] still Yisrael."

As Hashem promised,[6] *But also, even though there is (punishment) ... I will not hate them nor will I reject them to destroy them, to cancel My covenant with them, for I am Hashem their G-d.*

Historic evidence notwithstanding, human nature seems to demand a more personal method of developing a recognition of Hashem in our daily lives, especially when we pray. The *Mesillas Yesharim*[7] suggests: "When you pray, know before Whom you are praying, and that you are really standing before the Creator, His Name should be blessed. Although no eyes have seen Hashem, and it appears very difficult to have a genuine picture in a person's heart, and the senses do not assist in this at all, surely, one who has the proper understanding and intellect, with some observation and insight, is able to establish in his heart the truth of the matter, and he can come to actually connect with Hashem."

With these words to guide us, we can go forward into our daily lives with a new purpose — perceiving, absorbing, appreciating, and responding to the thousands of ways Hashem reveals Himself to us. By doing that, we will know and feel before Whom we stand.

---

5. *Sanhedrin* 44a. See *Daas Tevunos, Siman* 160, p. 181, s.v. *V'heenei.*
6. *Vayikra* 26:44
7. Ch. 19, *Chelkei HaChassidus.*

100 PERCENT
SPIRITUALITY

*E*ven a person who is burning with a desire for spiritual growth has to wonder: Can I find Hashem here in this office, behind a keyboard? On a highway full of fumes and noise? In a sink full of dirty dishes?

The *Mesillas Yesharim's* advice to "establish in his heart the truth of the matter and ... actually connect with Hashem" would seem simpler to follow if a person could live in a world of peace, surrounded only by spirituality, kindness, and beauty.

Yet David HaMelech, whose life was rife with war, betrayal, and pain, sought a continuous connection with Hashem from the midst of his all-too-real life struggles:[1] *One thing I ask of Hashem, and that is what I seek: that I may dwell in the House of Hashem all the days of my life.*

How could David HaMelech, let alone any ordinary individual, really seek to dwell in the House of Hashem *all the days* of his life? What time does that leave for the day-to-day routines — earning a livelihood, caring for children, sleeping, eating, and all the other mundane tasks that fill our days?

The Gemara[2] states: "What is a short verse upon which all the fundamentals of Torah depend? It is:[3] *In all your ways you must know Him, and He will straighten your paths.* The Rambam[4] maintains that *In all your ways you must know Him* teaches that all of one's activities must be

8 Cheshvan

9 Shevat

8 Iyar

9 Av

---

1. *Tehillim* 27:4.
2. *Berachos* 63a.
3. *Mishlei* 3:6.
4. *Hilchos Dei'os* 3:2-3.

performed for the sake of Heaven. This means that when one is occupied with any mundane physical activity, such as eating, drinking, sleeping, household chores, or even engaging in business, he must act with the intention to serve Hashem.

Rav Dessler explains that working toward our material needs is not an activity outside "the House of Hashem" when we acquire these Heavenly gifts as "tools" to help us in our pursuit of sanctity.[5]

Indeed, *Chazal* refer to the table of a Torah scholar as a *mizbe'ach*, altar, because his meal can be compared to an offering brought in the Holy Temple.[6] This is because the Torah scholar regards food to be used for spirituality, so he eats to gain strength to be able to learn Torah and to do mitzvos.[7]

The words of the *Ben Yehoyada* further illuminate this concept:[8] *In all your ways you must know Him* is a great rule in the Torah, for even when involved in material matters, one's purpose should be for the sake of Hashem. And this is what David HaMelech meant when he said:[9] *'I will walk before Hashem in the land of the living.'* At all times, I perceive myself before Hashem, even while standing in the marketplace, since my sole intention is to serve Him.

On our own level, we can strive to see ourselves as standing in Hashem's Presence — even when buying food in the supermarket — since all of our material possessions can be tools with which to serve Him. With this new perspective, the everyday details of our lives are transformed

---

5. *Michtav MeEliyahu*, Vol. 1, pp. 5-6. Also see *Rambam, Hilchos Teshuvah* 9:1.

6. See *Berachos* 55a and *Mesillas Yesharim*, Ch. 26. See also *Rama, Siman* 167, *Se'if* 5, "It is a mitzvah to bring salt onto all tables before one breaks [the bread], for the table is analogous to the Altar and eating to an offering, and it is stated, *With all your offerings you should offer salt.*"

7. See *Mishnah Berurah, Siman* 167, *Se'if Katan* 31, which states that eating is analogous to an offering "since a person eats in order to fortify his strength, so that he will have the health and vitality to serve Hashem."

8. *Yoma* 71a, s.v. *Es'haleich lifnei Hashem.*

9. *Tehillim* 116:9.

from possible detours on our spiritual journey into essential parts of the engine that get us where our souls want to go.

Points to Ponder

▸ *David HaMelech expresses the desire to live in constant connection with Hashem.*

▸ *Material benefits that one pursues in order to serve Hashem strengthen one's spiritual connection to Hashem.*

WITH JUST A THOUGHT

*F*rom there (the midst of exile) *you will seek Hashem, your G-d, and you will find Him, if you search for Him with all your heart and all your soul,* the Torah promises.[1] The words "from there," according to the Baal Shem Tov, indicate that Hashem meets a person at his own level, provided that the person is seeking Him.[2]

As we learned previously, one who is seeking Hashem can find Him, even in the details of everyday life. The mind-set with which one approaches his tasks in life is an important aspect that distinguishes a person who feels connected to Hashem from one who cannot move past the physical, material demands of living.

> The Chofetz Chaim once expressed his great envy to a pharmacist regarding his occupation, which gave him myriad opportunities each day to dispense medication and thereby save lives. The pharmacist rejected the praise, confessing that his real purpose was not saving lives, but rather, earning a living. The Chofetz Chaim advised him that he should not waste the great spiritual potential of his profession. "When you dispense medication," he advised, "do so with the intention that 'I am fulfilling a mitzvah of chesed (kindness) and saving lives.' Earning a profit does not devalue the mitzvah, as long as you have the proper intentions."
>
> The pharmacist followed the Chofetz Chaim's advice. He became an important communal leader whose guidance was eagerly sought.

9 Cheshvan

10 Shevat

9 Iyar

10 Av

---

1. *Devarim* 4:29.
2. Cited in *Living Each Day — Tishrei-Cheshvan* by Rabbi Abraham J. Twerski, M.D. (ArtScroll/Mesorah Publ.), p. 19.

Years later, he acknowledged that the merit of the intentions of chesed with which he performed his responsibilities as a pharmacist earned him his special status.[3]

Why do one's thoughts have such power?

It is because they derive their strength from the place of their origin — the *neshamah*, soul, which is the highest level of the human spirit. The *neshamah* is both the source of a person's thoughts and the part of him that strives to connect to Hashem; in fact, it is derived from Hashem's Heavenly Spirit.[4] As the Rambam writes,[5] "Wisdom and intellect are from Hashem and they are the link binding humans to Hashem." The brain is the part of the human body that is said to provide a home for the *neshamah*.[6] As Rav Dessler comments,[7] "The thoughts (of a person) personify the person."

This makes "thought" the most powerful spiritual force in existence for mankind, capable of transforming a chore into a mitzvah, and elevating the rote performance of a mitzvah into a more sacred act.

When a person dons *tefillin* or sits in a *succah* without any consciousness of serving Hashem, his mitzvah is "a body without a soul."

Moreover, even if a person has only the will to perform a mitzvah — it exists solely in his thoughts — but he is prevented from performing it, he is considered to have fulfilled the mitzvah.[8]

Our thoughts are a two-way channel. Through our *neshamah*, our minds can receive the electrifying spiritual energy that Hashem radiates into our world. And through our *neshamah*, Hashem can receive the love and devotion in our hearts.

Once a person feels, even to a small degree, the spiritual power that surges through this channel, he will strive to

---

3. *Kuntres Chaim V'Chesed*, p. 9; *Derech Sichah*, p. 26.
4. *Michtav MeEliyahu*, Vol. 5, p. 195.
5. *Moreh Nevuchim*, Vol. 3, Ch. 51.
6. *Sefer HaZikaron L'Baal Michtav MeEliyahu*, Vol. 2, p. 139.
7. Ibid. p. 116.
8. *Kiddushin* 40a.

remove all obstacles and keep it open, bringing his prayer to new heights of power.[9]

---

9. *Sefer HaZikaron L'Baal Michtav MeEliyahu*, Vol. 2, p. 146; *Michtav MeEliyahu*, Vol. 5, p. 195. Also see *Derech Chaim, Torah*, p. 96, which states that when a person increases his involvement in learning Torah and performing mitzvos, he will come closer to Hashem, thus enabling him to beseech Hashem with *kavannah*.

THE DEEP SLEEP

*O*ne can look at a newborn, relish the beauty of a sunset, experience the amazing capability of an up-to-date computer, place a call to a loved one 6,000 miles away while riding in a car, hop on a jet and deplane the same day on the other side of the globe, and still not see evidence of Hashem. It is as if his soul is asleep.

10
Cheshvan

11
Shevat

10
Iyar

11
Av

This spiritually comatose state has unfortunately become almost the norm in modern times. It is no coincidence that this development has coincided with many fabulous breakthroughs in medicine, technology, and the sciences. Rav Dessler[1] explains that Hashem has facilitated these discoveries because as spirituality declines, He allows more of the world's secrets (i.e., medical, technological, and scientific advances) to be revealed: "You see, the [great] secrets of creation are revealed for everyone to think about, and anyone who is disposed to observe and ponder a little is compelled to draw near to belief [in Hashem]."

Nonetheless, while Hashem puts the wonders of creation on display, even the people who are best equipped to comprehend the amazing complexity of it all — the physicians, researchers, and scientists — fail to see the hand of the Creator. No matter how miraculous a development people witness, they are quick to categorize it as "a part of nature."[2]

To illustrate this mind-set, Rav Dessler[3] contrasts perceptions of the "natural" growth of crops with the "mirac-

---

1. *Michtav MeEliyahu*, Vol. 5, p. 273.
2. *Sefer HaZikaron L'Baal Michtav MeEliyahu*, Vol. 2, p. 124; *Michtav MeEliyahu*, Vol. 5, p. 24. See also *Chochmah U'Mussar*, Vol. 1, p. 165, s.v. *V'agaleh lachem.*
3. *Michtav MeEliyahu*, Vol. 1, p. 177.

Points to Ponder

▸ In general, people are inured to miracles of nature that speak of Hashem's Presence.

▸ Life's difficulties awaken us to Hashem's overseeing of our lives.

ulous" resurrection of the dead: "We are not accustomed to the resurrection of the dead, yet [we are accustomed] to the everyday growth of produce; if only it would be the opposite, we would call the resurrection of the dead, nature, and the growth of produce … a wondrous miracle."

With this in mind, Rav Dessler[4] proposes that just as a field must be plowed before it is planted, an emotional awakening — resulting from either affliction or joy — is needed in order to open up a closed heart and to then plant seeds of change.

David HaMelech was forced to wander in uninhabited areas, hiding from his enemies who chased him incessantly. His fugitive life caused him to long for normalcy — for the ability to walk undaunted among people in the streets and marketplace. From this longing arose the words,[5] "Es'halech lifnei Hashem b'artzos ha'chaim" — *I will go before Hashem in the lands of the living.* The Gemara[6] explains that "the lands of the living" refers to the marketplace, an area where a person can readily obtain all his needs. Since David HaMelech was deprived of this basic privilege, he felt compelled to pray to Hashem for it.

For any longing or need that arises in the human heart, the answer is the same. A person must first recognize, in the depths of his soul, that there is only one Source for all that he wants and needs. Once he has made that concept real to himself, he is equipped to turn to Hashem to seek the help that only He can give.

---

4. Ibid. Vol. 5, p. 12. See also *Sefer HaZikaron L'Baal Michtav MeEliyahu,* Vol. 2, p. 149.
5. *Tehillim* 116:9.
6. *Yoma* 71a.

A RUDE AWAKENING

For those who find the comforts of a warm, soft bed to be a little too alluring, being "awakened" by Hashem may not seem to be much of a kindness. Both figuratively and literally, there are those who would rather be left to slumber undisturbed, existing happily in their own dream world. Nonetheless, Hashem's wake-up call is indeed the greatest kindness, for without this awakening, Hashem cannot begin to lavish upon a person the other benefits He has in store. Even the most forgiving king will not reward his servant if the servant refuses to get out of bed and attend to his job.

The beautiful *tefillah*, *Nishmas Kol Chai*, which is recited at the completion of *Pesukei D'Zimrah* every Shabbos morning, demonstrates the kindness inherent in the often unpleasant circumstances Hashem uses to wake us up. "Ha'meorer yeshaynim, v'ha'meikitz nirdamim, v'ha'maysiach illmim, v'ha'matir asurim, v'ha'someich noflim, v'ha'zokef kefufim" —*[Hashem] Who awakens the sleeping, alerts the drowsing, heals the mutes, releases the prisoners, supports the fallen, and straightens the bent ones.* Clearly, the mute, the prisoner, the fallen, and the bent ones appreciate the kindness that Hashem does when He alleviates their plights. Far less clear is the inclusion of "the sleeping" and "the drowsing," who are not usually seen as tragedies in need of Divine remediation, at the top of this list.

Metaphorically, "sleeping" and "drowsing" refer to people who are spiritually asleep.[1] The other plights listed in the *tefillah* comprise various means Hashem may use to rouse the sleeping person. An individual may encounter illness, a sense of imprisonment in his life's situation, a

---

1. See *Rambam, Hilchos Teshuvah* 3:4.

▸ *People
who are
spiritually
asleep are
sometimes
comfortable
in their state
and do not
wish to be
awakened.*

▸ *The tefillah
Nishmas Kol
Chai, which
recounts
Hashem's
kindness,
includes
the act of
awakening
those
who are
spiritually
asleep.*

▸ *Until a
person
"wakes up"
spiritually
and acknow-
ledges
Hashem, his
difficulties
may not be
alleviated.*

fall from high status, or burdens that bend his back with strain. All of these are, among other things, Hashem's efforts to awaken the "sleeping" and alert the "drowsing" so that they may ultimately recognize and connect to Him.

Having succeeded in prompting the person to awaken — to examine his life and wholeheartedly turn to Hashem, He may then alleviate the hardships that burden the individual. As the *tefillah* conveys, the awakening comes first, followed by the healing, the support, and the relief for those who are bent with strain.

> *When a mother comes to wake her child for school in the morning, she knows she is about to wrench him from his peaceful, warm cocoon. Out of her love for the child, she wishes she could let him lie there comfortably until his eyes open on their own. Nevertheless, there is much to accomplish and no time to lose. She wakes up the child, and that is an expression of an even deeper love.*

A LITTLE SHAKE

*T*hey did not always arrive happy and they did not always arrive fully alert, but counselor Moshe's bunk arrived at Shacharis on time every day of the camp season. "First he sticks his head in the door and sings a loud wake-up song," one of his campers related to his friends. "The next time he comes in, if you're not up, he pulls off your blanket. The next time, he comes in and dumps cold water on your head. Anyone who is still in bed five minutes after that gets the mattress pulled out from under him." The wise camper would obviously get out of bed at the sound of the first blast of music.

The counselor's technique is loosely adapted from the pattern set by Hashem in awakening the Jewish souls that He so closely and lovingly supervises. Often times, Hashem does not begin the process with a "rude awakening," but rather, with "a little shake." It comes in the form of life's small frustrations and inconveniences. One of its purposes is to cause a person to look around and feel that Hashem is there. These frustrations rattle one's assumption that things flow smoothly on their own, alerting a person to the need to acknowledge Hashem for the myriad details He oversees for him each moment of his life.[1]

The Gemara[2] teaches: "One does not stub his toe on earth, unless this was first declared upon him from (Heaven) Above."[3] The seemingly insignificant occurrences

Sidebar dates:
- 12 Cheshvan
- 13 Shevat
- 12 Iyar
- 13 Av

---

1. See *Chochmah U'Mussar*, Vol. 1, p. 165, s.v. *V'agaleh lachem*.
2. *Chullin* 7b.
3. See *Tosafos, Niddah* 16b. Also see *Sefer HaChinuch*, Mitzvah 546 (*Mitzvas Maakeh*). While this does not exempt a person from taking standard precautions to avoid injury and illness, we should pay attention to the minor, commonplace pains and frustrations that we experience daily.

**Points
to
Ponder**

▸ *In His effort
to awaken
us, Hashem
attempts
to "shake
us up"
using minor
frustrations.*

▸ *When we
perceive
Hashem's
message
in these
frustrations,
they bring
us closer to
Him.*

which tend to frustrate a person make it obvious that one
has no real control over his life. They force a person into
an instant understanding of Who is actually in control.
Each individual has the opportunity to reorient himself
to this reality through an endless variety of incidents that
might otherwise elicit nothing more than a slammed fist
or a sharp word. Consider what a person's standard response would be to some of these situations:

▸ You repeatedly try to send a fax and it will not go
through.
▸ You are about to rush off to an appointment when you
notice that your car has a flat tire.
▸ You are at a Shabbos Bar Mitzvah *seudah* and your
neighbor accidentally knocks a glass of soda into your
lap.
▸ You stand at the baggage carousel in the airport watching as everyone but you claims his luggage.
▸ Along with four other cars, you drive through a yellow
light, and only you are pulled over for a summons.

These are the small trials in life, "the little shake." When
a person sees bad luck and persecution in them, he misses
the real message. It's a loving message, sent from Above,
that says, "Wake up. I'm here for you." [4]

---

4. Also see *Sichos Mussar* (Rav Chaim Shmulevitz), *Shaarei Chaim,
Maamar* 18, p. 77, "*Chavivim Yissurim*" (5732, *Maamar* 14).

A LITTLE SHAKE, PART II

While one naturally turns to Hashem when desperate needs arise, doing so in response to smaller frustrations may generally not be the norm. However, a person who learns to awaken to Hashem's "little shake" can use these opportunities to feel Hashem's Presence and improve the quality of his life.

The "little shake" can be very little indeed. The Gemara[1] seeks to define the parameters of the term "suffering" to understand how minute an inconvenience could fall within the definition. Rabbi Elazar says one could be said to be suffering if he has a garment woven for himself but it does not fit him properly. The Gemara[2] counters that the term covers frustrations "even smaller than that; if they intended to mix one's wine in hot water for him, but they mixed it in cold water," that is classified as suffering.

Other examples include putting on one's shirt the wrong way so that it needs to be removed and put on again, and extending one's hand into one's pocket to take out three coins, but withdrawing only two. The necessity of putting one's hand back into the pocket to retrieve the third coin qualifies as "suffering."

The Gemara[3] asks: "Why is it important to know all this?" The answer is, so that one can understand the application of these words: "Whoever goes forty days without suffering has received his eternal reward on this world." If a person experiences even minor inconveniences, as the above Gemara illustrates, he is considered to have suffered. He can be assured, therefore, that his eternal reward still awaits him.

13 Cheshvan

14 Shevat

13 Iyar

14 Av

---

1. *Arachin* 16b.
2. Ibid.
3. Ibid.

▸ *Small
annoyances
serve as a
reminder
that
Hashem's
blessing
is needed
in every
endeavor, no
matter how
small.*

▸ *To provide
atonement
for sin,
Hashem
sends small
doses of
frustration
that a
person can
endure,
rather than
larger, more
devastating
occurrences.*

▸ *Hashem's
"little
shakes" are
meant to
prod one to
a spiritual
awakening.*

Why must suffering be part of the equation at all? We learn[4] that every single deed a person commits has its Heavenly consequence. Hashem's accounting is absolutely precise and just, and neither a mitzvah nor a sin falls through the celestial cracks. However, Hashem knows that if a person were to bear the full brunt of his atonement in one massive dose, he would be laid so low that he could not rise up again. Instead of sending a boulder-sized affliction that would crush the individual, Hashem breaks the affliction into small pebbles — bearable aches and pains, mishaps and small misfortunes[5] — that ultimately serve the same purpose.

There is no human being who can live without suffering, for it is one of the means by which one is purified from sin, and as Shlomo HaMelech observes, sin is part of the human condition:[6] *For there is no man so righteous on earth that he only performs good and never sins.*

> *A toddler sits innocently on his father's lap in the waiting room of the doctor's office. Soon, his father carries him into the examining room, where he trustingly allows himself to be undressed and examined. Suddenly, the father grasps the child's tiny hands tightly, immobilizing his arms, as a nurse pricks him with a needle. The little boy begins to cry, looking with bewildered misery at his father, who has seemingly betrayed him and subjected him to this momentary sting. Just seconds later, however, the child is clinging to his father's shoulder for comfort. He cannot understand why his father had to do this to him, but he knows intuitively that this man — the one who holds him and plays with him and tells him bedtime stories — always loves him.*

---

4. See *Devarim* 32:4; *Bava Kamma* 50a; *Yam Shel Shlomo, Bava Kamma*, Ch. 5, *Siman* 23; *Mesillas Yesharim*, Ch. 4.
5. See *Maharsha, Shabbos* 77b s.v. *Mai taima*.
6. *Ecclesiastes* 7:20.

PREVENTIVE MEDICINE

T he annoying inconveniences that occur in every life, almost every day, also possess the power of a highly effective "preventive medicine." They can prompt a person to recognize Hashem's Presence in his life and prod him to pray each day with a sense of urgency, for important matters may also be in jeopardy at any given moment. This message of the small frustrations is that one must always turn to Hashem in prayer, for His blessings are constantly needed to maintain a happy, healthy life.

The Gemara[1] advises us: "A person should always ask for mercy from G-d that he not become ill, for should he in fact become ill, [the Heavenly Tribunal], as it were, says to him: 'Bring us a merit and you will be set free.'" As long as a person is in good health he does not require a special merit to remain healthy. However, should he become ill, he will return to good health only if he has a persuasive basis for his improvement.

Once illness, poverty, family discord, or other difficulty sets in, one requires far greater merit to repair the situation than he would have required to simply avoid it in the first place. However, one who prays to be spared from troubles before they have even occurred builds the most effective barrier possible between himself and the gravest difficulties. Salvation is far easier to achieve before the affliction arrives.[2]

As the Ritva[3] advises: "When one needs to annul a judgment [against the person], one requires more prayer and

---

1. *Shabbos* 32a.
2. See *Beis Elokim L'HaMabit, Shaar Ha'Tefillah,* Ch. 12, s.v. *U'maalas kedimas hatefillah* for an additional reason why prayer is more effective before a *tzarah* occurs.
3. *Berachos* 5b.

supplication. However, when it is prior to a decree one does not require as much in the way of prayer."

This is the implication in the words of Iyov's friend when he asks:[4] *Did you arrange your prayer so that no trouble befall you?* The question conveys an answer: Had Iyov prayed to Hashem to show mercy to his family and spare his belongings before his troubles began, the troubles that caused him so much anguish might not have materialized.[5]

Chazal[6] advise that "*l'olam yakdim adam tefillah l'tzarah*" — a person should attempt to pray before trouble occurs [to prevent it from occurring]. The Gemara[7] presents an example of the efficacy of this type of prayer, citing the *tefillah* Avraham prayed when he was situated between Beth El and Ai.[8] This was the venue of the confrontation, many generations later, between Joshua and the forces of Ai. Had Avraham not prayed when he did, the Gemara states, there would have been no survivor from Israel in this battle, Heaven forbid.

If one knew in advance what great challenges lay ahead, praying in advance to prevent them would be a simple matter. Under normal circumstances, however, how does one pray to avert difficulties he cannot even see on the horizon?

A person does not need the ability to predict the future; he only need internalize the understanding that everything is given to him by Hashem moment by moment. Even the aspects of life that are in perfect working order today may fall into disrepair in a day or even in a moment. Yet, one's prayers have the power to prevent unforeseen developments from occurring. In the words of the *Meiri*,[9] "A person should run after prayer constantly, and not only

---

4. *Iyov* 36:19.
5. See *Rashi, Sanhedrin* 44b, s.v. *Hayaaroch.*
6. *Sanhedrin* 44b.
7. Ibid.
8. *Bereishis* 12:8, and see *Rashi* ibid. s.v. *Va'yeeven shom mizbe'ach,* who writes that Avraham prayed where his descendants would be faced with potential devastation because of the sin of Achan.
9. *Sanhedrin* 44b.

in time of trouble but every day, as it says 'l'olam yakdim adam tefillah l'tzarah.'"

Not only can prayer protect one's personal life, but for the Jewish people as a whole, prayers offered in times of tranquility can protect against the tragedies that might in the future befall the nation. Jewish history has proven that the tide can change quickly, turning a Golden Age into an Inquisition, an exile, or a Holocaust. One need not stretch his imagination to understand that even our daily security is a matter requiring constant, ardent prayer.

The Satmar Rebbe writes:[10] "All the afflictions that the Jewish nation has endured during *chevlei Mashiach*, the birth pangs of Mashiach ... had they [the Jewish nation] preceded their troubles with prayer, perhaps they would have been answered and spared in the merit of prayer which is *accepted even more* when offered *before* trouble occurs."

If a person is wise enough to heed the smaller frustrations in life as the loving message of a Father reminding His children of their sacred relationship, he will respond to the message by praying with the necessary sense of urgency. In doing so, he can prevent further, more disturbing reminders from entering his life.

To avoid being buffeted by the harsh winds Heaven can generate, one must learn to respond to the gentle breezes.

10. *Divrei Yoel, Parashas Shemos*, p. 60.

Points to Ponder

▸ One who heeds the message of the minor difficulties in life may avoid the necessity of greater afflictions.

▸ It is easier to avert difficulties by praying in advance, than to achieve salvation from troubles that have already occurred.

15 Cheshvan

16 Shevat

15 Iyar

16 Av

*T*he birth was over. The baby was cleaned and wrapped in a soft cotton blanket, and the nurse placed the child in his mother's arms. *She was spent but elated — the exhausted winner of a marathon. She gazed into the child's eyes and marveled that, only hours earlier, this person was a mystery, more a part of herself than a distinct, unique human being. "Nice to meet you," she told him softly, thinking of all the possibilities embedded in this tiny human being.*

Observing his perfect little features, she began to realize — nine months of development, countless stages of growth, chemicals, hormones, and molecules had all blended and balanced correctly. The perils of childbirth had been safely traversed, with mother and baby alive and well. Countless details could have gone wrong, but instead, they went right. She could think of only one response, David HaMelech's response, "Give thanks to Hashem for He is good; His kindness endures forever."[1]

As explained earlier,[2] a person may not change unless his heart is open. Both joy and affliction are tools Hashem uses to prepare the heart to accept the seeds of change. For those who find their connection to Hashem through joy — through gratitude and love for the Source of goodness in their lives — the need to experience suffering is lessened. Those who choose to keep their eyes open to Hashem's kindness will find it everywhere.

The physical world of nature is one vivid expression of Hashem's kindness that can, according to Rav Dessler[3]

---

1. *Tehillim* 118:1.
2. See Day 40, "The Deep Sleep."
3. *Michtav MeEliyahu*, Vol. 5, p. 12.

open the heart to spiritual growth. The medium does not have to be the great, sweeping miracles of nature, either. It can be in something as simple as food and drink. For example, wine and delicacies play an important role in Yom Tov observance because these pleasures provide a physical vehicle for the soul's expression of joy.

The Torah[4] tells us that when Jews made the pilgrimage to the Holy Temple during the three annual festivals, they were enjoined not to *appear before Me empty-handed* and were required to bring an *"olas re'iyah,"* (a special elevation-offering of appearance) in honor of the occasion.

There would seem to be no need to require such an offering, because a visit to the Holy Temple was in itself an unparalleled spiritual uplift. There, one could see with his own eyes the revelation of the *Shechinah*, along with a host of other patent miracles. Rav Dessler[5] explains that the offering was in fact necessary, because a person needs to "do something" in order to turn inspiration into something real and enduring in his heart.[6]

Rav Dessler further comments: "The objective of creation is action," as the Torah, in describing the process of creation, states:[7] ... *Which Hashem created to make.* Rav Dessler continues: Not only are one's great actions a benefit to him, but also his small actions.[8]

In our daily lives, we are all blessed with good fortune, great and small, and thus subconsciously recognize that every blessing comes from Hashem. To establish that realization in our heart, we must turn it into action, which can (at a minimum) be in the form of saying two simple words: *"Baruch Hashem."*

The following examples warrant a heartfelt *"Baruch Hashem."*

▸ You are sending a fax, and it goes through on the first try.
▸ On your way to an important appointment, you get into the car and arrive without difficulty.

---

4. *Shemos* 34:20.
5. *Michtav MeEliyahu*, Vol. 5, pp. 29, 453.
6. *Sefer HaZikaron L'Baal Michtav MeEliyahu*, Vol. 2, p. 39.
7. *Bereishis* 2:3.
8. *Sefer HaZikaron L'Baal Michtav MeEliyahu*, Vol. 2, p. 40.

▸ At a Shabbos Bar Mitzvah, a glass of soda tips over and narrowly misses spilling into your lap.

▸ Your luggage is among the first bags to roll onto the conveyor belt at the airport's baggage claim.

Even potential frustrations that do not occur can, and should be, reason to feel blessed. Saying *"Baruch Hashem"* helps build a lasting sense in one's heart that Hashem is watching him, sparing him frustration, and smoothing his way.

When we train our eyes to see the kindness and good Hashem constantly grants us, we cannot help but be filled with gratitude and love. Our natural instinct, like the mother holding her newborn child, is to pray with feelings of gratitude and to sing the praises to Hashem overflowing in our hearts.[9]

---

9. *Rambam, Hilchos Yesodei HaTorah* 2:2.

CHAPTER 6:
THIRTEEN PRACTICAL STRATEGIES TO ACHIEVE KAVANNAH

16
Cheshvan

17
Shevat

16
Iyar

17
Av

etween knowing and feeling lies an ocean. Anyone who has given even a little thought to the concept of prayer knows that it is a conversation with the Almighty. Anyone who has pondered the concept of the Almighty knows that He is a King before Whom a person must stand in utter awe. Nonetheless, even with that knowledge, many people are perfectly capable of speaking the sacred words of *tefillah*, specifically the *Shemoneh Esrei*, without feeling a thing. We become expert at the mind-boggling feat of mouthing prayers while thinking about anything from the dinner menu to the weather.

Why — when we want to pray correctly, when we want to pray effectively, when we understand what all this means — is it still so frustratingly difficult?

Some comfort might be taken in the knowledge that this is a challenge of very long standing. The Gemara[1] states that the one sin an average person commits every day is *Iyun Tefillah*, which, according to *Tosafos*[2] and the Maharal,[3] refers to a lack of *kavannah* during *davening*.

Nevertheless, the requirement for *kavannah* still stands; a key axiom of the Torah says that Hashem does not demand the impossible, and therefore, *kavannah* must be within our reach. According to Rav Yehudah HaChassid[4] there is no single "magic formula"; each person must implement the ideas that attract him, based on his desires and abilities.

According to Rav Dessler, in general, when setting goals, a person should set a "minimum" and a "maximum" goal.

---

1. *Bava Basra* 164b.
2. Ibid. s.v. *Iyun tefillah*.
3. *Chidushei Aggados* ibid.
4. *Sefer Chassidim, Siman* 784.

The minimum goals give him a greater opportunity to gain strength from success, while the maximum goals give him a vision toward which to strive.[5] Rav Dessler[6] reminds us that a person who wants to succeed in climbing the spiritual ladder should set an initial goal to reach the spiritual height that is closest to his current level of free will; with a realistic goal in sight, he will have the motivation to climb to the next step.

A person must be able to envision himself clearly at the level toward which he is striving, Rav Dessler[7] adds. He must feel that it is relevant to him, that he is already connected to this level. Otherwise, he is setting himself up for despair. He is like a clerk who decides he will strive to become president of the multinational corporation for which he works. He would gain far more momentum for his climb if he first set his sights on the senior clerk's position.

As in every attempt at self-improvement, the key is to make a modicum of effort, and Hashem will help with the rest. To capitalize on even the smallest effort, however, it must be rooted in a sincere desire to change. This single factor is what distinguishes those who are able to improve themselves from those who spend a lifetime spinning their wheels.

The crucial factor of internal motivation is noted in the Gemara[8] when Reish Lakish states: "Self-reproach in the heart of a person is better than one hundred lashes, as it is stated:[9] *The humbleness from reproach is more evident in an understanding man than a hundred lashes in a fool.* Modern psychology heeds this truth in dealing with many types of emotional ills. Despite the plethora of techniques available to treat people's distress, it is recognized that success depends not on any specific technique, but on the person's resolve to change. Only when this is achieved can techniques be useful in treatment.

---

5. *Sefer HaZikaron L'Baal Michtav MeEliyahu*, Vol. 2, p. 155.
6. *Michtav MeEliyahu*, Vol. 1, Introduction, p. 24.
7. *Michtav MeEliyahu*, Vol. 5, p. 375.
8. *Berachos* 7a.
9. *Proverbs* 17:10.

▸ *One might
understand
that he
should have
kavannah
and still
have
difficulty
feeling the
need.*

▸ *A real
resolve to
change
is most
important
in changing
oneself.*

▸ *Techniques
for change
can assist
a person
who has the
resolve.*

Rav Dessler[10] suggests that before improvements can
be implemented, amends must be made for the past. Rejection of past habits, he explains, is the workman's tool
for spiritual growth. Moreover, the degree of this rejection
— which must be strong in order to last — influences and
creates the degree of change. This step, although perhaps
difficult, is necessary to achieving meaningful *tefillah*.

Rav Dessler[11] reassures us that when striving to reach
a worthwhile goal, a person will willingly work hard to
achieve it regardless of the obstacles that he may face.
Tefillah is a most worthwhile goal.

---

10. *Michtav MeEliyahu*, Vol. 5, p. 241.
11. Ibid. Vol. 1, p. 20, s.v. *Hinei*.

ONE RUNG AT A TIME

*I*t was 1991, just one day before the fiery opening bomb-blasts of the Gulf War. Dayan Aharon D. Dunner asked Rav Shach, "What should we tell the people of America, England, and Europe to do? They want to do teshuvah — they want to do something!"

"Tell them to make small and meaningful pledges that they will keep for the next three months," Rav Shach replied. He himself undertook for that period of time a commitment to recite Bircas HaMazon from a siddur (or bentcher) when dining at home.[1]

17
Cheshvan

18
Shevat

17
Iyar

18
Av

Why did Rav Shach advise such seemingly minor commitments to meet the peril of imminent war? Rav Dessler[2] explains that this is the true path toward growth. One cannot leap from a superficial level of spirituality and expect to land with secure footing upon the peaks of the profound. A successful climb entails small degrees of development each day, which carry one to higher and higher levels.

> Spiritual growth can be compared to ascending a mountain in a wagon. As long as there is forward movement — even if progress is marked by spurts and stops — the wagon is still considered to be advancing. However, if the wagon stops straining forward, it will not stand still; it will slide back down the slope.

Chazal teach that "*maaseh avos siman le'banim*"[3] — the actions of our Patriarchs are a model for the children. Yaa-

---

1. *Listen to Your Messages* by Rabbi Yissocher Frand (ArtScroll/ Mesorah Publ.), p. 142.
2. *Michtav MeEliyahu*, Vol. 5, p. 196.
3. See *Ramban, Lech Lecha* 12:6.

kov Avinu, a paradigm of truth, was shown "a ladder stationed on the ground with its head (the top rung) reaching the heavens" as a symbol of his life's task, to demonstrate that one cannot successfully ascend the spiritual ladder in one stride.[4] In our service of Hashem as well, a person must complete the tasks required by each level of growth; it is not possible to reach the top rung in one huge leap.

Rav Chaim Volozhin[5] explains this concept with a parable:

> A master who asks his servant to fetch an item from the attic will not be angry when the servant does not leap from the bottom rung of the ladder straight to the top. He understands that his servant can ascend the ladder only one step at a time.

Our Master is not disheartened by our slow progress in climbing the ladder to better *tefillah*; neither should we lose patience with ourselves. Every small step that we successfully take toward our goal is not just a pause upon a new, higher level; it is a springboard that energizes our continuing climb.

The Torah states,[6] *And These words that I have commanded you today shall lie on your heart.* The Rabbi of Kotzk explains the particular choice of words in the *pasuk* as follows:[7]

> Intellectual knowledge is similar to water that accumulates behind a wall. Eventually, the water will soften the wall and a crack will emerge, allowing all the water to surge through.

Even if the "words" learned about *kavannah* lie only on the surface of the heart, it is worthwhile to learn them, because at some moment in the future, a minuscule crack will emerge, and through it, all the accumulated wisdom will flow into the heart.

---

4. *Michtav MeEliyahu*, Vol. 1, p. 25. It is for this reason that Yaakov Avinu, upon awakening, immediately began to pray to Hashem.
5. *Ruach Chaim, Avos* 3:1.
6. *Devarim* 6:6.
7. Cited in *Living Each Day — Tishrei-Cheshvan* by Rabbi Abraham J. Twerski, M.D. (ArtScroll/Mesorah Publ.), p. 63.

Having laid that foundation, in the following days we will examine some practical strategies that can help a person pray with *kavannah*:

- Removing distractions (Day 48)
- Preparing oneself (Days 49 and 50)
- Actively approaching prayer (Day 51)
- Feeling need (Days 52 and 53)
- Understanding the words (Days 54 and 55)
- Praying from a *siddur* (Days 56 and 57)
- Mastering the mind — Controlling extraneous thoughts (Day 58)
- Changing negative habits (Days 59 and 60)
- Finding joy in prayer (Days 61 and 62)
- Feeling a sense of excitement (Days 63 and 64)
- Adding personal requests (Days 65 and 66)
- Designating a personal place (Days 67 and 68)
- Using visualization (Day 69)

Each of these methods offers a means to traverse the vast ocean that separates what we know about *tefillah* from what we feel as we pray. It is our desire to get to the other side, however, that guarantees the success of the voyage.

Points to Ponder

- *Spiritual growth must be approached in small, manageable steps in order to be successful and long-lasting.*

- *When we stop trying, we slide backwards rather than remain standing still.*

- *Hashem is patient with our step-by-step progress.*

STRATEGY 1:
QUIETING THE MIND

T he mind is never still. Either it focuses on the sounds and words spoken around a person, on the words he himself is speaking, or on the thoughts running through his head. Even in one's sleep, the mind is still busy producing words and images.

The first imperative for building concentration in prayer is get the chatter, both internal and external, to stop.

The necessity of blocking out distractions is illustrated in a discussion in the Gemara[1] of Hashem's Thirteen Attributes of Mercy. We learn that (as it were) Hashem, wrapped in a *tallis* as a *shaliach tzibbur*, a messenger of the congregation, passed before Moshe as he recited the Thirteen Attributes. Hashem told Moshe: When Israel sins, let them recite the Thirteen Attributes of Mercy before Me in this order and I will forgive them.

Through this episode, Hashem promises *Klal Yisrael* that their prayers for mercy will never be rejected when they recite the Thirteen Attributes. Rav Dessler[2] comments that Hashem wrapping Himself in a *tallis* as a *shaliach tzibbur* symbolizes the removal of all outside concerns — a crucial prerequisite to prayer.

If a person begins praying immediately upon entering the synagogue, his mind is often preoccupied by other thoughts. He is not settled, and consequently, he will be unable to concentrate properly and focus on his prayers.

It is not uncommon to "catch up on the news" by listening to the radio in the car. However, if a person does this on the way to shul, he may hear the news replaying in his head as he tries to pray. Perhaps the stock market dropped, or a political scandal has unfolded or — to

---

1. *Rosh Hashanah* 17b.
2. *Michtav MeEliyahu*, Vol. 5, p. 231.

his deepest chagrin — his favorite team has lost a big game. It is nearly impossible to digest such information, and then, minutes later, speak directly to Hashem.

For this reason Dayan Dunner of London advised his congregation several years ago not to listen to the radio on the way to shul.[3] With this simple, practical recommendation, he offered a prime example of something one can do toward removing the distractions that interfere with kavannah.

The *Shulchan Aruch*[4] recognizes the need for a person to reorient himself before praying. It rules that one should not hurry to pray immediately upon entering [*the beis haknesses*]; rather, "When a person enters a synagogue, he should walk into it a distance equal to the width of two doors and after that he may pray." As the *Mishnah Berurah*[5] explains, this to allow one to be settled and calm, and ready to pray with *kavannah*, "For when one begins to pray precipitously, immediately on entering, he is not yet composed."

The Rambam also advises in *Hilchos Tefillah*:[6] "How does one concentrate, and what constitutes proper intentions? One should empty his heart of all (foreign) thoughts and view himself as if standing in front of the *Shechinah*. Therefore, one must settle in a little before the *tefillah* in order to enable his heart to concentrate, and thereafter pray in peace and supplication."

This is an investment of just a few minutes, but they that establish the success of the entire venture. Like a diver who takes a few deep breaths before he goes underwater, one who pauses before immersing himself in *tefillah* will have what he needs to make the rest of the effort worthwhile.

Points to Ponder

▸ When appearing to Moshe wrapped in a tallis, Hashem demonstrated the need to isolate oneself from distractions during prayer.

▸ Pausing to reorient oneself and clear one's head helps a person to embark upon tefillah with concentration.

▸ Distractions prior to praying should be avoided.

---

3. As related by Dayan Dunner, speaker at Keynote Session, 5758 Convention of Agudath Israel of America.
4. *Siman* 90, *Se'if* 20.
5. Ibid. *Se'if Katan* 62.
6. 4:16.

STRATEGY 2: TAKE TIME TO PREPARE

*R*achel's future in-laws were coming to visit her parents' home. Rachel looked around the house and decided it was a complete embarrassment. "The curtains are dusty. The kitchen cabinets have fingerprints on them. There are piles of papers on every table and shelf. This is a disaster!"

Rachel dusted, polished, organized, and bought a huge bouquet of fresh flowers for the fireplace mantel. Her mother baked a wonderful variety of cakes, and her father purchased a bottle of fine schnapps. Meanwhile, Rachel's younger brother looked on in bewilderment. "You know, they're going to find out sooner or later that our house doesn't always look like this. I'll bet their house doesn't look like this either."

"No matter," his mother replied. "When you prepare for people, you make them feel important. How would they feel if they walked in and everything was flying? Like we didn't even care enough to make a good impression."

Preparation shows the value a person places on the event for which he is preparing. This is amply illustrated by the way in which many great scholars interrupted their studies to take part in preparations for Shabbos.

The Gemara tells us[1] that Rav Abba bought meat from thirteen butchers on Friday in order to have the finest selection available for Shabbos. Rav Abahu sat on a stool and fanned the fires used to cook the Shabbos meals. There are many more examples, both ancient and modern.

---

1. *Shabbos* 119a.

The *Mesillas Yesharim*[2] explains that by personally engaging in even the most ordinary of preparations, these *Amoraim* were displaying the ultimate love and respect for Shabbos. Moreover, any task of advance preparation for Shabbos — even purchasing meat or salting fish — is included in the actual mitzvah of *oneg Shabbos*.

In fact, every mitzvah requires careful preparation in order for one to perform it properly.[3] For example, it is customary to recite the words, "L'shem yichud kudsha," *For Your sake we set apart sacredness*, before performing a mitzvah. By taking the time to prepare, one demonstrates that the mitzvah is dear in his eyes, and certainly, it will then be performed with happiness and anticipation.

Similarly, Rav Dessler,[4] quoting Rav Yeruchem Levovitz, the Mirrer Mashgiach, points out that the essence of mitzvos and the wholeheartedness of their performance depend on the degree of preparation, which serves as a measure of the value that the person attributes to the mitzvah.

Preparing to pray not only shows Hashem that one values the opportunity to speak to Him; it instills in the person himself a sense of the importance of the occasion. It helps a person internalize what he knows to be true — that this is an opportunity not to be wasted.

Points to Ponder

▸ *Preparing for a mitzvah illustrates its importance to a person.*

▸ *Preparation is considered to be part of the mitzvah itself.*

▸ *A person who prepares for tefillah becomes attuned to its importance, and this enhances his kavannah.*

---

2. Ch. 19, *Chelkei HaChassidus*.
3. *Kedushas Levi, Parashas Beshalach.*
4. *Michtav MeEliyahu*, Vol. 5, p. 191.

DAY 50

| 20 Cheshvan |
| 21 Shevat |
| 20 Iyar |
| 21 Av |

Pausing to empty one's mind of foreign thoughts is the vital first step in preparing to pray. There is a second step as well, and that is to refill the mind with thoughts that arouse a person's longing to connect to Hashem. The Rambam[1] says that pausing before praying provides an opportunity to focus on the idea that one is about to stand in front of Hashem. Apparently, the Rambam is informing us of a *halachah* — that a person must prepare properly in order to have *kavannah.*

The spirit of this *halachah* would therefore be violated by arriving late for *Shacharis,* which results in no preparation time and a hasty struggle to don *tallis* and *tefillin;* [2] by arriving at the last minute to "catch a *Minchah*"; or by "flying" through *Maariv* in an effort to catch up. A late arrival simply rules out a properly prepared *tefillah.* [3]

The *Shulchan Aruch*[4] offers this guideline: "One must wait an hour, or at least a few moments,[5] before standing up to pray, in order to properly direct one's heart to Hashem."

> In 2001, several rabbis from the New York metropolitan area were granted a meeting with President George W. Bush. One rabbi later described the great amount of careful thought that went into preparing

---

1. *Hilchos Tefillah* 4:16.
2. *She'arim B'Tefillah,* p. 20.
3. See *Mishnah Berurah, Siman* 90, *Se'if Katan* 33, which states that a *chillul Hashem* may occur if the individual in question is a *talmid chacham* — i.e., one whom others look up to.
4. *Siman* 93, *Se'if* 1.
5. See *Mishnah Berurah* ibid. *Se'if Katan* 1, which states that "this requirement to wait one hour is only for the pious, but for the rest of the people it is sufficient if before they begin to pray they pause for a short period of time, which is the time it takes to walk eight handbreadths, as stated above in *Siman* 90, at the end of *Se'if* 20."

*meaningful remarks that could be conveyed to the
President in the few moments they had. Would only
a fraction of that preparation go into coming before
Hashem, one could not even imagine the massive increase in the power of the words of tefillah.*

If a person wishes to enhance his preparation in order
to improve upon his *kavannah*, there are techniques he
can develop. He might find it helpful to summon certain
thoughts, words, and images.

> *Rav Elimelech of Lizhensk would say the following
> words before entering the synagogue to pray: "Know
> where you are entering; what you will do there; Who
> is in this house; Whose house it is; and Who empow-
> ered you to enter this house."*[6]

Even in the midst of prayer, preparation is necessary. For
each of the *berachos* in *Shemoneh Esrei*, a person should
pause before *Baruch Atah Hashem* (at the end of the *berachah*) and think into the blessing he is about to recite.[7] For
example, before ending the *berachah* of "*binah*," understanding, one should reflect on the fact that Hashem is a
"*Chonein Hadaas*," *gracious Giver of knowledge.*[8]

> *The Chofetz Chaim wrote*[9] *that he personally used
> the following method of preparation: "Zimein li
> HaKadosh Baruch Hu k'tzas eitzah she'yesader be-
> daato heiteiv techilah mah ledaber — Hashem grant-*

---

6. Cited in *Nefesh Shimshon*, p. 35.
7. According to the *Baal HaTurim, Shemos* 40:33, the word *lev*, heart,
   in all its variations, appears in the Torah a total of 113 times; this is
   also the total number of words found in the final sentences of all
   the *berachos* of *Shemoneh Esrei* (e.g., "*Baruch Atah Hashem Magen
   Avraham*" is five words). From this connection, we learn that the
   concentration of our heart (*kavannah*) is what draws into our lives
   the many aspects of Hashem's goodness expressed by the *berachos*
   of *Shemoneh Esrei*.
8. See *Mishnah Berurah, Siman* 101, *Se'if Katan* 1; *Shulchan Aruch
   HaRav, Siman* 101, *Se'if* 1, which states that a person should get
   himself into the habit of saying at least the conclusion of every
   berachah of *Shemoneh Esrei* with *kavannah*. Also see *Roke'ach,
   Hilchos Chassidus, Shoresh Zechiras Hashem*.
9. Shown to Rav Mordechai Schwab, as related by Dayan Aharon D.
   Dunner, speaker at Keynote Session, 5758 Convention of Agudath
   Israel of America. See *Shem Olam*, "*hashmatos*" at end of *sefer*.

**Points
to
Ponder**

▸ Preparing
to pray
includes
directing
one's mind
to thoughts
that enhance
kavannah.

▸ One should
take time
before
praying to
focus on
what he is
trying to
accomplish,
before
Whom he is
standing,
and where
he is
standing.

ed me a little advice that in the beginning [of each
berachah] one should arrange well in his mind what
he is about to say."

In his will, Rav Naftali Amsterdam[10] left several suggestions for preparing to recite Shemoneh Esrei:
One method is to think about the sequence of the
berachos. Another is to stop periodically at appropriate points to focus on the fact that one is standing before Hashem, Who can grant any request. He
suggested "Atah Chonein" (fourth berachah), "Teka
B'Shofar" (tenth berachah), and "Retzei" (seven-
teenth berachah) as berachos particularly suited to
this thought.

It is true that preparation takes time — even if it is just
a few minutes. This small investment of time, however, is
crucial in insuring that the *rest of the time* spent on *tefillah*
is not undermined by a rushed, inattentive approach. By
taking the time to prepare, we not only change our state
of mind, we change our state of heart. From there, our true
kavannah — our soul's deep desire to feel connected to
Hashem — can freely flow.

---

10. See *Tenuas HaMussar*, Vol. 2, p. 302.

STRATEGY 3:
DO SOMETHING

A man enters a synagogue as a minyan is gathering. The moment the tenth man walks in, a blinding light shines forth from above the ark. The room fills with an unearthly scent circulated by a strong wind. The men clutch their tallesim and siddurim and begin to pray. Each time they utter Hashem's Name, the light begins shooting bolts all around the room. No doubt, there is no kavannah problem in this shul.

21 Cheshvan

22 Shevat

21 Iyar

22 Av

For the rest of the world, however, the senses do little to help in the effort to perceive Hashem's Presence. The *Mesillas Yesharim*[1] points out that our senses do not naturally help us pray with *kavannah*: "When you *daven*, know ... that you are really standing before the Creator, His Name should be blessed. Because one's eyes do not physically see Hashem, it appears very difficult to have a genuine picture in a person's heart, and the senses do not assist in this at all."

To counter this reality, one should actively engage his senses to the greatest possible extent during prayer. The *Shulchan Aruch* states, "One must not pray in his heart alone, rather, he must say the words so he can hear himself pray."[2] The *Yesod V'Shoresh HaAvodah*[3] suggests that

---

1. Ch. 19, *Chelkei HaChassidus*.
2. *Siman* 101, *Se'if* 2. However, see *Mishnah Berurah, Siman* 101, *Se'if Katan* 5 which states that *bedi'eved* as long as one actually uttered the words, he is considered to have prayed properly, even if he did not hear himself say them. Finally, see *Be'ur Halachah Siman* 101, *Se'if* 2, s.v. *B'libo*, which states that if he just thought of the words without pronouncing them, he has not fulfilled his requirement.
3. *Shaar* 5, Ch. 1. Also see *Mishnah Berurah, Siman* 51, *Se'if Katan* 20, which states that when reciting *Pesukei D'Zimrah*, to avoid skipping or swallowing words, one should enunciate them as if he were counting money.

one articulate the words of prayer as if counting money, pausing after saying several words. Another means of engaging one's heart and senses is to pray with a pleasant melody.[4]

How does articulating the words in these ways improve one's *kavannah*? The *Mesillas Yesharim*[5] suggests that in general, a person's outward behavior stirs an inner awakening. Focusing on the words of prayer, either through careful enunciation or through melody, serves this purpose.

> *Rav Yechezkel Levenstein advised his students to clearly enunciate and listen to the words they were saying in order to have kavannah when praying.*

Another way to "actively" pray is to sway back and forth ("shuckel"), for, as Rav Yaakov Emden[6] and the *Yesod V'Shoresh Ha'Avodah*[7] both wrote, the movement arouses the heart. The Rema[8] also mentions that it is customary for those who are meticulous in the observance of mitzvos to sway back and forth during prayer. However, the *Magen Avraham*[9] quotes other opinions that one should sway only during *Pesukei D'Zimrah* and stand erect while reciting *Shemoneh Esrei*.[10]

The *Mishnah Berurah*[11] embraces both opinions and concludes that whether or not one sways back and forth during *Shemoneh Esrei* depends on individual preference: "It all depends on one's own personal nature. If one applies himself well to his prayer by moving to and fro, he should in fact do so but, if not, he should keep still, so that he should be able just to apply his heart to the praying."

> *When someone once criticized Rabbi Levi Yitzchak of Berditchev for shaking ("shuckling") excitedly during prayer, he asked, "If you saw a person drowning, and*

---

4. *Sefer Chassidim, Siman* 158.
5. Ch. 7 (at end). Also see *Michtav MeEliyahu*, Vol. 5, p. 201.
6. See Introduction to the *Siddur of Rav Yaakov Emden*.
7. *Shaar* 5, Ch. 1.
8. Introduction to *Siman* 48, citing the *Abudraham*.
9. Ibid. *Se'if Katan* 4.
10. See Day 31, "Addressing the King."
11. Ibid. *Se'if Katan* 5.

he was motioning wildly in his desperate attempt to stay above water or attract help, would you criticize his behavior? When I try to concentrate on prayer, I too am fighting for my life to retain my *kavannah.*"[12]

---

12. *Not Just Stories* by Rabbi Abraham J. Twerski, M.D. (Shaar Press), p. 174. Also see *Mabit*, end of *Iggeres Derech Hashem*, who writes that one should shake his body a little as if he is fearful of reciting Hashem's Name, to remind himself to concentrate.

STRATEGY 4:
FEELING THE NEED

A young boy was straying from the path of Torah. His parents' terrible distress transformed their Shemoneh Esrei into a daily, tear-soaked plea to their Father in Heaven. Previously, the words "Who resurrects the dead" carried no relevant meaning. Now their heart cried out that their wayward child's soul be revived. When they prayed for wisdom, they desperately begged Hashem to show them which way to turn, what to say. When they prayed for salvation, they pleaded that every Jewish parent be spared such anguish. When they said "Grant peace," they said it with a longing for peace in their home, in their son's heart, and in their own. Suddenly, this age-old liturgy had become their own fervent prayer.

Need is one of prayer's most potent fuels. A person with no needs is crippled in his efforts to connect to Hashem. As explained earlier,[1] Hashem cursed the serpent[2] more than all the animals and beasts of the field — *and you shall eat dust all your life* — for convincing Chavah to eat the forbidden fruit. The Rebbe, Rav Bunim of P'shis'che,[3] points out that this curse was particularly severe because the serpent, supplied with a constant food source, no longer needed to connect with and beseech Hashem.

In contrast, the curse of man (the need to earn a livelihood) and woman (the pain of childbirth) was not as severe, because these struggles cause a person to connect with Hashem and to come before Him in prayer.

---

1. Day 16, "Filled With Dust."
2. *Bereishis* 3:14.
3. See *Kol Mevaseir, Bereishis* ibid.

As mentioned previously, the Gemara[4] states that our Patriarchs were infertile because Hashem desires the prayers of the righteous. Rav Dessler[5] further explains that their difficulties were ultimately for their benefit, since their inability to have children inspired them to reach more deeply into the depths of their souls to cry out to Hashem.

The *Shelah HaKadosh* teaches that when a person strongly feels a need — especially when he faces immediate danger — prayer becomes more relevant and filled with *kavannah*. On the other hand, a person who does not feel any need will find it difficult to pray with *kavannah* because he has no internal drive to reach out to Hashem.[6]

The motivating power of real need becomes clear when one contrasts the usual mode of daily prayer with the emotion that is aroused on Yom Kippur, or when there is a crisis in Israel, or when a loved one is sick. The piercing sensation of need spurs us to pray with greater *kavannah*, expressing our heartfelt hope and belief in Hashem's powers.

The Mishnah[7] tells us that when a fast day is proclaimed to pray for rain, "they send down to lead the prayers an elder, well-versed in prayer, who has children, and whose house is empty of food, so that his heart should be completely devoted to his prayer."

Rabbeinu Nissim[8] explains that because the elder is afflicted by his family's desperate need, he will pray with greater intensity. The *Me'iri*[9] comments that in general, all those in a situation of great need will be similarly immersed in prayer, which will come from the depths of their hearts.

> The disciples of Rabbi Shimon bar Yochai asked him why the manna did not fall just once a year for the

---

4. *Yevamos* 64a.
5. *Michtav MeEliyahu*, Vol. 5, p. 67.
6. Also see *Derech Chaim — Necessity*, which states that a person concentrates in accordance with the level of his need.
7. *Taanis* 16a.
8. Ibid 16b.
9. *Beis HaBechirah, Taanis* 16b, s.v. *HaMishnah ha'sheniah*.

**Points
to
Ponder**

▸ *Need causes
people to
pray with
greater
fervor.*

▸ *Hashem
desires our
prayers and
provides
us with
motivation
to reach out
to Him.*

*Jews in the desert, in the same way that rain falls in a
single season to make the crops grow. He answered
with a parable:* [10] *The king's only son, whom he loved
dearly, visited his father once yearly to collect his allowance. Longing to see his son more frequently,
the king decided that henceforth, the funds would
be distributed on a daily basis. He was then able to
have the pleasure of his son's company each and every day.*

Similarly, Hashem longed for the pleasure of the prayers
of his chosen people, and so He provided just one day's
portion of *manna* at a time. *Klal Yisrael* was thus motivated
to pour out their hearts in prayer every morning and evening.

Need strips away our illusions of self-sufficiency and
causes us to feel acutely our dependence upon Hashem.
Through it, the true potential of our prayers is revealed
to us, thereby awakening the "need" to pray with intense
kavannah.

---

10. *Yoma* 76a. Also see *Lev Eliyahu, Parashas Vayakhel*, p. 129.

STRATEGY 4: FEELING THE NEED, PART II

The power of pressing need to transform a person's prayers is the dramatization of a concept that — were one truly spiritually awake — would transform every prayer. When the rains do not fall and the house is empty of food, the natural response is to turn to Heaven, for everyone can clearly understand that Hashem alone gives rain. There is nothing a human being can do to make it happen.

People do believe, however, that their normal everyday needs are in a different category, more a human concern than the subject of Divine intervention. If people were to perceive that as much as the rain, each breath, blink of the eye, and beat of the heart is a gift direct from Hashem's hand, this acute sense of need would pervade their daily prayers as well.

The Gemara[1] teaches us that one's *tefillah* is not considered a plea if it has become habitual. Rabbah and Rav Yosef explain that this refers to the prayers of an individual who is unable to feel anything new in his prayer. The *Tosafos HaRosh*[2] questions this individual's failure to put his heart into his prayers; after all, prayers are necessary for (among other things) one's livelihood and Torah learning. One would think that an absence of "newness" in *tefillah* is impossible.

A person's health is completely dependent on Hashem, as the Rambam[3] states: "The preservation of a person's health is one of the ways of Hashem." Livelihood is in the hands of Hashem as well, as the Gemara[4] tells us: "What should a person do to become wealthy? ... Let him pray

23
Cheshvan

24
Shevat

23
Iyar

24
Av

---

1. *Berachos* 29b.
2. Ibid.
3. *Hilchos Dei'os* 4:1.
4. *Niddah* 70b.

▸ The sense of pressing need brings heartfelt passion to one's prayers by assuring that we reach out and seek a connection with Hashem.

▸ Even without pressing problems, one can fortify his kavannah by recognizing that he needs Hashem's compassion simply to live his normal, everyday life.

for mercy from Hashem to Whom are the riches." So too is wisdom in Hashem's hands, as the Gemara[5] says: "What should a person do to become wise? ... Let him pray for mercy from the One [Hashem] to Whom is the wisdom."

The Gemara refers to *prayer* in several places as "compassion." For example,[6] "Whoever is able to ask for compassion for his friend, and does not, is called a sinner"; and later,[7] "Whoever requests compassion for his sick friend does not have to mention his name."

By calling prayer "compassion," we remind ourselves that need is not just an occasional, dramatic occurrence, but rather, the human condition. The bottom line is that it is only because of Hashem's steadfast compassion that we have anything at all.

---

5. Ibid.
6. *Berachos* 12b.
7. Ibid. 34a. See *Mishnah Berurah, Siman* 119, *Se'if Katan* 2.

STRATEGY 5:
UNDERSTANDING THE MEANING

A small child doesn't know the difference between a hundred dollar bill and a scrap of green paper. If he were given the currency to hold, he might drop it out the window or cut it into pieces; he would never understand what he had lost. To value something, you have to know what it is and how much it is worth.

A person who prays with little understanding of what he is saying and what the words are supposed to accomplish is missing a vital source of inspiration and *kavannah*. Learning the meaning of the words of *tefillah* and the holy origins of the prayers are vital steps in developing *kavannah* and maintaining it during *davening*.

As early as the 14th century, the *Abudraham*[1] recognized that understanding the words of prayer is vital to having our prayers answered: "Most of the masses raise their voice in prayer before Hashem but are going about it like a blind man in darkness, and they do not understand the words they are saying ... When I saw that the gates of *tefillah* are locked, I decided to write this (his) *sefer* explaining *tefillah*."

The *Chovos HaLevavos* writes:[2] "Regarding *tefillos*, one should observe the words and their objective so that when he speaks them before Hashem he knows what the words mean and what his heart is asking." The *Yosef Ometz*[3] states: "It is evident that the responsibility to elucidate prayer comes before one learns any other learning."

---

1. *Abudraham HaShaleim*, Introduction.
2. *Shaar Cheshbon HaNefesh*, Ch. 3, *Cheshbon* 24.
3. *Siman* 26.

For example, much is added to a person's recitation of the *Baruch She'amar* prayer if he has knowledge of its meaning and origin. This prayer, recited at the beginning of *Pesukei D'Zimrah*, was instituted by the Men of the Great Assembly almost 2,400 years ago. The text is based on a script that literally dropped down from the Heavens. The *tefillah* contains 87 words equal to the *gematria*, or numerical equivalent, of the Hebrew word *"paz,"*[4] meaning "finest gold," suggesting that these words are as precious and pure as the finest gold. Knowing the lofty origin of *Baruch She'amar*, one can easily understand why one is required to stand when reciting it.[5]

After the *Pesukei D'Zimrah*, which speak of the glory and wonder of nature, we recite the blessing "Yotzeir HaMeoros," *Who creates the luminaries*. We then proceed to proclaim "Ahavas Olam" (or "Ahavah Rabbah")[6] in which we express our eternal love for Hashem, leading to a proclamation of Hashem's Oneness in *Shema*. Progressing along this path, we build a connection with Hashem that culminates in the recitation of *Shemoneh Esrei*.[7]

> Rav Shmuel Auerbach testified about the way his father, Rav Shlomo Zalman Auerbach, recited Shemoneh Esrei: "Every tefillah was recited with hislahavus, fervor ... His prayers were pleas, not rote utterances ... From beginning to end he recited them with kavannah ... And he said that what counts most is understanding the meaning of the words."[8]

Among the closing prayers is "Aleinu Leshabe'ach," which, according to the *Kolbo*,[9] is one of the earliest prayers whose words we know. It was composed by Yehoshua when he captured Yericho. The *Chidah*[10] comments that after the destruction of the *Beis HaMikdash*,

---

4. See *Shir HaShirim* 5:11.
5. See *The Complete ArtScroll Siddur, Baruch She'amar.*
6. See *Orach Chaim, Siman* 60 for a discussion of the correct *nusach*.
7. See *Nefesh Shimshon*, pp. 313 and 317.
8. *The Man of Truth and Peace* by Rabbi Yoel Schwartz (Feldheim Publ.), p.127.
9. *Simanim* 11 and 16.
10. *Machzik Berachah, Orach Chaim, Siman* 132, *Se'if* 2.

Rabbi Yochanan ben Zakkai instituted it as part of our daily prayers to strengthen the Jewish people's faith in Hashem at a time when they were dishonored and heartbroken.

The *Mateh Moshe*[11] says that when one stands to recite *Aleinu*, Hashem also stands with all the angels in Heaven and all say, *Praiseworthy is the people for whom this is so, praiseworthy is the people whose G-d is Hashem.*[12]

This holy prayer, said at the conclusion of *davening*, serves as protection over all our *tefillos* by declaring our faith in Hashem's Oneness.[13] By focusing on the special lot Hashem has assigned to His chosen people, *Aleinu* also girds a person for the challenges to his faith that might emerge in the business day ahead. If he happens to see a non-Jew prosper, he will not contemplate following in his ways.[14]

Rav Sheftel Horowitz, in *Vavei HaAmudim*,[15] wrote:

> "When I was the head of the beis din (Jewish Court) and the yeshivah in Frankfurt, I instituted a great establishment whereby groups would gather to study all the tefillos from the beginning of the year to the end. They learned at least the meanings of the words so that their prayers would go up to the One Above. Praiseworthy is the one who listens to my words and sees to it that the meanings of the tefillos are fluent in his mouth."[16]

Points to Ponder

▸ Understanding the meaning of the words of prayer is a key to kavannah.

▸ Understanding the origins and purposes of prayers also increases kavannah.

▸ Rav Shlomo Zalman Auerbach said that understanding the meanings of the words in Shemoneh Esrei is of utmost importance.

---

11. Cited in *Nefesh Shimshon*, p. 449.
12. *Tehillim* 144:15.
13. *Nefesh Shimshon*, p. 450.
14. *Bach, Orach Chaim, Siman* 133.
15. *Amud HaAvodah*, Ch. 10.
16. Cited in *Pathway to Prayer* by Rabbi Mayer Birnbaum (ArtScroll/ Mesorah Publ.), p. 13.

DAY

55

STRATEGY 5:
UNDERSTANDING
THE MEANING,
PART II

*I*f a person had no sense of taste, what would motivate him to bite into a juicy rib steak? What would entice him to tackle a messy bowl of spaghetti? Why would he subject his mouth to the freezing sensation of ice cream? If people ate for the sake of nutrition alone, simply because "it's good for you," most people would be wasting away.[1] This is borne out by research that indicates that many people neglect to take important medication because the medicine has no taste.

25
Cheshvan

26
Shevat

25
Iyar

26
Av

In prayer, the "taste" is in the meaning.

Certain prayers, although very meaningful, are written in language that some find difficult. One such *tefillah* is the *Yekum Purkan*, which is recited each Shabbos after reading from the *Sefer Torah*. If one simply takes the time to understand the meaning of this prayer, however, one sees instantly that it is not obscure at all, but close to every person's heart. It asks for children who study the Torah and observe its laws scrupulously, and for health and long life.

Another somewhat difficult *tefillah* is *Av HaRachamim*, an elegy for the beautiful communities of devout, G-d-fearing Jews whose lives ended with their sanctification of Hashem's Name. In our time when, tragically, Jews still die for being Jews, should a person not stop for a moment and think about the meaning of these words? Anyone who grasps their meaning cannot help but feel his emotions aroused by the loss of the rich spiritual life that has been torn from our midst. One cannot help but feel comforted by Hashem's promise to avenge their spilled blood.

---

1. Cited in *Tallelei Oros on Seder HaTefillah*, "*Taam Tefillah*," from the Alter of Kelm.

Yet another prayer written in language that one may find challenging is *Machnisei Rachamim*. Composed by *Rishonim*, it is recited at the end of *Selichos*. Phrased as a prayer addressed to the angels, it is actually an expression of modesty and humility addressed to Hashem. One who recites, *Angels of mercy, servants on high, appeal to Hashem with the best pronouncement — perhaps He will have mercy on a poor people,*[2] puts himself in the role of a supplicant who feels unable to speak directly to the King.

Of the many means to find inspiration in one's prayers, understanding their meaning is among the most easily accomplished in our times. The bookstores and shuls are filled with beautifully translated and annotated prayer books that offer everything from simple translation to mystical insight. Taking one word at a time, one verse at a time, anyone can learn to speak the language of prayer.

Points to Ponder

▸ *Some prayers that appear difficult to understand have very clear and relevant messages for us.*

▸ *Translated and annotated siddurim make understanding prayer accessible to everyone.*

---

2. *Sdei Chemed, Hilchos Rosh Hashanah* 1:2. See also *Maharal, Nesivos Olam*, Vol. 1, *Nesiv HaAvodah*, Ch. 12; *She'eilos U'Teshuvos Chasam Sofer, Orach Chaim, Siman* 166; *She'eilos U'Teshuvos Yehudah Yaaleh*, Vol. 1, *Orach Chaim* 21.

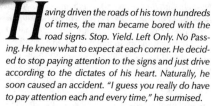

STRATEGY 6:
PRAYING FROM A
SIDDUR

26
Cheshvan

27
Shevat

26
Iyar

27
Av

*H*aving driven the roads of his town hundreds of times, the man became bored with the road signs. Stop. Yield. Left Only. No Passing. He knew what to expect at each corner. He decided to stop paying attention to the signs and just drive according to the dictates of his heart. Naturally, he soon caused an accident. "I guess you really do have to pay attention each and every time," he surmised.

Prayer is no less demanding a skill. To maintain one's focus, absorb the meaning of the words and form a live connection to them, one has to pay attention each and every time. The road signs in this journey are the words of the *siddur*, and surprisingly, the more expert the "driver," the more careful he is to read the signs.

The Vilna Gaon recommended reciting every word of the prayers from a *siddur*. He finds an interesting allusion to the importance of praying from a *siddur* in *Megillas Esther*, which states:[1] "Uv'voah lifnei hamelech amar im hasefer yashuv machashavto." Literally: *When she* [Esther] *appeared before the king* [Achashveirosh], *he commanded by means of letters that* [Haman's] *wicked scheme should be overturned.* Homiletically, the Gaon translates these words as follows: "When one appears before the King [Hashem] in prayer, he should recite the words from a *sefer* (*siddur*), [for in that way] he will cast aside any inappropriate thoughts."[2]

Similarly, the *Magen Avraham*[3] tells us that the Arizal *davened* exclusively from a *siddur*. This practice was also exemplified and advised by the Maharal, the Chofetz Chaim and more recently, by Rav Moshe Feinstein. In fact,

---

1. 9:25.
2. *Even Sheleimah*, Ch. 9, fn. 2.
3. *Orach Chaim, Siman* 93, *Se'if Katan* 2. However, *Kaf HaChaim* in *Siman* 95, *Se'if Katan* 10 states that the Arizal *davened* only *Pesukei D'Zimrah* and *Krias Shema* from a *siddur*, and *davened Shemoneh*

the Chofetz Chaim stated that using a *siddur* was one of the foremost priorities for proper *tefillah*.[4]

> *While davening from a siddur, the Alter of Kelm once walked to the back of the shul to glance into another siddur and then returned to his regular place. When questioned, he explained: "A word was missing from the siddur I was using. Because I always daven from a siddur, I felt compelled to find the missing word and to read it from a siddur."[5]*

> *The Manchester Rosh Yeshivah, Rabbi Yehudah Zev Segal, who was known for the power of his tefillah, was a compassionate messenger for thousands of Jews who, throughout his lifetime, asked him to be- seech Hashem on their behalf. He not only prayed from a siddur, but was often seen pointing with his finger to each word he uttered, in order to guarantee his exclusive focus on the meaning.[6] Even the bera- chos he recited were always read from either a siddur or a printed card.*

By praying from a *siddur*, one discovers new shades of meaning in the words of the *tefillos*. In addition, see- ing the words provides another sensory channel through which the words can penetrate the heart. Simply put, pray- ing from a *siddur* enhances *kavannah*.

Points to Ponder

▸ Torah luminaries throughout the ages prayed from a siddur.

▸ Seeing the words helps maintain a person's focus.

▸ Seeing the printed words as they are said provides new shades of meaning.

Esrei with his eyes closed. The *Sefer HaYashar, Shaar* 13, comments that one should close his eyes when praying because that will help him concentrate.

See *Mishnah Berurah, Siman* 53, *Se'if Katan* 87, citing the *Pri Megadim*, which states that it is proper for an individual to pray from a *siddur* and the *chazzan* should certainly pray looking inside a *siddur*. The *Magen Avraham* concludes that it is up to one's indi- vidual preference whether or not to *daven* from a *siddur*. Also see *Aruch HaShulchan, Siman* 93, *Se'if* 8.

4. *Shem Olam,* "hashmatos" at end of *sefer.*
5. *Moreshes Avos.*
6. *Along the Maggid's Journey* by Rabbi Paysach J. Krohn, (ArtScroll/ Mesorah Publ.), p. 125.

STRATEGY 6:
PRAYING FROM A
SIDDUR, PART II

hen a person looks at the words in a *siddur*,
he is literally keeping Hashem's Name before
his eyes. That alone can create a noticeable
impact on the power of his prayer. The Steipler Gaon says
that praying from a *siddur* helps a person recite Hashem's
Name with *kavannah* befitting this momentous utterance,[1]
and also enhances concentration in the vital first *berachah*
in *Shemoneh Esrei*.

The level of concentration that can be reached by focusing on the *siddur* as one prays is illustrated in this story:

> One year R' Kalman Krohn traveled to the Manches-
> ter Rosh Yeshivah for Rosh Hashanah and Yom Kip-
> pur. Shortly after Rosh Hashanah, R' Kalman came
> across a list of commitments the Rosh Yeshivah had
> taken upon himself for that year. It included a reso-
> lution to increase *kavannah* during the *berachah*,
> "Atah Chonein," the blessing for wisdom in Shem-
> oneh Esrei. One evening, R' Kalman wrote his name
> alongside the blessing "Atah Chonein" in the Rosh
> Yeshivah's personal siddur, hoping that the Rosh Ye-
> shivah would include him in his prayer.
>
> Before returning to America several nights later,
> R' Kalman regretted having written his name in the
> Rosh Yeshivah's siddur without first asking permis-
> sion. He asked the Rosh Yeshivah's forgiveness;
> however, the Rosh Yeshivah told R' Kalman that
> there was nothing to forgive. "I did not even notice

---

1. Rav Aryeh Tzvi Fromer, Rosh Yeshivah Yeshivas Chachmei Lublin
(following Rav Meir Shapiro), wrote in *She'eilos U'Teshuvos Eretz
Tzvi, Orach Chaim, Siman 45*, that he has seen many *tzaddikim*
praying from a *siddur* when reciting Hashem's Name.

your name written in my siddur," said the Rosh Yeshivah. *"You see, when I daven, I don't even look
out of the line."* [2]

So often, using a *siddur* reveals itself to be the tool of the
intellectual giant, not the crutch of the intellectually weak.
The more one understands and masters *tefillah*, the more
one demands the constant reinforcement of the *siddur*.

> *During the ominous years leading up to World War
> II, one of the key figures in Europe at that time, Rav
> Chaim Ozer Grodzenski, wrote down his resolu-
> tions for the New Year. The following words, writ-
> ten on Erev Yom Kippur 5694 (1934), were found
> among his writings: "To concentrate deeply when
> praying or reciting blessings; especially, to recite
> from a text."* [3]

Did Rav Chaim Ozer need the siddur to jar his memory?
Rav Shach relates the following telling incident:

> *Rav Chaim Ozer kept a notebook listing all the de-
> posits and expenditures made for various orphans
> and widows. Once, the ledger was misplaced and
> could not be found. Rav Chaim Ozer's wife became
> distraught, worrying about the loss of so much infor-
> mation that was vital to so many people. When Rav
> Chaim Ozer heard about the loss, he said to his wife,
> "Don't worry about it! Please bring a new empty
> notebook." Within several hours he had reconstruct-
> ed the entire record book, with all its numbers and
> information, all from memory.*
>
> *The original book was found a short time later, and
> all the information in it corresponded exactly to Rav
> Chaim Ozer's reconstructed ledger.*

Rav Shach observed, "One who never met Rav Chaim
Ozer can have no idea how phenomenal his memory was."
Rav Shach drew a lesson from this episode: "Despite his

---

2. *Along the Maggid's Journey* by Rabbi Paysach J. Krohn (ArtScroll/
Mesorah Publ.), p. 127.
3. *Reb Chaim Ozer: The Life and Ideals of Rabbi Chaim Ozer
Grodzenski of Vilna* by Rabbi Shimon Finkelman (ArtScroll History
Series), p. 247.

Points to Ponder

▸ *Praying from a siddur enables a person to better concentrate and focus.*

▸ *The sharpness of a person's memory does not mitigate his need to use a siddur.*

tremendous memory, Rav Chaim Ozer never davened or bentched without looking in a siddur."[4]

Praying from a *siddur* is not of minimal importance, as we see from the fact that this was what the great Rav Chaim Ozer chose to focus on in the face of the gravest of circumstances. The world needed the full force of prayer then, as it does now; this requires not only pronouncing the holy words and understanding their meaning, but keeping them before one's eyes.

---

4. *Harav Shach — Conversations,* compiled by Rav Asher Bergman (Feldheim Publ.), p. 221.

STRATEGY 7:
MASTER THE MIND

She was three-quarters of the way through Shemoneh Esrei when she realized that she had no idea how she had gotten there. While her mouth was saying the appropriate blessings, her mind had rambled across an astounding range of subjects. At the moment, she had been considering ideas for a family vacation, bowing in thanks to Hashem as she mulled it over. Realizing that she was indeed lost in thought, she pulled herself back to the words of the siddur, dismayed at how her tefillah was turning out.

28 Cheshvan

29 Shevat

28 Iyar

29 Av

Many people find their prayers derailed by "foreign thoughts" that are disconnected from the content of their prayers. Rav Dessler[1] explains: "What we call 'foreign thoughts' are (those) which ascend into our brain and disturb our prayer, meaning they are foreign to prayer. However, they are not foreign to the person himself, rather they are aspects of his personal essence."

For this reason, a person is advised to exercise great care regarding that which ultimately becomes a part of himself, for it is liable to intrude in the midst of his holiest thoughts. *Orchos Tzaddikim*[2] says that being careful with speech "is a means to being able to pray with *kavannah*, since most distractions emanate from idle talk that becomes entrenched into a person's heart." *Reishis Chochmah*[3] recommends that, to preserve the integrity of one's prayers, one should lower his eyes, because everything a person sees stays in his mind and may resurface when he is praying.

---

1. *Michtav MeEliyahu*, Vol. 5, p. 200.
2. *Shaar 21, Shaar HaShtikah*, s.v. *Klalo shel davar*.
3. *Shaar 8, Shaar HaKedushah*.

Rav Elyah Lopian observed that Hashem hears with equal clarity both one's thoughts and one's spoken words during *Shemoneh Esrei*, but gives more credence to thoughts because they reflect the true focus of the mind. Thus, if a person thinks about what to eat for breakfast instead of concentrating on the words of *tefillah*, Hashem pays more attention to the menu. Clearly, this is not the result for which one is aiming when he sets out to pray. How, then, can a person eliminate such thoughts and maximize *kavannah*?

The *Raavad*[4] introduces a very important concept that offers some guidance in avoiding distractions. "A person is not capable of concentrating on two things simultaneously." Therefore, focusing on the words of prayer will help prevent inappropriate thoughts from surfacing.

As previously discussed, understanding the meaning of the words so that the mind is actively engaged with them, and praying from a *siddur*, can go a long way toward keeping a person focused upon the words of prayer. However, if foreign thoughts do intrude during prayer, one should just stop and remain quiet until the thoughts go away.[5]

Rav Moshe Sternbuch[6] suggests that foreign thoughts during prayer are a consequence of a person's *aveiros*, sins. When one sins, angels of destruction are created which act as "clouds" that obscure one's connection to Hashem and keep one's prayers from entering the Heavens.[7] Therefore, a wonderful means to counteract this difficulty is to reflect on one's actions before beginning to pray. The Mishnah[8] relates that "the earlier pious ones waited one hour before praying," which, according to Rav Sternbuch, refers to this process.

Another solution to the problem is to internalize an absolute belief that foreign thoughts are unacceptable during prayer.

---

4. *Hilchos Parah* 7:3.
5. *Tur, Orach Chaim, Siman* 98.
6. *She'eilos U'Teshuvos Teshuvos V'Hanhagos,* Vol. 4, *Orach Chaim, Siman* 27.
7. See *Maharsha, Shabbos* 32a, s.v. *Eilu;* 119b, s.v. *Echad tov;* and *Makkos* 10b, s.v. *B'derech,* which state that when a person does a mitzvah or an *aveirah* an angel is created on his behalf.
8. *Berachos* 30b.

Does a person dream of having wings so he can fly, or desire to run at the speed of sound? Hope to swim the Atlantic Ocean? Certainly not, for a person only desires that which is achievable. Flying is humanly impossible, and running at such speeds, and swimming such distances, are unfeasible.

In a discussion regarding how one can control his thoughts to enable him to obey the Torah's command: *You shall not covet in your heart that which another person has,*[9] the Ibn Ezra explains[10] that a person has the power to create unassailable mental boundaries. He expounds that a person who truly believes that another individual's possessions are not meant to belong to him will never desire them.

One can conclude from this that a person who concedes no allowance for irrelevant thoughts during prayer will eliminate contemplating them.

As mentioned at the beginning of this chapter, internal motivation is the essential ingredient in personal growth. If we truly savor the opportunity prayer gives us to come before Hashem, and we recognize our constant need for His care, then we can fully understand what we lose when our prayers are not focused. This awareness is powerful motivation to pray with *kavannah,* and in such a state of mind, foreign thoughts have no space to intrude and no room to wander.

Points to Ponder

▸ *Foreign thoughts originate from one's inner essence and are difficult to eliminate.*

▸ *Hashem pays greater heed to what a person thinks than what he says during prayer.*

▸ *Praying from a siddur and understanding the meaning of the words of prayer help keep the mind focused.*

▸ *Foreign thoughts can be the result of sin; taking an accounting before prayer can provide an effective antidote.*

9. *Shemos* 20:14.
10. Ibid.

STRATEGY 8:
REVISE OLD HABITS

*T*wo patients suffering from the same ravaging disease lie in their beds. The first patient recovers, rises from his bed, and resumes a healthy, vigorous life, while the other grows weaker each day.

Two suspects charged with the same capital crime stand before the court; one walks out a free man and the other is led off to prison to await a death sentence.

The Gemara[1] asks, "Why was one patient cured while the other was not? Why was one suspect freed while the other was not? The patient who was cured, and the suspect who was freed, prayed and were answered, while the patient who was not cured, and the suspect who was not freed, prayed and were not answered. And why was this one's prayers answered? Because the one who was answered prayed a 'complete prayer,' while the other one who was not answered did not pray a 'complete prayer.'"

Rashi[2] defines a "complete prayer" as one prayed with *kavannah*. In the context of this Gemara, however, is it possible that a person facing death by illness or decree would not pray a "complete prayer"?

A person who prays three times a day says *Shemoneh Esrei* almost 1,100 times a year. This constant repetition can breed a mindless recitation that becomes deeply ingrained in a person's habits of prayer. As a result, a person might even have difficulty praying with *kavannah* when the sword is at his throat.

---

1. *Rosh Hashanah* 18a.
2. Ibid.

Understanding the tremendous benefits one reaps by praying with *kavannah*, most people want dearly to achieve it. Force of habit, however, can create a mighty impediment to that goal. A person's mind naturally clicks into a neutral mode as the familiar words rattle off his tongue, and even a plea for his own life manages to transport itself from the *siddur* page to his mouth without passing through his heart.

These old habits, however, do not have to reign forever. They can be overthrown and replaced with new habits of care, attentiveness, and emotional involvement in the words of prayer. Just as habit can drain a person's prayer of life, it can be the tool that refills it to overflowing.

Points to Ponder

▸ Since prayers are repeated so often they become rote.

▸ People fall into negative habits of praying without *kavannah*.

▸ Habits can be reworked to become the tool to more meaningful prayer.

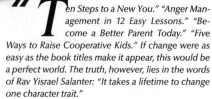

STRATEGY 8:
REVISE OLD HABITS,
PART II

"*Ten Steps to a New You.*" "*Anger Management in 12 Easy Lessons.*" "*Become a Better Parent Today.*" "*Five Ways to Raise Cooperative Kids.*" If change were as easy as the book titles make it appear, this would be a perfect world. The truth, however, lies in the words of Rav Yisrael Salanter: "It takes a lifetime to change one character trait."

Force of habit is just that — a force. It is in fact a tremendous force with which every person must reckon whenever he sets out to improve himself. In the realm of prayer, the first step is for a person to recognize the negative impact of habit. Until he understands the problem, he cannot attempt to find practical solutions. Even with recognition, however, he may not be able to see any escape route leading away from the habits in which he has become entrapped.

One solution is to harness the power of habit and use it to serve Hashem. In fact, one prays for such a habit every day after the morning blessings: "She'targileinu b'sorasecha" — *that you accustom us to study Your Torah.*

Positive habits, while more difficult to acquire, are every bit as powerful as their negative counterparts. Setting a goal is the first step. A person can then begin taking small steps toward that goal, repeating each step until it becomes a new habit. For example, a person who wishes to avoid speaking *lashon hara* can begin by purposefully refraining for as little as 15 minutes daily. If he is consistent, restraint will gradually become second nature, and he can then incrementally expand his new practice into a greater portion of his day. The key to success lies in tackling the project gradually.[1]

---

1. See *Michtav MeEliyahu*, Vol. 1, p. 25. Also see *Shemiras HaLashon*, Introduction, Days 7-9.

196 / PRAYING WITH FIRE

Many have attempted to learn the entire Talmud and have been defeated by the scope of the project after a very short while. Rav Meir Shapiro, the innovator of learning "Daf Yomi," advised that one who aspires to study the entire Talmud (with its voluminous commentaries) and undertakes to learn one folio a day and then another the following day and so on, will attain his goal. Little could Rav Shapiro have envisioned that eighty years later his seemingly simple idea has taken the Jewish world by storm.

Applying this principle to *tefillah*, a person who wishes to overcome difficulties with *kavannah* should cultivate positive habits of prayer gradually. The process requires a great deal of patience, but the success it generates is immensely rewarding.

To begin, a person can recite the first *berachah* of *Shemoneh Esrei* with *kavannah*, just once a day. Once this habit takes root, it will strengthen with every passing day. He can then extend his new habit to the same *berachah* during the other two daily *tefillos*. Each new step may be difficult, but after repeating it day after day over time, it will become ingrained. Through this gradual progress, a person can eventually reach the great goal of saying every *berachah* with *kavannah* .

Momentum is the element that gives habit its strength. Each time a person repeats an action, he builds a driving force behind it that moves it forward on its own power. Like a strong wind at a sprinter's back, momentum can propel a person to the finish line with far greater speed and ease than his own efforts could produce. For both good and bad, *Chazal* teach, "hergel naaseh teva" — *habit becomes second nature*. It can be the malady or the remedy. We make the choice.

Points to Ponder

▸ Habits must be changed gradually.

▸ To develop kavannah in prayer, start with the first berachah of Shemoneh Esrei, once a day.

▸ Once the new habit takes root, undertake a new step.

▸ Habits are strengthened by the force of momentum.

STRATEGY 9:
FIND JOY

J oy and boredom cannot coexist. If a person is filled with joy at the prospect of being received by his Father with open arms, he cannot possibly be mumbling distracted praises to Him at the same time.

The Gemara[1] describes the right frame of mind for prayer: "One should not rise to pray *Shemoneh Esrei* neither from sorrow, nor from laziness, nor from laughter, nor from previous conversation, nor from levity, nor from idle chatter, rather from the joy, *simchah*, of performing a mitzvah."

The *Iyun Yaakov*[2] explains that all these moods — sorrow, laziness, laughter, conversation, and levity — cause a person's mind to wander during prayer, resulting in a complete loss of *kavannah*. The Rambam[3] adds that *Shemoneh Esrei* should not be said after a quarrel or when a person is angry. According to Rabbi Yehudah HaChassid,[4] a person should refrain from conversation even before the start of *davening*.

As the Gemara explains, a person should enter *Shemoneh Esrei* filled with the "joy of performing a mitzvah." What is the source of that joy? The Rambam[5] says that a person will find the right level of joy from learning the words of Torah because learning Torah generates happiness. *Tosafos*[6] adds that the requirement to feel joy explains why the order of *tefillah* starts with the exultant words of *Pesukei D'Zimrah* and *Ashrei*. The Rema[7] concludes: "One

---

1. *Berachos* 31a.
2. Ibid.
3. *Hilchos Tefillah* 4:18.
4. *Sefer Chassidim, Siman* 158.
5. *Hilchos Tefillah* 4:18.
6. *Berachos* 31a, s.v. *Rabbanan.*
7. *Siman* 93, *Se'if* 3.

should rise ... to approach to pray with a feeling of happiness, for *the injunctions of Hashem are just and gladden the heart.*"[8]

The *Mesillas Yesharim*[9] explains that anyone who feels truly privileged to be able to pour out his heart in prayer to Hashem will naturally experience the desired sense of joy.

> *While standing in a corner praying, people overheard the "Bendiner Rav," Rav Hersh Henach Levine, saying in Yiddish: "Oy, Ribbono Shel Olam, ich hob Dier azoy lieb," meaning, "O Master of the Universe, I love You so very much."*[10]

Rav Shimshon David Pincus[11] comments that a person untouched by joy as he prays must be lacking in his perception of Who Hashem is. On the other hand, a person who truly feels in his heart that he is addressing the One Who has the answer to all his problems and the desire to fulfill his needs, rises to his feet with enthusiasm, joyful at the opportunity he has been given.

Points to Ponder

▸ Joy is included by many sources as an essential ingredient in reciting Shemoneh Esrei.

▸ Joy is derived from recognition of Hashem's greatness, from Torah learning, or from the ability to serve Hashem.

▸ Understanding Who Hashem is and what prayer achieves, creates a sense of joy.

---

8. *Tehillim* 19:9.
9. Ch. 19, *Chelkei HaChassidus.*
10. *Rav Schwab on Prayer* (ArtScroll/Mesorah Publ.), p. 118.
11. *She'arim B'Tefillah*, p. 49.

STRATEGY 9:
FIND JOY, PART II

3
Kislev

3
Adar

3
Sivan

3
Elul

*I*t is the standard plot to every drama: The situation is desperate. All hope is lost, and then, help arrives! This is a real-life drama that plays out in some form in almost every person's life. Through the emotions inherent in this drama — the anxiety, the longing, the rejoicing — one can learn to pray.

How does one understand the joy a person is to experience upon approaching Hashem in prayer? Imagine:[1]

▸ A person is stricken with an illness, and all the doctors in his small town have given up hope. Suddenly, word spreads that a world-renowned specialist in this disease has arrived in town for a visit. Knowing that someone is there within reach, someone who has healed others like him, ignites a great surge of optimism within the patient.

▸ In a last-ditch effort to find a livelihood, a person seeks a substantial loan to implement his plans to start a business. He believes that if he could present his proposal to the bank manager, he could convince him to grant it. Unfortunately, the manager's secretary will not put through his calls.

One day, a casual conversation with a stranger on the bus leads to an impassioned description of his business proposal. Upon reaching his stop, the stranger exclaims, "Thank you for speaking to me about this! I am the bank manager and I would like to finance your plans." The man feels his heart swell with joy, as he marvels at the opportunity he had been handed to bring his case before the one person who could help him.

---

1. Paraphrased from *She'arim B'Tefillah*, p. 49.

When a person recites *Shemoneh Esrei*, he must realize that he is praying to the One and only One Who can, and will, help him. If he consciously connects to that truth, he will be overwhelmed with joy at having been handed the longed-for opportunity to express his needs to the One Who can answer them. In the words of Rav Pincus:[2]

"So it is, when a person speaks to his Creator, and mentions His Name, if he would only think for a moment about the meaning of Hashem's Name,[3] at that moment an enormous happiness would shine inside … Specifically, the One he 'meets' in shul in the *Shemoneh Esrei* prayer, the One to Whom he is now speaking, He has the ability to help the person who is about to *daven Shemoneh Esrei*. And He (Hashem) assists all who sincerely ask Him for help."

Our quest is to see Hashem's Presence, hear His message and feel His loving guidance in every aspect of our lives. When we develop this perspective, we infuse ourselves, our lives, and our prayers with the indispensable ingredient of joy.

Points to Ponder

▸ *The opportunity to approach Hashem with one's needs is the source of the joy a person must feel when he prays.*

▸ *The more a person seeks to recognize Hashem's Presence, the more he will feel joy in his ability to pray.*

---

2. Ibid. p. 53.
3. Hashem - *Master of All, Who always was, is, and will be.* When one mentions the Divine Name, he should have in mind the meaning of the Name as it is *read*, referring to His Mastery and that He is the Master of all creation. See Day 28, "The Merit of Our Fathers."

STRATEGY 10: A SPIRIT OF EXCITEMENT

DAY 63

4 Kislev

4 Adar

4 Sivan

4 Elul

*I*t was a day before the boy's 13th birthday. His father came home bearing a package. Finally! They came! His tefillin were completed. He opened the package and reverently removed the smooth, polished leather boxes from their case. The next morning, with his father by his side, he carefully donned his new tefillin, feeling as if he were already standing upon a whole new, higher rung of spiritual life. He knew this tefillah had to be different. He wasn't a little boy anymore. Now it was "for real."

It was, of course, equally real two years later. However, the inspiration emanating from those sacred boxes had long ceased to move him. He could put the tefillin on as mechanically as he would don his socks. The newness was gone, and with it went the tefillin's power to move him.

It is because of this trait of human nature that the *Shema,*[1] specifies *And these words that I command you today* shall be upon your heart. "Today," Rashi[2] explains, means that the words of the Torah "should *not* be in your eyes like an old law to which a person does not attach importance; rather, they should be like a new one to which everybody runs."

Newness has a unique power to excite one's heart, and that excitement provides the power for higher levels of achievement.[3] In fact, Rav Dessler[4] explains: "The root of

---

1. *Devarim* 6:6.
2. Ibid.
3. See *Chochmah U'Mussar*, Vol. 2, Maamar 196.
4. *Sefer HaZikaron L'Baal Michtav MeEliyahu*, Vol. 2, p. 13.

enjoyment by mankind is built on newness and change ... The greater the change or newness, the greater is one's satisfaction and pleasure."

The Gemara[5] reveals this concept through a statement that seems to contradict common sense. It states that to relearn something that has already been studied and forgotten is more difficult than to learn something new.

The *Chochmah U'Mussar*[6] poses the obvious question: Should it not be easier to relearn familiar material than to tackle something completely new? The answer offers insight into human nature. A person naturally experiences a sense of excitement when striving to comprehend a new lesson or skill, and therefore, he does not need to expend great effort. Relearning old lessons, on the other hand, is devoid of the thrill of newness. It is an act of pure self- discipline and will, which requires tremendous effort.

Even miracles can seem routine. The *Midrash*[7] notes that Avraham Avinu was not told that his descendants would miraculously subsist on *manna* in the desert. Had Avraham been given this information, it would have been passed down through the generations and been known by the Jews who were redeemed from Egypt. When it finally came to fruition, it would have failed to impress them. "We already knew about the *manna* while in Egypt by the table of Pharaoh," they would have said. Rav Chaim Shmulevitz[8] explains that the lesson in this *Midrash* is that even an open miracle loses its impact if it is not perceived as something new and unanticipated.

Because of the innate desire for newness, prayers that one recites and mitzvos that one performs *regularly* are prone to losing their vitality. To the extent that a person can heed the Torah's words to accept Hashem's commandments "today" — each day anew — he can inject the spirit of freshness into his prayers. Otherwise, he becomes like

---

5. *Yoma* 29a.
6. Vol. 2, *Maamar* 219.
7. *Devarim Rabbah* 1:11.
8. *Sichos Mussar, Maamar* 1, 5731, p. 4; *Sichos Mussar, Shaarei Chaim, Maamar* 38, p. 160.

the boy in the opening story, listlessly regarding a precious gift that has been given to him with love — a gift that truly is the best thing he has.

STRATEGY 10:
A SPIRIT OF
EXCITEMENT, PART II

DAY 64

"*O*h, hi," said the man to his friend, whom he had met in the same spot every morning for the past twenty-two years. His voice was a perfect monotone as he recited the same words he said each time. "Nice to see you. You're great. I'm desperate. Think you could give me and my family a day of life again today? How about some breakfast? Well, whatever."

5 Kislev

5 Adar

5 Sivan

5 Elul

One can hardly call this a plea for compassion. Rather, it is a half-hearted repetition of a formula that has lost its urgency, even though the content is of life-and-death significance. The person speaking obviously doesn't feel that his life is at stake; apparently, he has received his day of life and his breakfast for the past twenty-two years, and doesn't expect things to change today.

The Gemara[1] states that if a person makes his *tefillah* fixed and regular, it ceases to invoke compassion. What exactly is meant by this fierce condemnation of praying by rote?

Rashi[2] explains that this refers to the manner and content of a person's prayer — today's is the same as yesterday's and tomorrow's will inevitably be no different. Such a *tefillah* is not *tachanunim* — a plea. According to the *Me'iri*,[3] it becomes so humdrum that eventually it is beyond repair: "He hurries through the *tefillah* according to his habitual way, so that even if he wishes to add something new, he is unable to."

---

1. *Berachos* 29b (according to Rabbah and Rav Yosef). Also see *Avos* 2:13.
2. *Berachos* 29b, Rashi s.v. *L'chadeish boh davar*.
3. *Beis HaBechirah*, *Berachos* 29b. Also see *Bach, Orach Chaim, Siman* 98.

How can one counteract the powerful tendency to become overly accustomed to words that are repeated three times a day, every day? How can verses and phrases this familiar take on the quality of newness in a person's eyes?

The Alter of Kelm[4] teaches that the words of the *Shema* mentioned in yesterday's lesson — *and these words that I command you today shall be upon your heart* — apply to prayer as well as to Torah. In the same way that the Torah yields a new understanding every time it is studied, the words of prayer provide a person with new insights, and therefore, new feelings and experiences, every time he prays.

To reinforce this sense of newness, a person can make some occasional, practical changes. Rav Shmuel Kamenetsky suggests that one change his *siddur* every once in a while to feel a freshness when praying.[5] The *Mekor Chaim*[6] comments that while it is better to pray from a *siddur* … once in a while the best way is to pray by heart because the habit of using a *siddur* will eventually cause a person's *kavannah* to lessen. Rav Yeruchem Levovitz,[7] the Mirrer Mashgiach, suggested to his students that they consider changing their regular place for prayer in order to regenerate enthusiasm.[8]

The most basic change, however, is an internal one. That is, to bring to mind every time we pray that we are asking Hashem for compassion, literally praying for our lives. If we would take this fact to heart and truly believe it, then every new day of life would give rise to a fresh, impassioned, new day of prayer.

The Mishnah teaches:[9] "Rabbi Shimon said: Be vigilant when saying *Shema* and the prayers. And when you pray, do not make your prayer routine. Rather it should be a plea for mercy and compassion before Hashem, as the

---

4. *Chochmah U'Mussar,* Vol. 1, p. 165.
5. Heard from Rav Shmuel Kamenetsky.
6. 90:4.
7. Cited in *Michtav MeEliyahu,* Vol. 5, p. 24.
8. *Shulchan Aruch, Siman* 90, *Se'if* 19, states that one may deviate from a *makom kavu'a,* set place, if there is an imperative reason, such as for a mitzvah or a pressing need.
9. *Avos* 2:13.

verse says,[10] *For He is gracious and compassionate, slow to anger, exceedingly kind ...*"

Rabbeinu Yonah[11] explains the Mishnah as follows: "Every person must plead for his life because there is no person who does not sin." Even though things may be fine today, this does not prove that all will be well tomorrow.

Rav Matisyahu Salomon[12] explains Rabbeinu Yonah in the following manner: "We are all living on credit. Our Creditor can call in the loan at any time and force us into bankruptcy in a moment, not only in business but in everything else as well, Heaven forbid. We have no choice but to beg Him for an extension.

"If we would realize this, that we are not living by our own account but on credit G-d has extended to us, we would not be complacent when we pray. We would grasp that we are in a crisis situation ... If we understand this, we would pray like beggars standing at the door."

---

10. *Yoel* 2:13.
11. *Avos* 2:13, s.v. *Ukeshe'atah mispalleil.*
12. *With Hearts Full of Faith* by Rabbi Matisyahu Salomon (ArtScroll/ Mesorah Publ.), p. 96.

STRATEGY 11:
PERSONAL REQUESTS

A person who needs a job doesn't pray for his livelihood in a distracted manner. His heart aches with need. His mind focuses sharply on the words he speaks. His prayer is saturated with sincere emotion. Personal needs move one's prayers from the abstract to the concrete, providing a powerful connection to the person's innermost self.

The blessings of *Shemoneh Esrei* relate to every area of human aspiration, both material and spiritual. Each blessing offers an opportunity to present one's personal requests to Hashem. Rabbi Yehudah HaChassid states,[1] "When you pray, add to each *berachah* which is relevant that which pertains to it for your needs, because that will prepare the heart to pray with proper concentration."

There are several places throughout *Shemoneh Esrei* in which one may insert personal requests: in each of the middle blessings, in the *berachah* of *Shema Koleinu* or in *Elokai Netzor*. There are specific *halachos* regarding how to add these personal requests.

Middle Blessings: This portion of *Shemoneh Esrei* starts at the blessing *"Atah Chonein,"* the blessing for wisdom, and ends after *"Es Tzemach David,"* which refers to the times of Mashiach. The *Shulchan Aruch*[2] rules that a person may add a personal request corresponding to any of the middle blessings; however, one should be concise in his requests.[3] Thus, he may ask for mercy for someone who is ill in *"Refa'einu,"* the blessing for health and heal-

---

1. *Sefer Chassidim, Siman* 158.
2. *Siman* 119, *Se'if* 1.
3. Ibid. *Se'if* 2; *Mishnah Berurah* ibid. *Se'if Katan* 12. However, at the conclusion of *Shemoneh Esrei*, before the (second) *"Yihyu Leratzon,"* one may make any personal requests and need not be concise.

ing. One in need of sustenance may ask for it in *"Bareich Aleinu,"* the blessing for prosperity. In response to violence in Eretz Yisrael, one may add a personal request for Hashem to alleviate our suffering in *"Re'ei Na V'anyeinu."* If a person has a family member who is suffering from a spiritual setback, he can ask Hashem to arouse the person to *teshuvah* in the blessing of *"Hashiveinu."* If he has a difficult time learning Torah, he can ask Hashem to help him in *"Atah Chonein L'adam Daas."* All of these requests can even be made in the person's own language if he has difficulty reciting them in Hebrew.

However, the *Mishnah Berurah*,[4] citing the *Pri Megadim*, rules that one may add a personal request to a middle blessing only if it is for a current need, rather than a possible future need. For example, one may pray for the recovery of a person who is currently ill, but he cannot pray that a healthy individual be spared illness in the future. Similarly, only a person who is currently lacking sustenance may add a plea for a livelihood; he may not, however, ask that he be provided for in the future. According to this ruling, a person may not add a request in the middle blessings that Hashem guide his children onto the right path in life, since this is a general request.

The *Rema*[5] comments that when adding a personal request to a middle blessing, a person should begin with the wording of the *berachah* first, and then continue with his own request before the conclusion of the *berachah*. He should not make the addition first and begin the wording of the *berachah* afterward.

The *Pri Megadim*[6] writes that when adding a personal request to any of the middle *berachos,* one is required to precede the request with a complete phrase from the topic of the blessing. For example, if one wishes to ask that Hashem give him knowledge, he should precede his entreaty by saying, *"Atah chonein l'adam daas,"* You have endowed man with knowledge (and not just with the word *"Atah"*), then proceed to make his specific request.

---

4. *Siman* 119, *Se'if Katan* 1.
5. *Siman* 119, *Se'if* 1.
6. *Siman* 119, *Se'if Katan* 3.

Points to Ponder

▸ *Personal requests turn prayers from abstract to concrete.*

▸ *One should study the halachos of where and how to add personal requests in Shemoneh Esrei.*

According to *Rabbeinu Yonah* (cited in *Shulchan Aruch*)[7] when a person is making a request on behalf of *all the Jewish people* (he says it for the sake of many), he should phrase it in the plural and he should add it only at the end of the *berachah*,[8] before he has said the words, "*Baruch Atah Hashem*."[9]

Rabbeinu Yonah permits one to insert his request in the middle of the blessing when praying for *his own needs*, such as for a sick member of his household. In that case, he should express himself in the singular.[10]

Once a person learns how to tap into the opportunity to add personal requests to his prayers, he will find that each occasion to pray takes on new meaning. It is his time to unload his burdens, speak his heart, and find the inner peace that Hashem provides to all who trustingly turn to Him.

---

7. *Siman* 119, *Se'if* 1.
8. See *Mishnah Berurah* ibid. *Se'if Katan* 8, which states that when one requests the needs of the many in the *middle* of the blessing it appears as if he is adding to the formula of the *berachah* devised by the Sages.

    It should be noted, however, that this ruling applies only when an *individual* prays. When a *congregation* prays it is permitted. That is why we say *Selichos* (forgiveness prayers) in the middle of the blessing "*Selach Lanu*."
9. See *Mishnah Berurah* ibid. *Se'if Katan* 7, who cites the *Pri Megadim*, *Siman* 122, in the *Mishbetzos Zahav*, that "one may do so only before he has said the words *Baruch Atah Hashem*, but after he has said them it appears that it is forbidden (however, see there that he is not certain about this statement)."
10. See *Mishnah Berurah* ibid. *Se'if Katan* 9, which states that if he will say it in the plural it will appear as if he is adding to the formula of the *berachah* devised by the Sages.

STRATEGY 11: PERSONAL REQUESTS, PART II

DAY 66

There are places in *Shemoneh Esrei* that are essentially an open letter to Hashem. In these places, a person can pour his heart out regarding any matter that is of importance to him, present or future, personal or communal, spiritual or material. Those who utilize these opportunities to their full potential do not have to force themselves to engage in prayer; on the contrary, they bemoan any occasion for *tefillah* that they miss.

Shomei'a Tefillah: The personal requests added to the blessing of *Shomei'a Tefillah* may encompass any and all needs.[1] Here a person may seek help for the future, asking that a healthy person remain healthy, or that his children be guided on the right path in life.[2] The *Mishnah Berurah*[3] adds that this is also an appropriate time to confess one's sins. The only limitation is that one should be concise in his requests.[4]

Shomei'a Tefillah provides an opening into which one can insert his deepest yearnings. To help people articulate some of the common longings of the Jewish heart, Torah scholars throughout the ages have prepared special formulations through which one can state his requests. The Chazon Ish[5] composed a prayer for the success of a child in Torah study:

"Yehi ratzon milfanecha, Hashem Elokeinu Velokei Avosainu, she'teracheim al b'nee (child's name and the mother's name) v'sahafoch es livavo l'ahavah ul'yirah Shemecha v'lishkod b'sorascha hakedoshah. V'saseer

7
Kislev

7
Adar

7
Sivan

7
Elul

---

1. *Siman* 119, *Se'if* 1. See *Yaaros Derush*, Vol. 1, *Derush* 1. Also see *Mabit, Beis Elokim, Shaar HaTefillah*, Ch. 3.
2. *Mishnah Berurah, Siman* 119, *Se'if Katan* 1.
3. Ibid. *Se'if Katan* 4.
4. *Siman* 119, *Se'if* 2; *Mishnah Berurah, Siman* 119, *Se'if Katan* 12.
5. *Kovetz Igros Chazon Ish*, Vol. 1 #74.

milfanav kol hasibos hamonos oso mi'shkidas Torascha hakedoshah v'sachin es kol hasibos hame'vios l'sorascha hakedoshah, ki Atah shomei'a tefillah ..."

May it be your will, our G-d and G-d of our fathers, that You have mercy on my child (name and the mother's name) and turn his heart to love and fear Your Name and to dedicate himself to the study of Your holy Torah; and remove all the factors which prevent him from Torah study, and prepare all the factors which will bring him closer to learning Your holy Torah.

Elokai Netzor: This personal prayer of Mar the son of Ravina is said at the conclusion of *Shemoneh Esrei.*[6] The Tzlach[7] explains that these personalized prayers were added there to dismiss any notion that *Shemoneh Esrei* is recited in a forced or perfunctory way. Thus, *Elokai Netzor* serves as a place for one to add personal requests to *Shemoneh Esrei.*

The *Mishnah Berurah*[8] adds that this is an appropriate time for everyone, rich or poor, to beseech Hashem for sustenance. It is also a time for a father and mother to pray that their children develop into Torah scholars with fine character traits. This is a prayer that should be continually upon a parent's lips whenever the opportunity arises.

Yaaros Devash[9] observes that the recitation of *Elokai Netzor* is a most fitting place for asking Hashem for all our needs — nothing is too petty to bring to His attention. Neither is anything too large; no request, however seemingly unattainable, is ignored when accompanied by heartfelt, tearful prayer. The *Chayei Adam*, emphasizing the importance of adding personal requests to *Elokai Netzor*, states:[10]

"It is appropriate and worthwhile for every person to pray each day specifically for his own financial needs, and other practical parts of life, and that his children should be Torah scholars and that all his descendants should be G-d-

---

6. *Berachos* 17a.
7. Ibid.
8. *Siman* 122, *Se'if Katan* 8.
9. Vol. 1, *Derush* 1.
10. Cited in *Mishnah Berurah*, *Siman* 122, *Se'if Katan* 8.

earing people ... And if he cannot phrase these thoughts in the Hebrew language of prayer, let him say his thoughts in his own language, as long as they come from the depths of his heart."

Is any one of these places in *Shemoneh Esrei* preferable for the insertion of personal requests? The *Mishnah Berurah*[11] offers the following guidance: "It is better for one to insert the prayers for all those matters of which he is in need after he has finished saying all *Shemoneh Esrei's* eighteen blessings (i.e., in *Elokai Netzor*), rather than to introduce them into the blessing *Shomei'a Tefillah*, so that when it is necessary for him to respond to *Kaddish* or to *Kedushah,* he will be able to respond."[12]

Personal requests warm the heart with all the emotions of human need and longing. This warmth can turn rock-hard ice into a flowing river of spiritual feeling. Every word of prayer is carried along this powerful current, imbuing one's entire *tefillah* with an intensity and sincerity that might otherwise remain out of reach.

Points to Ponder

▸ *In Shemoneh Esrei, Shomei'a Tefillah and Elokai Netzor are where any request can be inserted.*

▸ *The kavannah inspired by personal requests impacts the rest of one's Shemoneh Esrei.*

---

1. Ibid.
2. However, if one prays alone, or where saying *Kedushah* or responding to *Kaddish* is not an issue, see *Ishei Yisrael*, Ch. 23, fn. 195, that it is better to insert personal requests where they correspond to any of the middle blessings.

STRATEGY 12:
A PERSONAL PLACE

8
Kislev

8
Adar

8
Sivan

8
Elul

As any small child knows, "Hashem is here, Hashem is there, Hashem is truly everywhere." It would seem then that a person could pray with equal effectiveness anywhere — at home or at shul, in the front row or the back, in the living room, or the study, or the backyard.

Our Forefathers, however, set a different precedent. Through numerous episodes that recount their moments of prayer and inspiration, these ancestors, who are credited with establishing the practice of praying three times a day, demonstrated that prayer imparts holiness to a place and a holy place imparts power to one's prayers.

Avraham Avinu was the first of our Forefathers to demonstrate the importance of a set place; after concluding his plea to Hashem to save the inhabitants of Sodom, the Torah[1] relates that *Avraham arose early in the morning to the place where he had stood [in prayer] before Hashem.*

Yitzchak Avinu, too, acknowledged the value of a fixed place to pray. A later verse[2] recounts that Yitzchak, who lived in the south, returned there from *Be'er Lachai Ro'i.* Why had he gone to *Be'er Lachai Ro'i?* The *Ramban*[3] states: "It is likely that Yitzchak Avinu always went to this place [*Be'er Lachai Ro'i*] because it was to him a place of prayer due to the appearance there of the Angel."

The *Sforno*[4] explains that Yitzchak went there because it was the place where Hagar's prayers were answered, and it was there that Yitzchak decided to go to pray for a wife.

---

1. *Bereishis* 19:27.
2. Ibid. 24:62.
3. Ibid.
4. Ibid.

The location (Be'er Lachai Ro'i) is mentioned again in a verse[5] that relates, *And it was after the death of Avraham that G-d blessed Yitzchak his son, and Yitzchak settled near Be'er Lachai Ro'I.* It appears that Yitzchak favored that location since it was there that, through prayer, he experienced the sense of Hashem's goodness and achieved a spiritual awakening.

Finally, we find that Yaakov Avinu also made an effort to pray in a place previously sanctified by prayer. When Yaakov traveled from Be'er Sheva to Haran, he passed Beis El, which was also known as Har HaMoriah [the future site of the *Beis HaMikdash*], but did not stop to pray. However, when he arrived in Haran, Yaakov said, "Is it possible that I passed the place where my fathers [Avraham and Yitzchak] prayed and I did not pray there?"[6]

He immediately decided to go back, and a miracle occurred. In an instant, the ground between Haran and Beis El contracted and Yaakov found himself in Beis El.[7] Yaakov recognized that Avraham and Yitzchak's prayers had infused this place with holiness. Har HaMoriah forever became the site from which prayers are more easily accepted — the perfect location in all the world for the establishment of both the First and Second *Beis HaMikdash*.

The holiness of our Forefathers left its imprint on the sites where they prayed, transforming these locations into holy places. Even in our times, the concept remains vibrant. Each and every Jew can strive to pray in a way that brings holiness to a place, and enables him to achieve his direct connection with Heaven.

Points to Ponder

▸ A person should have a specific place to pray.

▸ The Forefathers demonstrated the importance of praying in a specific place.

▸ Praying sincerely in a specific place imbues it with holiness and that, in turn, enhances one's kavannah.

---

5. Ibid. 25:11.
6. See *Rashi, Bereishis* 28:17.
7. *Chullin* 91b.

DAY
68

STRATEGY 12:
A PERSONAL PLACE,
PART II

A Rav recently traveled to Vilna. When it was time for Minchah, he entered a small shul to daven. As he began to pray, he suddenly felt a tremendous spiritual uplift, almost as if he were praying "Neilah" on Yom Kippur. Why, he wondered, did this particular Minchah prayer move him so deeply?

When the prayer was finished, he asked the local people if they knew of any extraordinary feature of the shul that would account for his experience. They told him that this was the shul in which the Vilna Gaon had davened whenever he was in the city. When the Rav asked, "Where was the Vilna Gaon's makom kavu'a," they pointed to the exact place where the Rav had davened Minchah that day. These few square feet in this small, simple shul still radiated the holiness of the gadol who had prayed there 200 years earlier.[1]

9
Kislev

9
Adar

9
Sivan

9
Elul

The Rambam[2] names eight important precepts regarding proper prayer, and designating a *makom kavu'a* is among them. In fact, the *Shulchan Aruch*[3] states that a person should choose a fixed place to pray and should not deviate from it unless there is an imperative reason, such as to perform a mitzvah[4] or because he was compelled to do so.[5]

The Gemara[6] relates the importance of each of us establishing a *makom kavu'a*,[7] a set place to pray, and says of

---

1. *Derech Sichah*, p. 55.
2. *Hilchos Tefillah* 5:1,6.
3. *Siman* 90, *Se'if* 19.
4. See *Tur, Siman* 90.
5. *Aruch HaShulchan, Siman* 90, *Se'if* 23.
6. *Berachos* 6b.
7. See *Mishnah Berurah, Siman* 90, *Se'if Katan* 60, which states that within four cubits is considered one place. See ibid. *Se'if Katan* 59,

a person who does so, "The G-d of Avraham is his helper." It states further that "when this individual dies, people will say about him, 'Where is the pious man, where is the humble man? [He] is one of the students of Avraham.'"

The Tzlach[8] asks why the Gemara describes someone who establishes a *makom kavu'a* as humble. The answer provided by the Tzlach offers a profound insight. The main reason to establish a *makom kavu'a*, he explains, is to gain the benefit of the sanctity that the designated place acquires. The person who maintains this habit is humbly acknowledging that his prayers alone are inadequate; they need the added spiritual power of a holy place to assist them in penetrating the Heavens.

Conversely, when a person does not pray in a *makom kavu'a*, he seemingly proclaims that his prayers are good enough on their own. He apparently feels that he is capable of generating enough holiness all by himself, wherever he should stand to pray.

If the right location can enhance prayer, it makes sense that, in equal measure, the wrong location can harm it. Thus, one should not pray in a place where concentration will be difficult, such as in the presence of children who have not yet reached the age of *chinuch*.[9]

Noise is not the only factor that constitutes a distraction. One should also avoid praying where there are distracting odors or sights that are not conducive to prayer.[10]

The *Sefer Chassidim*[11] warns against praying next to a wicked person for two reasons: The neighbor's influence

---

which states that one must establish a *makom kavu'a* even when praying at home. See *She'arim Metzuyanim BaHalachah, Siman 12, Se'if 10, Kuntres Acharon*, which states that it appears one must establish a *makom kavu'a* only for reciting *Shemoneh Esrei*.

8. *Berachos* 6b.

9. *Mishnah Berurah, Siman 98, Se'if Katan 3*. According to the *Shelah HaKadosh*, "These children play and dance in the shul and profane the sanctity of the shul and also muddle the minds of those praying. Furthermore, when the children grow older, they will also not desist from the bad practice in which they were educated in their childhood, to run around and show disrespect to the sanctity of the shul."

10. See ibid. *Se'if Katan* 4 and 7.

11. *Siman* 770.

will inspire negative thoughts in one's mind, and also, the *Shechinah* will remove itself from the evil man's presence, making the prayer a fruitless endeavor. In such a situation, *Chazal* declare,[12] "*Oy l'rasha oy lish'cheino*" — Woe is to the wicked person, woe is to his neighbor.

Even the presence of a *minyan* gathered for prayer cannot override the impurity that pervades a place that has been defiled. As Rav Moshe Feinstein ruled,[13] one may not pray in such a place:

"A place where detestable things occur is not a pleasing place for prayer at all, as it is hated by Hashem. And it is better to pray in a place which is loved by Hashem ... and that the *Shechinah* should be with them through prayer itself ... We see that one is forbidden to pray in a place established for repulsive behavior and one should pray alone (if need be) in his house and not in the detestable place even if a *minyan* is present."

A person's surroundings exert a powerful influence upon him. Our Forefathers, Sages and Rabbis have taught us to use this power — to create a cocoon of holiness for ourselves, from which our prayers can emerge transformed and take flight.

---

12. See *Rashi, Bamidbar* 3:29; *Succah* 56b.
13. *Igros Moshe, Orach Chaim,* Vol. 1, *Siman* 31, and Vol. 2, *Siman* 30.

STRATEGY 13:
THE POWER OF
VISUALIZATION

*T*he Gemara[1] relates this incredible scene: As R' Akiva was being tortured to death by the Romans, he calmly began to recite the Shema with complete joy.[2] His students were astounded by R' Akiva's serenity and exclaimed, "Our teacher, how can you remain so calm and concentrate on Shema when you are being tortured?"[3] R' Akiva answered, "My entire life I was troubled by the verse,[4] 'You shall love Hashem ... with all your soul.' I said to myself — when will the opportunity arise that I may fulfill this verse? And now that it has come to pass, should I not fulfill it?"

Rav Dessler[5] explains that R' Akiva reacted with such flawless composure because he had perfected the capacity to transcend all pain for the sake of his love of G-d. His method for achieving this level was to visualize himself — every time he recited this verse in *Shema Yisrael* —being tortured to death for the sanctification of Hashem's Name, giving up his life with joy for his love of the Creator.

Indeed, had this (torture and execution) been forced upon me suddenly, said R' Akiva, I would have been unable to recite the *Shema* properly. That is what he meant by, "My entire life I have been waiting for this moment." Ultimately, this exercise of daily visualization gave him the strength to withstand the ultimate final test.

---

1. *Berachos* 61b.
2. *Yerushalmi Sotah* 5:5.
3. See *Ben Yehoyada* on *Berachos* 61b, who explains that the students' question did not occur when R' Akiva was put to death. Rather, it occurred at an earlier time when the Romans were torturing him and he was reciting *Shema*.
4. *Devarim* 6:5.
5. *Michtav MeEliyahu*, Vol. 4, pp. 252-253.

The technique of visualization is so powerful that it can help a person overcome a great many obstacles. Rabbi Zelig Pliskin relates the following story to illustrate the practical results that this mental exercise can achieve, even for a trivial pastime:

> During the Vietnam War, an American prisoner of war spent several years in solitary confinement. In order to preserve his sanity, he spent four hours of every day visualizing himself mastering his game of golf, with every swing of the club pictured in minute detail.
>
> After his release, he eventually returned to the golf course and found his score greatly improved. All those years of visualization had actually succeeded in improving his game.[6]

This potent mental capacity is there for a person to use in his effort to develop the ability for the most important and difficult daily tasks as well.

> Rabbi Pliskin[7] describes an eye surgeon who mentally visualizes each operation in advance of the procedure. He reviews the entire process in his mind and imagines various difficulties that may arise and how to deal with them.

We, too, can utilize this approach to overcome the obstacles we face in reciting *tefillah* with *kavannah*. The following are some suggestions:

(1) Visualize possible obstacles to *kavannah* that you may encounter during *davening*. Then imagine yourself as having the necessary conviction and persistence to meet the challenge.

For example, picture a friend approaching to engage you in conversation during *davening* and mentally practice how to deflect him without hurting his feelings. Or, imagine that you are reciting *Shemoneh Esrei* and your mind begins to wander. Then envision how you would force away the foreign thoughts so that you would be able to continue the *tefillah* with *kavannah*.

---

6. *My Father, My King* by Rabbi Zelig Pliskin (ArtScroll/Mesorah Publ.), pp. 322-323.
7. Ibid. p. 276.

(2) The *Mesillas Yesharim*[8] writes that as no human eyes have seen Hashem, it is difficult for us to internalize the fact that we are standing before the Creator. To overcome this impediment, visualize a telephone conversation; although you cannot see the person to whom you are speaking, you know that he is listening. Summon this image to perceive the sense that Hashem listens to you when you pray.[9] For example, in *Shemoneh Esrei*, all agree that *"Atah"* — You, Hashem — recited a total of thirty-three times — refers to the fact that we beseech Hashem directly.

> The *Chazon Ish*[10] offers the following technique for arriving at the correct kavannah: "The task of a person during tefillah is to visualize that Hashem is listening to every word of the prayers that are uttered by human lips and scrutinizing the thoughts of those who pray to Him."

(3) Most people find it difficult to summon the self-discipline needed to stick with a productive routine. Distractions and temptations inevitably throw them off track. If a person practices visualizing himself arriving at shul on time, avoiding extraneous conversation, preparing before prayer, and looking inside the *siddur* while praying, these behaviors will gradually become a part of his routine.

Visualization is a means through which a person can see himself as he wishes to be — as he *can* be. It's not just wishful thinking, it's purposeful thinking that helps a person establish high expectations for himself, and then fulfill them.[11]

Points to Ponder

▸ A person can develop a desired behavior or skill by visualizing it.

▸ One can improve tefillah by imagining himself praying with kavannah and overcoming distractions and obstacles.

---

8. Ch. 19, *Chelkei HaChassidus*.
9. See *Berachos* 28b: R' Eliezer said, "When you pray, know before Whom you are standing." *Rashi* explains: "So that you will pray with fear and concentration."
10. *Kovetz Sichos Maamar Mordechai*, Vol. 1, p. 126.
11. For more on the power of visualization, see *Motivation That Works* by Zev Saftlas, pp. 90-103.

CHAPTER 7:
FINDING ANSWERS TO UNANSWERED PRAYERS

UNCOVERING THE DEPTHS

INTRODUCTION

"**K**i mi goi gadol asher lo Elokim krovim eilav, kaHashem Elokeinu b'chol kareinu eilav" — *For which is a great nation that has a G-d Who is close to it, as is Hashem, our G-d, whenever we call to Him?*[1]

Tefillah, as this verse indicates, is the very definition of the close bond between Hashem and the Jewish people. As previous chapters have proven, prayer is the key to all that an individual wants and needs in his life, and all that the Jewish people yearn to achieve as a nation. Nonetheless, it is an undeniable fact played out in Jewish history, as well as in countless personal lives, that sometimes prayer does not bring about the prayed-for salvation.

> *A person is suffering. The prayers that are sent to Heaven on behalf of this person are tear-drenched, heartfelt pleas for mercy. However, the suffering continues, leaving the aching question of "Why?" Why does Hashem sometimes allow His beloved children to continue struggling, despite their prayers?*

This is a question whose complete answer will be known with clarity only at the end of days. Nonetheless, there are Divine principles at work in such a situation, and understanding them is an essential foundation stone in bolstering one's relationship with Hashem through prayer. One or more of the following may be at work in any given situation:

- Prayers may go unanswered in order to motivate a person to reach greater heights in the *kavannah* of his prayers. (Day 70)

11
Kislev

11
Adar

11
Sivan

11
Elul

---

1. *Devarim* 4:7.

- One may be praying for something which, if granted, will prevent him from fulfilling his *tafkid*, mission. (Day 71)
- Those whose mouths are tainted (i.e., with *lashon hara*) produce tainted prayers that cannot reach Heaven. (Day 72)
- Hashem, in His perfect wisdom, knows that the person is praying for something that will ultimately be detrimental. (Day 73)
- The person is judging the situation as it appears at that moment. By waiting for the larger picture to emerge, one will see that the denied request eventually brings a positive result. (Days 74 and 75)
- All sincere prayers are answered, either for the person who makes the request or for his future generations in their time of need. (Days 76 and 77)
- Everything that goes successfully, safely, and smoothly in life is the result of Hashem answering a person's prayers and preventing many setbacks from ever occurring. (Day 78)

It is vital for one to understand these concepts, so as to never fall under the damaging misconception that Hashem is ignoring or deaf to one's heartfelt pleas. Although Divine wisdom is beyond man's capacity to comprehend, Divine love can never be placed in doubt.

And now let us begin finding answers to the issue of unanswered prayers.

❦ ❦

Every day, the father pleads with Hashem to help him find a cure for his young child's condition. Yet every day, the patient grows weaker. David HaMelech promises that Hashem is close to all who call upon Him, to all who call upon Him sincerely,[2] and yet at times sincere prayers seem to go unanswered.

To resolve this perceived difficulty we must turn for insight to the Gemara[3] that says: *Why were our Patriarchs infertile? Because Hashem desires the prayers of the righ-*

---

2. *Tehillim* 145:18.
3. *Yevamos* 64a.

teous. As Rav Dessler[4] explains, our Patriarchs and Matriarchs benefited from their intense suffering, since it caused them to reach deeply into their souls and cry out to Hashem that He bless them with children.

Similarly, Rav Tzadok HaKohen[5] explains: "It is well known that one reaches the essence of prayer through feeling pain, suffering, and loss, because then one prays from the depth of one's heart with the sensation of the loss. This itself (the loss) is from Hashem. And all pain and suffering which Hashem dispatches our way, Heaven forbid, is to awaken, arouse, and alert us to pray properly."

One may still wonder why it was necessary for our holy Forefathers to suffer so much. After all, they fully understood the significance of prayer; it was they who conferred upon *tefillah* its pivotal role in our daily lives.

Rav Dessler teaches us a critical lesson: It was a great kindness of Hashem to bring pain to our Forefathers. Their desperate predicament spurred their already heartfelt prayers onto a new intensity of *kavannah.* This demonstrates the enormous value, in the eyes of Hashem, of each measure of additional *kavannah* in prayer. As the *Abudraham*[6] teaches, "According to the level of concentration will prayer be accepted."

Had our Forefathers not felt this void in their lives, they may have prayed with what they believed to be their full capacity, yet in reality, their full capacity may have remained untapped. Likewise, we may believe that we are praying with every ounce of *kavannah* we can find within ourselves, yet Hashem sees far more in us than we can perceive. Embedded within the troubles He sends us is a loving message: "I know you and care about you, and I know there is a depth to you that you have not yet tapped." The unanswered prayer may really be Hashem's call to us, urging us to uncover the powerful emotions and *kavannah* in the deeper recesses of our hearts.

One who prays can be compared to a person digging a ditch. The deeper he digs, the more the pit can hold.

---

4. *Michtav MeEliyahu,* Vol. 5, p. 67.
5. *Resisei Lailah,* Os 11.
6. P. 92 (end).

"Digging" deep into our souls to create a better *tefillah* increases our capacity to draw close to Hashem and to merit His abundant blessings.[7]

Misfortune and difficulty — whether related to health, finances, children, family, or even spiritual issues — are a part of every life. When these troubles serve as the spark that ignites our passion and sincerity in prayer, then we transform those troubles into "the beginning of our salvation."

▸ Sometimes, we feel that our sincere prayers have not been answered.

▸ Hashem sends misfortune to help us access our deeper levels of kavannah and passion in prayer.

▸ Using misfortune as a tool to come closer to Hashem transforms difficulties to spiritual elevation.

7. *She'arim B'Tefillah,* p. 140.

EQUIPPED FOR THE MISSION

*I*f a fish were able to pray, perhaps it would pray to be given legs so that it could walk the earth and feel the warmth of the sun. The cow's prayer might be that Hashem allow it to fly — to escape its plodding existence and soar among the clouds.

As appealing as these gifts might seem, the fish would not be a better fish if it were to acquire legs, nor would the cow be a better cow, were it equipped with wings. In fact, those appendages would stand in the way of the creatures' fulfillment of their distinct roles in creation.

Sometimes, a person prays for something that he perceives as an essential need in his life. He prays with all his heart, with full concentration, from the deepest depths of his being — and yet, his prayer is not answered. In some cases, Hashem does not fulfill the prayer because if He were to do so, He would be defeating the person's *tafkid* — his Divinely ordained mission in life.

> *A rebbi with a large family is struggling to earn a living and pay his overwhelming monthly bills. He pours out his heart in prayer every day, begging Hashem to somehow increase his income to enable him to support his family while continuing to spread the word of Torah. However, his financial situation does not improve.*[1]

Perhaps this rebbi's *mazal* is to struggle throughout his life to earn a decent living. We have learned, however, that it is possible to change one's *mazal* through a great merit,[2]

---

1. See *Michtav MeEliyahu*, Vol. 4, p. 99, fn. 3; also cited in *Sefer Sifsei Chaim, Pirkei Emunah V'Hashgacha*, Vol. 1, p. 263.
2. *Shabbos* 156a, *Tosafos*, s.v. *Ein mazal*.

which is prayer.[3] Thus, the rebbi's fervent *tefillos* should change his *mazal* and improve his plight.

However, *Tosafos* conclude that "sometimes *mazal* cannot be changed." Rav Dessler explains that each and every person has a unique *tafkid* in life and is faced with a different set of challenges.[4] The nature of a person's mission may limit his ability to change his *mazal* through prayer.

Is the *tafkid* of this rebbi to serve Hashem by disseminating Torah or is it to accept the will of Hashem that he live in abject poverty, regardless of his occupation? If his primary mission is to spread Torah, then his prayers can ease his financial struggles. However, his specific task may change; he may, for instance, obtain a more lucrative position in teaching, or enter the business world and use his newfound means to disseminate Torah.

Alternatively, his life's mission may be to serve as a paragon of self-sacrifice by sanctifying the Name of Hashem while living in poverty. If so, even the most sincere prayer will be unable to change his financial situation, for as *Tosafos* said, "Sometimes *mazal* cannot be changed." This is not to say, however, that his prayers are "unanswered" or are of no benefit, as we will shortly see.

Why does Hashem assign poverty to one person as a mere tool in his mission, and yet give that same degree of poverty to someone else as his fundamental life mission? The answer to this question, says Rav Dessler, is beyond human comprehension: "It is impossible to reveal the reason in this world at all … and it [will not be] revealed until … the end of time. Just as no two people have the same face … [so too] every person has a particular place in revealing Hashem."[5]

The Ramchal[6] adds that the assignment of a particular soul to a person is part of the decree of Heaven, and is not even comprehended by prophets. Rav Chaim Friedlander

---

3. *Ritva* ibid., *Ran*, cited in *Sifsei Chaim, Pirkei Emunah V'Hashgachah*, Vol. 1, p. 263; *Tosafos Yom Tov, Kiddushin*, Ch. 4, Mishnah 14. Also see *Rabbeinu Bachya, Devarim* 31:14.
4. *Michtav MeEliyahu*, Vol. 4, p. 100.
5. Ibid. p. 313; ibid. Vol. 5, p. 214.
6. *Daas Tevunos*, Siman 168, p. 189, s.v. *V'amnam*.

▸ Some
  prayers,
  even though
  emanating
  from the
  depths of a
  person, do
  not invoke
  the desired
  answer.

▸ Even though
  prayer can
  change
  mazal, mazal
  cannot
  always be
  changed.

▸ Prayer will
  not bring
  change
  where the
  change
  interferes
  with a
  person's
  performance
  of his
  Divinely
  ordained
  purpose.

▸ Even if
  prayer does
  not bring
  change, it
  still brings
  blessing.

writes that if we understood the reasons for Heaven's decrees, and their essence were revealed to us, this knowledge would cancel out our tests in life and we would not
be subject to reward and punishment.[7]

Not only is each person assigned a specific role in revealing Hashem's honor, according to the Ramchal,[8] but
each individual must also complete his intended task as
determined by Hashem in His supreme wisdom.

Ultimately, regardless of a person's *tafkid*,[9] Hashem
cherishes his prayers and answers them with good.

---

7. Ibid. fn. 466.
8. Ibid. *Siman* 128, p. 117.
9. See *Vilna Gaon* on *Yonah* 4:3, who states that it is possible for one to
   discern his *tafkid*. Generally, sins which a person is drawn to most
   are likely to be the area which he must correct in this life in order to
   fulfill his *tafkid*. Also see *Nesivos Shalom, Parashas Re'eh*, p. 75.

UNDELIVERED PRAYERS

*H*e should not profane his word; whatever comes from his mouth he shall do.[1] The simple meaning of the verse is that one should fulfill his promises. There is another layer of meaning, however, that reveals the intimate relationship between a person's power of speech and the power of his prayer.

Dayan Aharon D. Dunner[2] relates the explanation of the *Chidah*: If a person is careful with his words, then what "comes from his mouth" — his prayers — "He, [Hashem], shall do." Care with one's power of speech is an essential factor in having one's requests of Hashem granted.

What is the basis of this relationship? Is it simply a matter of sin and punishment, that one sins by using his power of speech improperly, and therefore, Hashem rejects his request? That does not fully explain what is happening. There are many sins into which a person might stumble; why do sins of speech, such as speaking *lashon hara*,[3] or giving bad advice,[4] have a specific impact on the ability to be answered from Heaven? The explanation is not that Hashem is punishing the person for the sin; it is that the person himself, by using his mouth improperly, is tainting the mechanism that produces his prayers.

> In today's world, a revealing allegory is the computer virus. A person sends his message through cyberspace believing that it will arrive at its destination intact. He does not know that the entire program has become infected, and that every transmission carries contamination with it. His messages are distorted, destructive, and unwelcome.

13
Kislev

13
Adar

13
Sivan

13
Elul

---

1. *Bamidbar* 30:3.
2. Keynote Session, 5758 Convention of Agudath Israel.
3. *Shemiras HaLashon, Shaar* 1, Ch. 7.
4. *Machzor Vitri*, p. 725.

A person has many requests that he presents to Hashem every day. The tool that he uses to present his plea is the mouth. It is therefore critical to the success of one's prayers that one exercise great care when using this all-important tool.

> A doctor performs a delicate, lifesaving operation. He works meticulously, expending great effort and care to assure that every step of the procedure is completed perfectly. Although he does everything right, his patient is almost certainly doomed, because the instruments the doctor is using are contaminated. No matter how lofty the doctor's intent, and how great his skill, he cannot succeed with unclean tools.

The essential first step in any effort to improve the effectiveness of one's prayers is to purify the mouth that produces them. When one prays without apparent result, it is imperative that he examine his habits of speech. Although mastery of this area is an ongoing challenge, one must at least recognize where he has stumbled and concede to himself that his improper speech may be impairing his prayers. He has at his disposal the mighty power of *teshuvah* to help him correct this fatal flaw in his ability to pray (See Day 87, "Rebuilding Burned Bridges"), but first, he must identify and admit to the problem.

Just as damaging to the efficacy of one's prayers as speaking *lashon hara*, is the habit of talking during *chazaras hashatz* — the *chazzan's* repetition of the *Shemoneh Esrei*. Speaking during *chazaras hashatz* is condemned by the *Shulchan Aruch*[5] using the harshest language seen in any discussion of transgression. One could almost conclude from this admonition that there is no worse sin: "One should refrain from speaking profane words during the time the *chazan* repeats *Shemonah Esrei*. And if one spoke, it is a sin, **and the sin is too great to bear.** "

Why does this sin merit such strong disapproval?

Rav Matisyahu Salomon, Mashgiach of Beis Medrash Govoha,[6] explains that the sin of speaking during *chazaras*

---

5. *Siman* 124, *Siman* 7.
6. During a large gathering for *Teshuvah*, Elul 25, 5761. See also *Sefer Matnas Chaim*, pp. 192-194.

hashatz is not, in reality, more egregious than eating on Yom Kippur or desecrating the Sabbath. Rather, the level of condemnation reflects the message being expressed by the person who is engaged in conversation. He shows his great disrespect for prayer and demonstrates his innermost feeling that it is meaningless to him, for it is pre-empted by a conversation with his friend.

> *Such behavior severs the unique bond that prayer forges between man and the Almighty. It is this severed relationship that is "too great to bear," for who can bear life without a relationship with Hashem? Furthermore, should a tragedy strike this person, causing him to turn to the potent power of prayer, it will not be available, because he no longer enjoys that special connection with Hashem.*[7]

The message in these concepts is a stark one: The manner in which a person uses his power of speech can incapacitate the mouth in its most essential task. The message is, however, a comforting one as well, for it tells us that it may *not* be the incomprehensible machinations of Heaven that are denying us an answer to our prayers. It may be that *we ourselves* are tainting our own prayers. That leaves us with an avenue of hope; we can examine our habits, correct what is wrong, and make a fresh attempt at beseeching Hashem for our needs.

Points to Ponder

▸ *The mouth is the instrument with which we present our prayers.*

▸ *A tainted tool produces a tainted product. Thus, a mouth that speaks lashon hara or speaks during prayer cannot produce effective prayers.*

▸ *If one does not receive an answer to his prayers, he should examine his speech habits and do teshuvah so that his prayers will be effective.*

---

7. See Day 85, "*Chazaras Hashatz* — Sending the Message, Part II."

20/20 FORESIGHT

I magine a world in which a mitzvah was clearly and immediately rewarded right here in this world, for all to
see. Rav Huna's words in the Gemara[1] present such a
world, in which certain mitzvos come with an assurance of
certain tangible rewards.

If his description played itself out precisely, every woman who lights her Shabbos candles correctly would have
Torah scholars for sons. Every house that bears *mezuzos*
that are kosher and properly placed would be a beautiful home. Every man who is careful to wear kosher *tzitzis*
would own impressive clothing, and all those who observe
Shabbos carefully would possess a winepress overflowing
with wine. These are the assertions given by Rav Huna,[2]
and they are stated unequivocally. Any person who looks
around him, however, will quickly note that there appear
to be a great many exceptions to these statements.

The *Shevet HaMussar*[3] explores the question of why
the rewards that are linked to certain mitzvos do not seem
to accrue to all those who scrupulously perform them. For
example, the Gemara[4] states that the pious people living in
the times of R' Yehudah bar Ila'i had only one garment to
cover six scholars when they studied Torah. They were unquestionably careful in their performance of the mitzvah
of *tzitzis*, and yet the stated reward for that mitzvah did
not accrue to them. The answer given in *Shevet HaMussar*
is that even where reward is merited, "At times, Hashem
sees that the individual will most benefit if He withholds

14
Kislev

14
Adar

14
Sivan

14
Elul

---
1. *Shabbos* 23b.
2. Ibid.
3. Ch. 40.
4. *Sanhedrin* 20a.

the reward in this world and grants it instead in the World to Come."

> Ben's uncle was opening a branch of his successful real estate business in the local neighborhood. Uncle Chaim would need someone to manage the new office, a position Ben knew would be lucrative. He had the right experience for the job, and so he prayed to Hashem to lift him out of his current mediocre career and give him a new, high-paying job with Uncle Chaim. Despite the fervor with which he prayed, the job went to someone else. Ben felt that his prayers had gone unanswered, and a good thing had slipped through his fingers.

> What Ben did not realize, however, was that the job that was so appealing to him was in fact not "a good thing." Ben could not imagine that life in a higher economic class could be anything but wonderful. Hashem, however, knew that Ben would misuse his wealth. In denying Ben the job, Hashem saved him from the overindulgences on which he would have wasted his time. He saved Ben from the heartbreak of watching his children falter in school as they became distracted by the ever-increasing inventory of electronic toys that would have filled their home. He rescued Ben from the lost learning time that would have been sacrificed to vacations and entertainment, and from the emotionless prayer that would have emanated from his complacent heart.

As in Ben's case, the reward which a person merits is not always something he is equipped to use to his benefit. Hashem does not reward a person in order to trap him in a test he cannot withstand or burden him with choices he is not equipped to make.

For example, wealth can be a great test, and it is a test that many people are not prepared to pass. That is why Shlomo HaMelech said,[5] *Give me neither poverty nor wealth; provide me my allotted bread.* The *Metzudas David*[6] and

---

5. *Mishlei* 30:8.
6. Ibid.

Points
to
Ponder

▶ *Even though
certain
mitzvos
are linked
to specific
rewards,
people do
not always
receive
those
rewards.*

▶ *Hashem
foresees
whether
or not
rewards are
beneficial for
a person at a
specific time
— and may
set them
aside until
such time as
they will be
beneficial.*

▶ *Sometimes
a reward is
not granted
until the
person
reaches the
World to
Come.*

Ibn Ezra[7] explain that the verse asks Hashem to give a person that which he requires for sustenance, but no more. If wealth will cause a person to stumble, Hashem may withhold it rather than drag him down to a spiritual low-point.

> *"Be careful what you ask for," goes the popular saying. For a Jew, however, Hashem is the arbiter of rewards. In Him we can trust absolutely, knowing that what He gives is for our good, and what He withholds is equally for our good.*

Ultimately, even if one does not receive what he asked for, Hashem cherishes his prayers and answers them with good.

---

7. Ibid.

DESPERATE PLIGHT

*O*ne could almost feel the heavy gloom that had settled upon the family's house. Whatever broke remained broken. The formerly brightly lit rooms were now bathed in darkness in an effort to lower the electric bills. The children who played in the yard looked unkempt, for their mother could not muster the strength to maintain appearances.

It had been six months since her husband brought home his last paycheck — six months of job interviews that went nowhere, six months of battles with creditors and utilities, six months of ever-increasing despair. "What do I ask for, Hashem?" she pleaded, her heart twisting inside her. "Just to be able to raise my family, to send them to school, to make a Shabbos without worry. Please give my husband a job, please!"

The words of the *Shevet HaMussar*, that "At times, Hashem sees that the individual will most benefit if He withholds the reward in this world and grants it instead in the World to Come" can satisfy one who is praying for something he wants, but may not really need. A person can understand that the excess he hopes for may cause him to lose sight of Hashem and become ensnared in his newfound status. The person himself, were he able to perceive Hashem's view, would not want his request granted.

The explanation is more difficult to understand, however, when the matters about which one is praying are matters of survival. Human beings cannot conceive of any ultimate benefit that would result from being kept in a state of desperate poverty or dire illness. They may even see their spiritual level declining as a result of their preoccupation with their pressing troubles. Why, then, are their fervent prayers not being answered?

One of the great *Tannaim*, who was a teacher of R' Akiva, is known as *Nachum Ish Gamzu*. He acquired this name because his response to any difficulty was "Gam zu l'tovah" — *This too is for good*. Rav Chaim Shmulevitz[1] explains that his greatness lay in his ability to view events in their overall context. By applying the words "this too" to events that clearly appeared, at the moment, to be troublesome, he declared that everything that happened belonged within Hashem's script of goodness for His world. Although man does not have the ability to perceive this script from its beginning to the end, if he knows the nature of the Author, he knows that all that happens in the script is good.

> The Gemara[2] relates that R' Akiva was once traveling to a city. He was refused lodging in the city and was forced to spend the night in a field. He had brought with him a rooster to awaken him in the morning, a donkey upon which to travel, and a candle to provide light. As he settled himself for the night, a strong wind extinguished the candle. A cat appeared and ate the rooster. Finally, a lion emerged and demolished the donkey. Nevertheless, R' Akiva cried out: "Gam zu l'tovah."
>
> That night an armed band of robbers invaded the city. Upon hearing this, R' Akiva stated: "Did I not tell you that all that Hashem does is for the good?" Rashi[3] explains: Had the candle remained lit, the rooster crowed, or the donkey brayed, R' Akiva would have been captured along with the people of the city.

In a letter to his family, the Vilna Gaon[4] echoed R' Akiva's teachings: "Remember … about that which you cry today you will laugh tomorrow." The Gaon was cautioning

---

1. See *Sichos Mussar, Shaarei Chaim*, Maamar 13, p. 53, "Gam zu l'tova"; [5732 Maamar 9].
2. *Berachos* 60b.
3. Ibid.
4. Cited in *Sichos Mussar, Shaarei Chaim*, Maamar 13, p. 54.

his family not to judge events in the context of the "here and now," for the goodness inherent in every event may only become apparent at the end of one's life, or it may even wait until the World to Come.

Each day when a Jew awakens he recites the *Birchos HaShachar, morning blessings.*[5] One of the blessings is: "Blessed are You, Hashem, our G-d, King of the universe, Who has provided me with my every need." Rav Moshe Schwab, Mashgiach in Gateshead,[6] teaches that this blessing represents a Jew's faith that Hashem provides him with his every need, and that Hashem has the ability and desire to bestow upon His children all that they need to live.

When a specific prayer goes unanswered, it may indicate that, despite the difficult circumstances, Hashem has determined that the request is not what the person needs. While a person can and should continue to pray for salvation, his greatest merit comes from his acceptance of Hashem's judgment, and his recognition that "this too," however difficult it may be, "is for the good."

Ultimately, even if one does not receive what he asked for, Hashem cherishes his prayers and answers them with good.

▸ *Difficulties cannot be assessed on a day-to-day basis –but only as part of the "complete picture."*

▸ *Ultimately, even if he did not receive what he asked for, Hashem cherishes his prayers and answers them with good.*

---

5. See *Mishnah Berurah, Siman* 70, *Se'if Katan* 2, which states that from the wording of the *Tur* and the *Shulchan Aruch* in *Siman* 46, *Se'if* 4, and especially the corresponding wording of the *Levush*, women are likewise required to recite the *Birchos HaShachar*. Also see *Halichos Bas Yisroel*, Ch. 2, *Se'if* 5 and fn. 12.
6. *Maarchei Lev*, Vol. *1, Yamim Noraim*, p. 47.

DESPERATE PLIGHT, PART II

16
Kislev

16
Adar

16
Sivan

16
Elul

B y attuning one's perceptions to the ways of Hashem, a person can see the concept of "Gam zu l'tovah, *this too is for good*" at work throughout his life. It is this outlook that allows a person to see opportunity where others see disappointment, to see a blessing where others see a burden.

The ability to see the good that emerges from troubles — even tragedies — is a hallmark of those whose lives are steeped in Torah. Three great luminaries exemplified this concept through great difficulties they endured.

> In the 1930's, Rav Yaakov Kamenetsky[1] was Rav of a small, sixty-family community in a town called Tzitevian. His family lived in dire poverty and he could not even afford to buy a suit for his son Binyamin for his bar mitzvah.
>
> Unable to subsist on the income he earned, Rav Yaakov applied over the course of several years for rabbinical positions in larger towns. The last one for which he applied was in Vilkomir, the third largest Jewish community in Lithuania. After several interviews, Rav Yaakov was offered the position. He returned home to tell his wife the great news, and the household erupted in jubilation; finally their crushing poverty would be alleviated.
>
> Three weeks later, the jubilation turned to grief when Rav Yaakov received news that the position had gone to someone else. The rebbetzin cried bitter

---

1. Paraphrased from *Reb Yaakov, The Life and Times of HaGaon Rabbi Yaakov Kamenetsky*, by Yonoson Rosenblum (ArtScroll/Mesorah Publ.), pp. 108-110.

tears over the loss of the rabbanus in Vilkomir, recognizing that it virtually ensured that Rav Yaakov would have to seek some means of support abroad.

The failure to win that position, as well as the others, profoundly affected Rav Yaakov's own strong sense of Divine Providence. The successful candidates and their families eventually fell into the hands of the Nazis. "In counseling people undergoing difficult tests, Rav Yaakov would often point to his own experience as an example of how that which is perceived at the moment as the greatest tragedy may, with the passage of time, be revealed to be the greatest salvation."[2]

A few years earlier, a similar chain of events occurred in the life of another great Torah leader, Rav Eliyahu Eliezer Dessler.

In 1928, just a few years after Rav Dessler married, he was forced to leave his home in Kelm and travel to London with his ill father, whose business had recently collapsed.

Rav Dessler was alone in London, without his wife and children, and cut off from the spiritual wells [Kelm] from which he had drunk all his life ...[3]

Ultimately, Rav Dessler's entire family would be saved by virtue of his being forced to go to England. But at the time, he could not possibly have known that. All he knew was that he had been uprooted from an environment of the most intense spiritual striving imaginable and set down in a strange land ...[4]

In America, a few years later, a similar story was being played out.[5]

In 1936, Rav Pam sought a position in Torah Vodaath, but none were available. Being proficient in a num-

---

2. Ibid. p. 109.
3. Paraphrased from *Rav Dessler* by Yonoson Rosenblum (Artscroll/Mesorah Publ.), p. 110.
4. Ibid. p. 115.
5. Paraphrased from *Rav Pam* by Rabbi Shimon Finkelman (ArtScroll/Mesorah Publ.), p. 57.

ber of languages, he applied for a position as a court interpreter. He was highly qualified, and scored highest on the exam. However, the judge gave his nephew the post.

He then applied for a rabbinical position in Pennsylvania. It was arranged that he would take a bus from Port Authority for an interview. Rav Pam, who was very punctual, missed the bus by minutes. The interview was never rescheduled.

Decades later, Rav Pam remarked that he was eternally grateful to Hashem for having led him to dwell in the tent of Torah all his life. He elaborated:

When one misses a bus for an interview, the natural reaction is, "Oh, I've missed my chance, my opportunity!" When I was a rebbi in Torah Vodaath and then a Rosh Yeshivah, I could look back and see the great chesed Hashem did for me by causing me to miss the bus.

One should never feel bad when an opportunity does not work out, for he never knows what lies ahead. There is a vast difference between focusing on the present and focusing on the broader picture as one relies on the Ribbono Shel Olam with the belief that "Gam zu l'tovah."

Only by understanding Hashem's perfection can a person comprehend that goodness is the final outcome of all the troubles and injustices he sees in the world. David HaMelech expresses this thought in the Song for the Shabbos Day:[6] The psalm offers praise of G-d:

How great are Your deeds, Hashem; exceedingly profound are Your thoughts ... a boor cannot know, nor can a fool understand this: when the wicked bloom like grass and all the doers of iniquity blossom, it is to destroy them till eternity ...

Rav Matisyahu Salamon, Mashgiach of Beis Medrash Govoha, explains that first one must recognize how great are Your deeds, Hashem; exceedingly profound are Your thoughts. With that underlying understanding, one knows

---

6. Tehillim 92.

with certainty that everything — including the instances *when the wicked bloom like grass and all the doers of iniquity blossom* — arises from Hashem's perfect wisdom.

- *Faith in the goodness of Hashem's deeds provides comfort in the face of an unanswered prayer.*

- *Often, the good that comes out of a seemingly terrible situation becomes apparent only many years later.*

DAY 76

THE BETTER GOOD

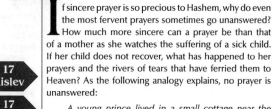

17 Kislev

17 Adar

17 Sivan

17 Elul

I f sincere prayer is so precious to Hashem, why do even the most fervent prayers sometimes go unanswered? How much more sincere can a prayer be than that of a mother as she watches the suffering of a sick child. If her child does not recover, what has happened to her prayers and the rivers of tears that have ferried them to Heaven? As the following analogy explains, no prayer is unanswered:

> A young prince lived in a small cottage near the king's castle. One day, bandits came and destroyed his home. Crying bitterly, the prince begged his fa-ther to rebuild his cottage, but the king took no ac-tion, despite his son's pleas.
>
> Disappointed, the prince asked his father why he refused to help him. The king answered, "On the contrary, I wish to help you and I will indeed do so. I have not rebuilt your cottage because I want to build you a palace in its place."[1]

In the same way, Hashem in His infinite wisdom chooses not to immediately fulfill a specific request. If that request comes to him in a sincere prayer, however, it ultimately will be answered, perhaps by something much better than what one has imagined. The answer may become appar-ent in this world, or it may await a person in the World to Come.

Two seemingly unconnected verses in *Parashas Vayeira*[2] illustrate the way in which Hashem stores "unanswered" prayers as a merit for the future: *And Hashem said, Shall I conceal from Avraham what I do (in Sodom)? And Avra-ham will surely be a great and mighty nation.*

---

1. Cited in *Keser Shem Tov*, p. 20.
2. *Bereishis* 18:17-18.

What is the connection between these two verses? The Dubna Maggid[3] explains that Hashem was deciding whether to inform Avraham of Sodom's impending destruction [*Shall I conceal from Avraham what I do?*] for even if Avraham were to pray on Sodom's behalf, Hashem knew that it must ultimately be destroyed.

Nevertheless, because *Avraham will surely be a great and mighty nation,* Hashem decided to tell him that Sodom would be destroyed. As a result, Avraham prayed for Sodom; these prayers became a tremendous benefit to Avraham's descendants many generations later.

Illustrating the same concept, the Dubna Maggid[4] explains the oft-quoted Gemara, *Why were our Patriarchs infertile? Because Hashem desires the prayers of the righteous.* Hashem, the All-Merciful, brought great suffering to the Forefathers, which caused them to pray, because He knew that when crisis would strike future generations of the Jewish people, they would desperately need the benefit of those heartfelt cries. Today, in a very real way, the Jewish people gain immensely from the prayers and tears of the Forefathers.

> The Steipler Gaon sometimes reflected on the phenomenon of a return to Judaism among Jews whose parents and grandparents could not even read Hebrew. He felt that this resurgence was due to the enormous merit of previous generations — the great-grandmothers who prayed and cried that their children would remain upstanding religious Jews. Although these supplications did not benefit their immediate offspring, Hashem kept the prayers and "used" them for the advantage of their descendants today.

Points to Ponder

▸ Some prayers seem not to evoke an answer from Heaven.

▸ Avraham's prayers for the inhabitants of Sodom did not help them, but were stored as a merit for his descendants.

▸ The return to Judaism of many assimilated Jews could be attributed to the prayers their great-grandparents said for their own children.

---

3. Cited in *She'arim B'Tefillah,* p. 143.
4. *Ohel Yaakov, Parashas Lech Lecha* 12:20.

PRAYER AND LOSS

S ometimes, unfortunately, despite sincere prayers, a seriously ill family member or close acquaintance passes away. There is a natural tendency in such a situation to feel that one's prayers were for naught. However, according to the Steipler Gaon, comfort should be drawn from the knowledge that our prayers do have a significant effect; the prayers remain a source of merit because through them Heavenly compassion was aroused. These merits will stand by the departed in the World to Come and may also protect their children in the future.

These prayers may also bring salvation to other individuals and to the community as a whole. At the End of Days, when all will be revealed, we will see the redeeming power of each and every *tefillah* that has ever been prayed.[1]

> *When Rav Shneur Kotler, Rosh Yeshivah of Beis Medrash Govoha of Lakewood, was suffering from his terminal illness, a group of his students and admirers journeyed to Bnei Brak, Israel, to implore the Steipler Gaon to intensify his prayers on Rav Shneur's behalf. They confided to the Steipler that they were discouraged because prayers were pouring from tens of thousands of Jewish hearts, yet the Rosh Yeshivah's condition continued to decline.*
>
> *The Steipler responded, "Do not be dismayed. There is no such thing as a sincere prayer that goes unanswered. Any heartfelt request addressed to G-d must be answered. It cannot be otherwise. If it is not answered today it will be answered tomorrow. If not tomorrow it will be answered in a week. If not in a week, in a month. If not answered in a month, it may*

18
Kislev

18
Adar

18
Sivan

18
Elul

---

1. *More Shabbos Stories* [*Toldos Yaakov*] by Rabbi Shimon Finkelman (ArtScroll/Mesorah Publ.), pp. 118-11.

> *be answered in a year, or in ten years, or in one hundred years or more. If your prayers are not answered in your lifetime, they will be answered for your children or for your children's children. We cannot say for sure when a prayer will be answered, but we can rest assured that every prayer will be answered somehow, someday."*[2]

Rav Shimshon David Pincus[3] explains that while each prayer evokes a corresponding reply from Heaven, Hashem alone perceives a situation in its full complexity. One cannot always understand the logic or justice in His response. Seemingly unanswered prayers are sometimes like the rain and snow. They appear to sink out of sight, accomplishing nothing, but in fact, they saturate the Heavens just as rain saturates the earth and brings forth its blessings. The bounty of Heaven, just like the bounty of earth, waits for its proper season.

Only Hashem knows when that season will be. For example, a loved one might be involved in a serious accident, G-d forbid. Nobody in the family knows of the accident as the ambulances race to the scene. No one is there to pray while the victim hangs tenuously onto life. In such a case, Rav Pincus says, Hashem "takes out" a heartfelt prayer that a family member uttered years ago — a prayer that was unanswered at the time — and showers its merit upon the current situation. That prayer, held in reserve for so long, may now become the injured person's salvation.

> *Reuven is a confident, energetic little boy who runs everywhere he goes. One morning, his mother calls him to come downstairs for breakfast, and he dashes to the stairs in his typical, high-speed style. This time, however, he trips on his shoelace and begins a headlong descent down the stairs. His mother hears the child's startled shout and then the sickening thump-thump of his body landing heavily on step after step. She runs to the scene just as he crashes to the floor.*

---

2. See *Chayei Olam*, Perek 28, p. 42; and *A Letter for the Ages* by Rabbi Avrohom Chaim Feuer (ArtScroll/Mesorah Publ.), p. 121.
3. *She'arim B'Tefillah*, p. 143. Also see *Nefesh Shimshon*, p. 339.

**Points
to
Ponder**

▸ *Even when
a person
passes
away, the
prayers for
his recovery
are not lost.*

▸ *Prayers are
stored and
answered in
the manner
and at the
time that
Hashem
deems best.*

▸ *All sincere
prayers are
answered
with good.*

*He lies perfectly still for a moment, and her heart fills
with cold fear. Just as she approaches him, he begins
to move. He gets up, adjusts his rumpled shirt, col-
lects his yarmulke and says, "What's for breakfast?"*

*The boy's mother has prayed many times for
many things, and sometimes, her prayers were not
answered as she had hoped. At this moment, however, she can appreciate that not one word has gone
to waste.*

We pray for certain aspects of good to come into our
lives, yet we have no real way of knowing if our vision of
good is accurate from the true perspective of Heaven. The
man praying to meet his household's expenses may
always have to struggle for money, but his prayers might
keep his children securely upon the path of Torah. The
couple praying for children may not ultimately succeed in
their quest, but the merit of their prayers may help save
their entire community from some terrible decree.

We do not always know what good a prayer will bring.
We do know, however, that all sincere prayer is answered
with good.

BEHIND THE SCENES

*L*ook at the world around you for a moment. The air is filled with microbes. The city streets harbor legions of felons. On the highways, drivers who are tired, distracted or just don't drive very well speed along at 70 miles an hour. It's a miracle that a person makes it through a day.

Looking at the world from a Jewish perspective, it is indeed a miracle — a miracle wrought by our daily prayers. The "answer" we are looking for when we pray is all around us, in the disasters that don't happen, the diseases that don't strike, the enemies that don't attack. Hashem answers us in ways we cannot readily perceive.

At the conclusion of *Bircas Avos* in our daily *Shemoneh Esrei*, we say that Hashem is a King, a Helper, a Savior, and a Shield.[1] Rav Dessler[2] explains that there are three levels of Heavenly Help a person may receive.

First, Hashem is an *Ozeir*, a Helper. At this level, a person is in the throes of an *existing,* immediate, and inescapable danger, and Hashem thwarts the harm or injury:

> *A man is accosted by a criminal who waves a gun in his direction and demands his wallet. Suddenly, a police officer on a routine patrol notices the crime in progress and rescues the victim.*

Hashem is also a *Moshia*, a Savior. At this level of help, He pushes aside an impending peril, canceling the danger that is *threatening* a person:

1. See *She'eilos U'Teshuvos HaRashba,* Vol. 5, *Siman* 115; *Bnei Yissaschar, Teves, Maamar* 41, *Os* 29; *Malbim on Yeshayahu* 12:2 for other interpretations of "a Helper, a Savior, and a Shield." Also see Day 30, "King, Helper, Savior, and Shield."
2. *Michtav MeEliyahu,* Vol. 4, p. 65.

A young man is innocently walking down the street, when he suddenly notices a commotion in an alley-way as he passes by. The police are in the process of arresting a pair of armed muggers who were lurking in the shadows awaiting their next victim.

Finally, Hashem is a *Magen*, a Shield. At that level, He prevents the trouble or misfortune from even approaching the person in the first place:[3]

A pedestrian decides to take the longer "scenic route" through the park to work. He'll never know that a gang of hoodlums had gathered along his usual route.

When we are in an obvious position of difficulty or danger, it is easy to perceive that Hashem is an *Ozeir*, Helper, or *Moshia*, Savior. We can clearly recognize when Hashem saves us from the potential consequences of a perilous situation. Recognizing that no damage or harm has ensued, we are moved to cry out a heartfelt "Baruch Hashem."

However, as a *Magen*, Hashem shields us completely, providing us with cover from potential harm. We have no knowledge or perception that we have been spared.

Imagine a huge corporation whose workers are blissfully unaware that a major downsizing is being considered as a means of improving the company's bottom line. The top executives huddle in a conference room secretly deciding the fate of their employees. At the last moment, they decide to sell off one of their overseas divisions and spare the staff of their home office the dreaded "axe."

A Jewish employee fervently praying for his livelihood in Barech Aleinu (of Shemoneh Esrei) on a daily basis has no idea that Hashem responded to his heartfelt prayers by enabling him to keep his job.

The *Bnei Yissaschar* explains the following verses with this important concept:[4] *Praise Hashem, all nations; praise Him, all the states! For His kindness has overwhelmed us,*

---

3. Sefer *Derech Sichah*, p. 659.
4. *Tehillim* 117:1-2.

and the truth of Hashem is eternal. Why would the nations praise Hashem for His goodness on our behalf? How do they even know of the favor that Hashem bestows on His people?

The fact is that the nations of the world are actually more aware than we of Hashem's kindness toward us, because they know of the plots being planned against us — schemes of which we are completely ignorant. That ignorance stems from Hashem acting as a *Magen*, a Shield, Who prevents the misfortune of those evil plots from even approaching us.

> *In July 1997, the evil plans of two Arabs were thwarted before being bought to fruition. They had plotted to place pipe bombs filled with nails in a subway station, in Brooklyn, N.Y., in a neighborhood primarily inhabited by Orthodox Jews. The plot was aborted at the last minute when a roommate of the Arabs became leery of their activities and told a policeman of his suspicions.*

As quoted earlier, the verse, *Hashem is close to all who call upon Him, to all who call upon Him sincerely,*[5] assures us that Hashem always responds to dignified prayers, recited with sincerity and *kavannah*.

When any aspect of life runs smoothly without drama and trauma, we are seeing the answer to our prayers.

Points to Ponder

- *Hashem helps people in various ways.*
- *When Hashem acts as a Helper or a Savior, taking us out of harm's way, we see clearly the answer to our prayers.*
- *When Hashem acts as a Shield, deflecting the harm altogether, we are receiving a powerful but less apparent answer to our prayers.*

CHAPTER 8
THE SPOKEN WORD: OUR DOWNFALL, OUR SALVATION

MANUFACTURING WORDS

Note: This chapter is not meant to criticize any member of the Jewish people; rather, it is a heartfelt attempt to help overcome an unfortunate reality. The phenomenon of talking during tefillah must be addressed so that we can truly unleash the awesome power of prayer, for the sake of every individual as well as for the Jewish nation as a whole.

All that Hashem created can be turned toward constructive or destructive purposes: "Zeh l'umas zeh asah HaElokim."[1] G-d has made the one as well as the other. The more powerful the force, the greater its impact.

Atomic power can fuel the entire world or destroy it. Rain can bring sustenance or floods. Fire can bring warmth or pain and ruin. Man's creative powers can yield marvelous inventions to help mankind, or evil plans capable of destroying civilizations.

Of all these forces, the spiritual power inherent in the human capacity for speech is perhaps the most powerful force of all, and therefore it possesses an unmatched potential for invoking either good or evil.

Rabbeinu Yonah[2] expresses this concept in the words of the *Yalkut*: "The Community of Israel is beloved through its voice, and hated through its voice. It is loved through its voice, as it is written:[3] *Let Me hear your voice, because your voice is sweet.* It is hated through its voice, as it is written:[4] *She raised her voice against Me, therefore I have*

---

1. *Koheles* 7:14.
2. Cited in *With Hearts Full of Faith* by Rabbi Matisyahu Salomon (ArtScroll/Mesorah Publ.), p. 150.
3. *Shir HaShirim* 2:14.
4. *Yirmiyahu* 12:8.

hated her. This is the meaning of that which is written:[5] *Death and life are in the power of the tongue and those who love [to use] it shall eat its fruit."*

The Gemara[6] discloses just how precious the pure, untainted mouth is in the eyes of Heaven. It states that the world continues to exist only in the merit of the breath that comes from the mouths of schoolchildren. This statement raises an objection from Rav Pappa. He asks Abaye: What about my breath and your breath? Is our Torah study not at least as meaningful as theirs? Abaye replies: A breath that bears the impurity of sin is not comparable to a breath that is free of the taint of sin.

How is it possible that schoolchildren's elementary words of Torah accomplish more than the profound Torah of the great Abaye and Rav Pappa? The answer is that the mouths of the great Rabbis are not as pure as those of schoolchildren. *Sefer Halkrim*[7] echoes this concept, stating that one who is not tainted with sin and serves Hashem at a lesser level is valued more than one who is tainted with sin and serves Hashem at a more advanced level.

The Talmud[8] relates that Rabbi Shimon bar Yochai wanted Torah to be learned uninterrupted. He said, "Had I been standing at Mount Sinai when the Torah was given to the Jewish nation, I would have asked Hashem that a person be created with two mouths: one mouth to continuously learn Torah, and the other mouth to perform all the necessities of life such as eating and drinking."

However, he came to the conclusion that had man been created with two mouths, the world would be unable to exist. Since the world cannot endure all the meaningless talk, combined with *lashon hara*, which is spoken with one mouth, then with two mouths (whereby one would always be available to speak such talk) the world would certainly be unable to exist.

For better or worse, a person has but one mouth, and that one mouth has to suffice for a multitude of uses.

---

5. *Mishlei* 18:21.
6. *Shabbos* 119b.
7. *Maamar* 4, Ch. 29, s.v. *V'yoreh*.
8. *Yerushalmi, Berachos* 1:3.

‣ *Hurtful or
meaningless
speech
taints the
mouth
which
produces
prayer.*

‣ *A tainted
mouth
cannot
produce
effective
prayer.*

‣ *Hashem
treasures
children's
learning
and prayers
because
they are
untainted by
sin.*

Clearly, the choices we make in this regard are critical to our ability to use our mouths for their G-d-given purpose — as the tools that enable our souls to do their work on earth, producing words of Torah learning and prayer.

TALKING DURING PRAYER

*P*raying with a minyan has become, for many people, the setting for a power struggle. The power of speech pulls in two directions simultaneously, and the mouth switches gears, gliding from idle chatter to holy words, over and over again: A friendly greeting to a late-arriving friend, then an "Amen." A few words about the morning's stock market quotes, then a catch-up on Pesukei D'Zimrah. Solemn silence during the "silent" Shemoneh Esrei, and then a full-blown political debate during the chazzan's repetition.

To our great misfortune, conversation during prayer has become an almost natural and even expected practice. The stringent halachic prohibitions against conversing during prayer appear to be overlooked by many people who may be extremely careful with adherence to *halachah* in many other areas.

Sometimes the problem rests with a misguided notion of what friendliness requires in meeting the demands of one's neighbors. In some communities, however, shul attendance has evolved into a social phenomenon, and community members have established a routine of meeting and socializing at various points of prayer. The social imperative is so strong that one might even be embarrassed to set himself apart by refraining from talking.

This is a heartbreaking situation, because the practice of talking during prayer is unimaginably destructive. The harm done by disturbing others is so substantial that the *Shulchan Aruch*[1] rules that to avoid disturbing others, a

---

1. *Siman* 101, Se'if 2.

person saying *Shemoneh Esrei* should not raise his voice in prayer. The *Mishnah Berurah*[2] applies this rule even to raising one's voice only slightly. If this is the *halachah* regarding voices raised in *tefillah*, one can surmise that there would be no tolerance for disturbances created by voices raised in casual conversation.

In a shul where talking proliferates, the harm extends beyond the individuals involved and creates a climate that threatens the existence of the shul itself. The *Mishnah Berurah*[3] cites the testimony of the *Eliyahu Rabbah* who writes in the name of the *Kol Bo*: "Woe to those people who speak during the prayers. For we have seen several synagogues destroyed as a result of this sin."

> During the Chmielnicki massacres of 1648-1649, when the Ukrainian Cossacks murdered thousands of Jews and destroyed many shuls,[4] the *Tosfos Yom Tov* revealed that he was told in a dream that the devastation took place because of talking during prayer in the synagogue. Therefore, he wrote a *Mi She'beirach* to bless those who refrained from talking during prayer:[5]
>
> He who blessed our Forefathers — Avraham, Yitzchak and Yaakov, Moshe and Aharon, David and Shlomo — may He bless everyone who guards his mouth and tongue and refrains from talking during the prayer service. May the Holy One, Blessed is He, protect him from every trouble and distress, from every plague and illness; may all the blessings written in the Torah of Moshe and in the books of the Prophets and Writings be applied to him; may he merit seeing

---

2. Ibid. *Se'if Katan* 6 and 10.
3. Ibid. *Siman* 124, *Se'if Katan* 27.
4. In 1648, the Cossack leader Bogdan Chmielnicki led a Cossack insurgency against the Polish aristocracy. After conquering the Polish army, his followers joined with the Polish peasants in attacking the Jews. Intermittent brutality continued for eight years. Over 10,000 Jews were killed; many more were tortured or mistreated (*The Routledge Atlas of Jewish History* by Martin Gilbert, Sixth Ed. Routledge Taylor & Francis Group, London and New York, p. 56).
5. Cited in various *siddurim*; *Matnas Chaim*, p. 193; and *Notrei Amen*, Vol. 1, p. 216.

his children alive and established; may he raise them to Torah, the wedding canopy, and good deeds; may he serve Hashem, our G-d, in truth and integrity; and now let us respond "Amen."

Rav Shimon Schwab felt that quiet during prayers is so essential that he encouraged his congregants at Congregation K'hal Adath Jeshurun to sign a pledge not to talk during davening. He rewarded them with the unique Mi She'beirach of the Tosfos Yom Tov.[6]

Rav Matisyahu Salomon,[7] Mashgiach of Beis Medrash Govoha, related that the Beis Yisrael[8] said that the Sephardi Jews in countries such as Spain were spared from the Holocaust because of one particular merit; unlike other Jewish communities, they did not converse during prayer and were blessed by the Mi She'beirach of the Tosfos Yom Tov many centuries earlier .

Can this ingrained habit of talking during prayer be changed? One need only look back at Jewish life in America fifty years ago, or even twenty-five years ago, to see that growth in learning Torah and mitzvah observance is occurring constantly. If we set ourselves the goal of repairing this situation, surely we can succeed.

Points to Ponder

▸ *It is unfortunate that conversation during prayer has become ingrained in many communities.*

▸ *The Mishnah Berurah cites idle chatter in shul as a damaging force.*

▸ *Both individuals and communities suffer from this destructive habit.*

---

6. *Rav Schwab on Prayer* (ArtScroll/Mesorah Publ.), Editor's Foreword, p. xxii.
7. Cited in *Matnas Chaim*, p. 193. Also cited in *Notrei Amen*, Vol. 1, p. 216, in the name of the *Imrei Emes*.
8. R' Yisrael Alter of Gur.

TALKING DURING PRAYER, PART II

or all that shuls and communities have suffered from the grievous habit of conversing during prayer, the individual who participates suffers tremendously as well. He loses his spiritual standing and is identified with the worst of sins.

The *Zohar*[1] identifies a person who speaks about worldly matters in *shul* as a "kofer b'ikar," *a heretic.* The *Roke'ach*[2] adds that one who talks during prayer is guilty of "masig g'vul," *stealing the sanctity of the shul.*

Rather than lowering himself to these levels and dragging others down with him, a person who habitually talks during prayer should stay home and pray alone, according to a halachic ruling issued by the *Kaf HaChaim*.[3] A person who comes to shul and talks to others has been referred to as a "chotei u'machti es harabim," *a sinner who causes others to sin,* who forfeits his portion in the World to Come.[4]

Finally, the *Aruch HaShulchan*[5] rules that one who talks during prayer is guilty of that severest of transgressions, "chillul Hashem," *desecrating the Name of Hashem,* since this habit reinforces the perception that non-Jews are more careful than Jews to maintain proper decorum in their house of worship. Rashi[6] explains *chillul Hashem* as: "A great person, from whom other people will learn, who is not careful with his actions. Perhaps, therefore, it is found that the smaller ones make light of the Torah because of him (the person they learn from) and say that (this great man) really understands that Torah and mitz-

22 Kislev

22 Adar

22 Sivan

22 Elul

---

1. *Parashas Terumah* 131a.
2. *Hilchos Teshuvah, Siman* 26.
3. *Orach Chaim, Siman* 151, *Se'if Katan* 8.
4. *Doveir Shalom*, p. 70.
5. *Siman* 124, *Se'if* 12.
6. *Shabbos* 33a. See also *Yoma* 86a; and *Mesillas Yesharim*, Ch. 11, *Middas HaNekius*.

vos have no substance. As a result, we find that Hashem's Name is desecrated."

The *Beur Halachah*[7] similarly warns that a *chillul Hashem* is frequently created by those who openly converse during the Torah reading in shul.

The impact of talking during prayer is sometimes perceived more keenly by newcomers to Judaism, who have not become desensitized to it. They cannot reconcile the great divide between what prayer truly is and how it is sometimes treated.

> A story is told of a baal teshuvah who joined a minyan that formed one morning in an Orlando hotel. Shacharis was completed at breakneck speed, with many in the group neglecting to properly say the Pesukei d'Zimrah. Commenting on the rapid pace of the prayer and the widespread talking, he exclaimed in frustration, "What I just saw is enough to make a person turn away from Judaism!"

If the chatter makes a bad impression upon a newcomer, imagine the deep and indelible impression it makes upon the *children* who consistently see adults talking during prayer. They are not in a position, like the *baal teshuvah*, to judge the situation. For them, it becomes established as the norm, and the importance of prayer is greatly diminished in their eyes.

All of this leaves us with a bitter irony. So many people undertake the obligation to arise early and pray with a *minyan* every day, yet their effort brings sin and spiritual disaster upon them, and perhaps upon their shul and community as well. This obviously cannot be their goal. We can settle for this sad status quo, or shake off old habits and reach much, much higher. We are electing the Jewish people's future, and every vote counts.

Points to Ponder

▸ One who talks during prayer is described with many dishonorable terms; many sins are ascribed to him, including chillul Hashem.

▸ Children who observe adults talking during tefillah will undoubtedly develop bad habits and attitudes.

---

7. *Orach Chaim*, Siman 146, s.v. *V'hanachon*.

Ideally, there should be no talking in shul from the beginning to the end of prayer. This should be the long-range goal of every congregation. Idle talk, which even includes conversation about one's livelihood or other essential needs,[1] is forbidden in shul even when prayers are not being recited.[2]

Nowadays, there is some room for leniency concerning such talk when prayers are not being recited, since some *Rishonim* rule that shuls are generally built with a precondition allowing them to be used for essential matters other than prayer.[3]

During certain portions of *tefillah*, talking is prohibited for additional reasons as well. From a halachic point of view, it is important to distinguish the reasons.

Sometimes talking is considered a *hefsek*, an interruption. If this *hefsek* occurs where not even a single word is permitted to be uttered regardless of need (e.g., *Birchos Krias Shema* and *Shema*, *Shemoneh Esrei*, *Kedushah*, *Hallel*), it may invalidate the portion of the *tefillah* that is being interrupted. At other times, talking is prohibited because the congregation must give its undivided attention to that portion of the prayer or because of shul decorum (e.g., *Kaddish*, *chazaras hashatz*). In those cases, an exception can be made when **a special need** arises, allowing one to

---

1. *Siman* 151, *Mishnah Berurah*, *Se'if Katan* 2.
2. *Siman* 151, *Se'if* 1.
3. *Aruch HaShulchan*, *Siman* 151, *Se'if* 5. Concerning shuls in Eretz Yisrael, see *Siman* 151, *Se'if* 11; *Mishnah Berurah* ibid. *Se'if Katan* 38 and *Beur Halachah* ibid. s.v. *Aval b'vatei kneisios*. Also see *She'eilos U'Teshuvos Shevet HaLevi*, Vol. 9, *Siman* 3; *and Orchos Rabbeinu*, Vol. 1, p. 75, who cites in the name of the Chazon Ish that such a precondition must be stated for shuls in Eretz Yisrael.

quietly murmur a few words.[4] It is important to note that, regardless of the portion of prayer being recited, according to the *Mishnah Berurah*,[5] one who is wearing *tefillin* should be scrupulous to refrain from idle talk at all times.

To avoid error, one must acquire knowledge of where and when interruptions are permitted, where and why they are prohibited, and to what degree. Below is a brief summary of this vital information, presented in the order of daily prayer:[6]

Between *Birchos HaShachar* and *Baruch She'amar*

There is no specific *halachah* which prohibits talking. However, during this section of *tefillah*, one should apply the previously mentioned general reasons for prohibiting talking.

During *Kaddish*

Talking is strictly forbidden, as one must pay full attention so that he can answer *Amen*, etc. properly.[7]

> The Tur cites the following illustrative story from Sefer Chassidim: After his death, a certain pious man appeared to another pious man in a dream. As the apparition's face was distinctly yellow, the other man asked him, "Why is your face so yellow?" The apparition answered, "Because I used to speak during Yisgadal (Kaddish)."[8]
>
> The Mateh Moshe[9] cites a Midrash which relates that a certain Torah scholar appeared to his pupil in a dream and the pupil noticed that the scholar had a stain on his forehead. The pupil asked him why this happened to him and he answered that it was be-

---

4. See *Salmas Chaim* 38 and written responsum by HaRav C. Kanievsky cited at the end of *Ishei Yisrael*, Number 206, based on *Mishnah Berurah, Siman* 125, *Se'if Katan* 9.
5. *Siman* 37, *Se'if Katan* 7.
6. The following compilation of laws is adapted from an article published in the *Yated Ne'eman, Parsahas Vayeishev*, for the week of December 1, 2004. Permission is granted by the author, Rabbi Doniel Neustadt, Rav of Young Israel in Cleveland Heights and principal of Yavneh Teachers' College in Cleveland, Ohio.
7. *Mishnah Berurah, Siman* 56, *Se'if Katan* 1.
8. Ibid., also cited in *Mishnah Berurah, Siman* 268, *Se'if Katan* 26.
9. *Siman* 411.

cause he did not avoid speaking while the chazzan said Kaddish.[10]

Both of these stories, while relating consequences suffered in the World to Come, actually speak of the here and now. They illustrate the spiritual disfigurement a person inflicts upon himself every time he speaks when he is prohibited from doing so. He may not see this blemish in the mirror when he arrives home from shul, but it is there nonetheless, and in the World of Truth it becomes apparent.

During *Pesukei D'Zimrah* (After *Baruch She'amar*)

Unless there is an emergency, it is forbidden to talk during this time as it would constitute an interruption between the blessing of *Baruch She'amar* and the blessing of *Yishtabach.*[11]

Between *Yishtabach* and *Borchu*

It is permitted to talk for a pressing mitzvah need only.[12]

Between *Borchu* and *Yotzer Ohr* (*Shacharis*) or *HaMaariv Aravim* (*Maariv*)

It is forbidden to talk.[13]

During *Birchos Krias Shema* and During *Shema*

It is forbidden to talk. It could be considered an interruption in the middle of a blessing, which may invalidate the blessing.[14]

Between *Gaal Yisrael* and *Shemoneh Esrei*

It is strictly forbidden to talk, since it would interrupt the crucial connection between *geulah* and *tefillah.*[15]

During *Shemoneh Esrei*

It is strictly forbidden to talk, as it constitutes an interruption in *tefillah.*[16] If one spoke inadvertently during one

---

10. Cited in *Mishnah Berurah, Siman* 56, *Se'if Katan* 1.
11. *Siman* 51, *Se'if* 4; *Mishnah Berurah, Se'if Katan* 6 and 7.
12. Ibid. *Siman* 54, *Se'if Katan* 6.
13. Ibid. *Se'if Katan* 13; ibid. *Siman* 236, *Se'if Katan* 1.
14. *Siman* 66, *Se'if* 1; beginning of ibid. *Mishnah Berurah.*
15. *Siman* 66, *Se'if* 8 and 9.
16. *Siman* 104, *Se'if* 1.

of the blessings of *Shemoneh Esrei,* he must repeat the blessing.[17]

After *Shemoneh Esrei* (Before *Chazaras HaShatz*)

It is forbidden to talk if it will disturb the concentration of others who are still praying.[18]

During *Chazaras HaShatz*

See Days 84 and 85, "*Chazaras HaShatz* — Sending the Message."

---

17. *Mishnah Berurah, Siman* 104, *Se'if Katan* 25.
18. See *Siman* 123, *Mishnah Berurah, Se'if Katan* 12. Also see *Siman* 101, *Se'if* 2; and *Mishnah Berurah* ibid. *Se'if Katan* 6 and 10 which state that if a person saying *Shemoneh Esrei* with a *minyan* should not raise his voice in prayer to avoid disturbing others, certainly one can derive that he should not do so in casual conversation.

TALKING DURING PRAYER, PART IV

The following is a continuation of the laws of talking during prayer.

During *Kedushah*

It is strictly forbidden to talk. Total concentration is essential.[1]

During *Nesias Kapayim* (*Bircas Kohanim*)

It is forbidden to talk or even to learn Torah or recite *Tehilim*,[2] as complete attention must be paid to the Kohanim.[3]

Between *Chazaras HaShatz* and *Tachanun*

It is inappropriate to talk, since there should be no interruption between *Shemoneh Esrei* and *Tachanun*.[4]

Between *Tachanun* and *Krias HaTorah,* the Reading of the Torah

There is no specific prohibition against talking. However, during this section of prayer, one should apply the previously mentioned general reasons for prohibiting talking.

During *Krias HaTorah*

It is strictly forbidden to engage in idle talk or even to utter words of Torah during *Krias HaTorah*.[5] One who

---

1. *Mishnah Berurah, Siman 56, Se'if Katan 1; Siman 125, Se'if 2.*
2. *Yosef Ometz, Os 807.*
3. *Siman 128, Se'if 26, Be'er Heitev, Se'if Katan 46; Mishnah Berurah, Se'if Katan 102.*
4. *Mishnah Berurah Siman 51, Se'if Katan 9; Siman 131, Se'if 1 and Aruch HaShulchan ibid. Se'if 3. Also see Kaf HaChaim ibid. Se'if Katan 4, who comments that according to the Zohar HaKadosh and the Arizal one is forbidden to speak.*
5. *Siman 146, Se'if 2 and Mishnah Berurah ibid. Se'if Katan 4 and 5.*

speaks at that time is called "a sinner whose sin is too great to be forgiven."[6] Some authorities prohibit talking as soon as the Torah scroll is unrolled.[7]

Between *Aliyos* of *Krias HaTorah*

There are several views: Some authorities prohibit talking totally,[8] others permit discussing words of Torah only,[9] while others are even more lenient and also allow the type of talk which is permitted in shul.[10]

During the *Haftarah* and Its Blessings

It is forbidden to talk, as one must pay undivided attention.[11]

Between *Krias HaTorah* and End of *Tefillah*

There is no specific prohibition against talking. However, during this section of prayer, one should apply the previously mentioned general reasons for prohibiting talking.

During *Hallel*

It is forbidden to talk. Doing so could be considered an interruption of *Hallel*.[12]

During *Kabbalas Shabbos* (Friday Night)

There is no specific prohibition against talking. However, during this section of prayer, one should apply the previously mentioned general reasons for prohibiting talking.

6. *Beur Halachah* 146, *Se'if* 2, s.v. *V'hanachon*, who severely criticizes such people.
7. *Mishnah Berurah* 146, *Se'if Katan* 4. However, see *Aruch HaShulchan* 146, *Se'if* 3, who disagrees.
8. *Siman* 146, *Se'if* 2; *Mishnah Berurah*, *Se'if Katan* 6 quoting *Eliyahu Rabbah*; *Kitzur Shulchan Aruch*, *Siman* 23, *Se'if* 8.
9. *Bach*, as understood by *Mishnah Berurah*, *Siman* 146, *Se'if Katan* 6 and many *poskim*.
10. *Be'er Heitiv* ibid. *Se'if Katan* 3, *Machtzis HaShekel* ibid. *Se'if Katan* 3, *Aruch HaShulchan* ibid. *Se'if* 3 *and Shulchan HaTahor* ibid. *Se'if* 1, maintain that the *Bach* permits even idle talk between *aliyos*. See also *Pri Chadash*, *Se'if Katan* 2, who permits conversing *bein gavra l'gavra*, between *aliyos*.
11. *Siman* 146, *Se'if* 3; ibid. *Mishnah Berurah*, *Se'if Katan* 16; *Siman* 284, *Se'if* 3.
12. *Siman* 422, *Se'if* 4 and *Beur Halachah*, s.v. *aval*; *Siman* 488, *Se'if* 1 and *Siman* 644, *Se'if* 1.

During *Vayechulu* and *Magen Avos* (Friday Night)

It is forbidden to talk.[13]

During *Chazaras HaShatz*, *Krias HaTorah* and *Haftarah* on Shabbos

Besides the prohibition against talking during *chazaras hashatz*, *Krias HaTorah* and the *Haftarah* cited above, talking on Shabbos during *chazaras hashatz* or during the blessings said over *Krias HaTorah* and the *Haftarah* may also render one unable to fulfill his requirement to recite 100 *berachos* daily.[14]

Normally one says even more than the required 100 blessings each day.[15]

However, on Shabbos, a person is thirteen blessings short of the required hundred. Consequently, he completes the total of 100 blessings by eating various kinds of fruit and delicacies. If he is unable to do so, he can fulfill his obligation by listening attentively to the blessings said over *Krias HaTorah* and the *Haftarah*, and responding *Amen* to them.[16] He may also fulfill his obligation by listening to *chazaras hashatz*.[17]

HaRav Shimon Schwab[18] sums up the Torah viewpoint on the subject of talking during *tefillah* as follows:

> For Hashem's sake, let us be quiet in the Beis Haknesses. Our reverent silence during the tefillah will speak very loudly to Him Who holds our fate in His hands.

---

13. *Siman* 268, *Se'if* 12; *Mishnah Berurah*, *Siman* 56, *Se'if Katan* 1.

14. *Siman* 284, *Se'if* 3; *Siman* 46, *Se'if* 3. Also see *Menachos* 43b. See ibid. *Mishnah Berurah*, *Se'if Katan* 14, who cites the *Tur*, which states that David HaMelech ordained that one should say 100 blessings daily to counter the fact that 100 Jewish people were dying each day. See *Magen Avraham* ibid. *Se'if Katan* 7, as to whether this requirement is Biblical or Rabbinic. Also see *Seder HaYom* regarding the greatness of reciting 100 *berachos* daily. Also see *She'eilos U'Teshuvos Shevet HaLevi*, Vol. 5, *Siman* 23, where it states that women are not required to recite 100 blessings daily.

15. See *Mishnah Berurah*, *Siman* 46, *Se'if Katan* 14, for a listing of the 100 blessings recited daily.

16. *Siman* 284, *Se'if* 3. However, see *She'eilos U'Teshuvos Teshuvos V'Hanhagos*, Vol. 2, *Orach Chaim*, *Siman* 86.

17. See *Mishnah Berurah*, *Siman* 46, *Se'if Katan* 14.

18. *Selected Writings* (C.I.S. Publishers, Lakewood N.J.), p. 230.

Communicating with Hashem is our only recourse in this era of trial and tribulations. There is too much ugly noise in our world today.

Let us find peace and tranquility while we stand before Hashem in prayer!

Points to Ponder

▸ There are many places during prayer in which talking is not permitted under any circumstances.

▸ Especially on Shabbos, listening to the blessings said for Krias HaTorah and the Haftarah, and chazaras hashatz, enables a person to fulfill the obligation to recite 100 blessings each day.

CHAZARAS HASHATZ — SENDING THE MESSAGE

alking during prayer, as the preceding days illustrate, ranges from a habit best avoided to a sin of unbearable proportions. The most serious impact, however, arises from conversing during the *chazzan's* repetition of the *Shemoneh Esrei*, known as *chazaras hashatz*. During this segment of prayer, talking is strictly forbidden.[1] The *Shulchan Aruch*[2] rules: "When the *shaliach tzibbur* repeats *Shemoneh Esrei*, the congregants are required to be silent and apply their minds to the blessings made by the *chazzan* and respond *Amen* to them."

The *Mishnah Berurah*[3] comments that "one should avoid saying supplicatory prayers or studying during the repetition of *Shemoneh Esrei*. Even one who applies himself to the end of the blessings of *Shemoneh Esrei*, enabling him to answer *Amen*, also acts improperly. If those who study Torah turn to their study then, other less learned individuals will learn from them not to listen to the *shaliach tzibbur* and will engage in idle talk, Heaven forbid. They will thus cause many people to sin."[4]

---

1. It is permitted, however, for a rav to answer a halachic question that is posed to him during *chazaras hashatz*; *Aruch HaShulchan, Siman* 124, *Se'if* 12.
2. *Siman* 124, *Se'if* 4.
3. Ibid. *Se'if Katan* 17.
4. See *Igros Moshe, Orach Chaim,* Vol. 4, *Siman* 19, which states that one should not study Torah during *chazaras hashatz*. The *Yaavetz* in *Siddur Yaavetz, Laws of Chazaras HaShatz* 2, warns that one should not recite *Tehillim* nor walk around during *chazaras hashatz*. See also *Reishis Chochmah, Shaar HaKedushah,* Ch. 14, *Se'if Katan* 39 through 41 and *Yeish Nochalin,* Ch. 1, *Os* 14, s.v. *V'hinei. Igros Moshe, Orach Chaim,* Vol. 5, *Siman* 20, *Os* 9, even prohibits speaking when the congregants or *shaliach tzibbur* say *piyutim,* liturgical hymns.

Talking during *chazaras hashatz* can also cause the *shaliach tzibbur's* recitation of the blessings of *Shemoneh Esrei* to be almost in vain. The *Shulchan Aruch*[5] rules: "If there are not nine people applying their minds to the *shaliach tzibbur's* recitation of the blessings of *Shemoneh Esrei*, they are almost blessings said in vain.[6,7] Therefore, everyone should act as if there will not be nine people doing so without him and apply his mind to the blessing the *chazzan* is saying."[8]

Rabbeinu Avraham, the son of the Rambam, said that his father considered those who speak during *chazaras hashatz* to have committed a great sin, because they show disdain for the honor of Heaven. Similarly, the *Shulchan Aruch HaRav*[9] comments concerning those who speak during *chazaras hashatz*: "Whoever speaks in the *beis haknesses* during the time the *tzibbur* is busy with the praise of Hashem (*chazaras hashatz*) shows that he has no portion in the G-d of Israel." Rav Shlomo Zalman Auerbach[10] wrote that this is a "*chillul Hashem*," as those who act this way, "sit in the Temple of the King and humiliate His Name."

---

5. *Siman* 124, *Se'if* 4.
6. See *Mishnah Berurah, Siman* 124, *Se'if Katan* 19, which states that in such an instance it is desirable to act as stated in the work *Shulchan Shlomo*, that the *shaliach tzibbur* should specify to himself that his *chazaras hashatz* is a "*tefillas nedavah*," a voluntary prayer.
7. See *Derishah, Siman* 124, *Se'if Katan* 1, which states that it is not truly a blessing in vain because it is no different than the *halachos* cited in *Siman* 55, *Se'if* 2: "If one began saying *Kaddish* or *Kedushah* when the required ten were present, but some of the ten went out in the middle, then the *Kaddish* or *Kedushah* which was already started should be completed, provided a majority of the ten remain."

   However, see *Halichos Shlomo (Tefillah)*, Ch. 9, *Halachah* 4, and *Igros Moshe, Orach Chaim*, Vol. 4, *Siman* 19, which state that if there are not nine people applying their minds to the *shaliach tzibbur's* recitation of *Bircas Avos* at the **beginning** of *Shemoneh Esrei*, the *berachos* of *Shemoneh Esrei* repeated by the *chazzan* are, in reality, blessings said in vain.
8. See *Mishnah Berurah, Siman* 124, *Se'if Katan* 18: "Accordingly, one should see to it initially that he applies himself to hearing the entire blessing and not only the end of the blessing."
9. *Siman* 124, *Se'if* 10.
10. *Keser Meluchah*, p. 402.

**Points
to
Ponder**

▸ *Talking
during the
repetition
of the
Shemoneh
Esrei
(chazaras
hashatz)
is singled
out as a
particularly
grave trans-
gression.*

Speaking during *chazaras hashatz* is condemned by the *Shulchan Aruch*[11] using the harshest language seen in any discussion of transgression. One could almost conclude from this admonition that there is no worse sin: "One should refrain from speaking profane words during the time the *chazzan* repeats *Shemoneh Esrei*. And if one spoke, it is a sin, **and the sin is too great to bear.**"

Nowhere else in *halachah* is the expression "and the sin is too great to bear" applied.[12] In fact, although all agree that it is a great sin to eat on Yom Kippur or desecrate the Shabbos, even in those cases the *halachah* does not state that "the sin is too great to bear."

Could it be that so many people blithely commit an act that the *Shulchan Aruch* describes in this way? By taking a deeper look at what happens when we speak during *chazaras hashatz*, we will be able to understand the great destructive forces with which we are dealing. With that understanding, we will gain the motivation to step back, away from the edge of disaster, and aim our words and hearts toward Heaven.

---

11. *Siman* 124, *Se'if* 7.
12. However, see *Beur Halachah* 146, *Se'if* 2, s.v. *V'hanachon*, who describes one who speaks during *Krias HaTorah* as "a sinner whose sin is too great to be forgiven."

CHAZARAS HASHATZ — SENDING THE MESSAGE, PART II

Y esterday we explained that if one talks during the *chazzan's* repetition of the *Shemoneh Esrei* — *chazaras hashatz* — the condemnation is harsher than any mentioned in all of *halachah*. Why does this sin merit such strong disapproval?

Rav Matisyahu Salomon, Mashgiach of Beis Medrash Govoha,[1] explains that the sin of speaking during *chazaras hashatz* is not, in reality, more egregious than eating on Yom Kippur or desecrating the Sabbath. Rather, the level of condemnation reflects the message being expressed by the person who is engaged in conversation. He shows his great disrespect for prayer and demonstrates his innermost feeling that it is meaningless to him, for it is preempted by a conversation with his friend.

Such behavior severs the unique bond that prayer forges between man and the Almighty. It is this severed relationship that is "too great to bear," for who can bear life without a relationship to Hashem? Furthermore, should a tragedy strike this person, *r"l*, causing him to turn to the potent power of *tefillah*, it will not be available, because he no longer enjoys that special connection with Hashem.

What is it about *chazaras hashatz* that is so unique that disregard for it causes such devastating results? The *Shulchan Aruch*[2] explains the purpose of *chazaras hashatz* as follows: "After the congregation has finished reciting *Shemoneh Esrei*, the *shaliach tzibbur* repeats the *Shemoneh Esrei* in case someone present does not know how to pray,

26 Kislev

26 Adar

26 Sivan

26 Elul

---

1. During a large gathering for *teshuvah*, Elul 25, 5761. See also *Sefer Matnas Chaim*, pp. 192-194.
2. *Siman* 124, *Se'if* 1.

[so] he can concentrate on the *shaliach tzibbur's* recitation and fulfill his duty (to *daven Shemoneh Esrei*)."[3]

Rabbeinu Avraham, son of the Rambam, states that recitation of this prayer should be contingent upon the congregation — on whose behalf it is being said — attending respectfully to the proceedings. He also comments that the *chazzan* can curtail *chazaras hashatz* if people are talking during the recitation, because the situation displays contempt for the honor of Heaven.[4]

The *Talmud*[5] equates the *shaliach tzibbur* who repeats the *tefillah* to the Kohen who brought the offerings in the Holy Temple. The *Shevet Mussar*[6] explains that since *tefillah* takes the place of the offerings brought in the Holy Temple, one is in effect beseeching the *shaliach tzibbur* to act on his behalf, just as one would say to the Kohen: "Please bring my offering for me!"

> *Because the shaliach tzibbur is entrusted with so vital a role, the prewar congregation of Frankfurt, Germany would designate only a worthy individual to perform this function. This was also the case in the Vienner Kehillah and in the yeshivos in prewar Europe, such as Mir and Kelm.*[7]

When one interferes with the recitation of *chazaras hashatz*, one interferes with the ability of the congregation to have its prayers answered. *She'arim B'Tefillah*,[8] quoting the Arizal, explains that *chazaras hashatz* has a greater preeminence than the silent *Shemoneh Esrei* because it fulfills the directive of the Gemara:[9] "If one sees that his prayers are not answered, he should repeat the *tefillah*." According to the Vilna Gaon, this refers to *chazaras hashatz*.

---

3. Although nowadays people usually are familiar with the Hebrew text of prayer, we still repeat *Shemoneh Esrei*.
4. Cited in *Halichos Shlomo (Tefillah)*, p. 373.
5. *Yerushalmi, Berachos* 4:4.
6. See *Aderes Eliyahu on Yerushalmi* ibid.
7. Cited in *Kovetz Sichos Maamar Mordechai*, Vol. 1, pp. 98-99.
8. P. 14. See also *Kaf HaChaim, Orach Chaim, Siman* 124, *Se'if Katan* 2, who cites the Arizal.
9. *Berachos* 32b.

The Vilna Gaon explains further that the essence of *chazaras hashatz* is the prayer of the assembly. The Gemara[10] states: "*HaKadosh Baruch Hu* does not spurn the prayers of the congregation, as it says:[11] *Behold, Hashem is vast* [in wisdom and mercy] *and He will not despise the numerous* [when they band together in prayer]."

The manner in which the *Shemoneh Esrei* is said reflects this concept. First, one prays quietly, like one who is afraid to display an expensive item he has in his possession. *Chazaras hashatz*, however, is said aloud, with confidence that the power of the assembly will protect it from any evil forces.

As previously explained, although it was originally instituted for those who did not know the text of the *Shemoneh Esrei*, *chazaras hashatz* remains the essence of *tefillah b'tzibbur*. Many halachic authorities[12] rule that one who recites *Shemoneh Esrei* at the same time as *chazaras hashatz* is considered to have prayed a *tefillah b'tzibbur*, since *chazaras hashatz* is said only because of the presence of a *tzibbur*. In fact, even when almost all those who are praying are knowledgeable in the *Shemoneh Esrei* prayer, it is still repeated on behalf of the entire congregation.[13]

The *Avodas Yisrael*[14] likens *chazaras hashatz* to the giving of the Ten Commandments. Just as the Jewish nation stood silently as Moshe repeated to them the words uttered by Hashem, those assembled for prayer should stand silently as the *shaliach tzibbur* repeats on their behalf the words of the *Shemoneh Esrei*.

The *She'arim B'Tefillah*[15] laments the widespread lack of awareness of the value of *chazaras hashatz*. He compares a person who is devoid of this understanding to someone

---

10. Ibid. 8a.
11. *Iyov* 36:5.
12. See *Kaf HaChaim, Orach Chaim, Siman* 90, *Se'if Katan* 63; *Orchos Rabbeinu* Vol. 1, *Siman* 162, and Vol. 3, *Siman* 208; and *She'eilos U'Teshuvos Chasam Sofer HeChadash, Siman* 3; *Halichos Shlomo* (*Tefillah*) Ch. 8, *Siman* 41. However, see *Igros Moshe, Orach Chaim*, Vol. 3, *Siman* 9.
13. See *She'eilos U'Teshuvos Yabia Omer, Orach Chaim* 2, *Siman* 7; *She'eilos U'Teshuvos HaRama Mipano, Siman* 102, Question 8.
14. *Avos* Ch. 5.
15. P. 14.

▸ *Talking
during
chazaras
hashatz
cuts us
off from
Hashem.*

▸ *The
shaliach
tzibbur
fulfills the
role of the
Kohen who
brought
offerings
on behalf of
the Jewish
people.*

▸ *As the
prayer of
the tzibbur,
chazaras
hashatz
carries the
strength
of the
multitude.*

who buys a powerful, high-performance sports car and, lacking an understanding of what it can do, never drives it faster than five miles an hour. *Chazaras hashatz* is a high-performance vehicle; we only have to learn how to unleash its full power.

BLOCKED ACCESS

The great question of unanswered prayers has been explored elsewhere in this *sefer*,[1] and throughout the ages by Torah scholars and lay philosophers as well. Many causes are beyond human capacity to understand, but there is one factor every person can address: speaking during *chazaras hashatz*.

As Rav Matisyahu Salomon has explained, one who talks during *chazaras hashatz* severs his special relationship with Hashem, to the point that even his future prayers are no longer accepted. He undermines the power of his own prayers to help him.

One can find a basis for this concept by examining the Gemara's[2] discussion of the causes of the devastation of the Land of Eretz Yisrael at the time of the destruction of the first *Beis HaMikdash*. "Why was the Land [of Israel] destroyed? This question was asked of the Sages, who could not explain. It was asked of the Prophets, who also could not explain. Hashem then explained it Himself: 'Because they have forsaken My Torah which I put before them.' Rav Yehudah said in the name of Rav: This means that they did not make the blessing on the Torah before they studied it."

Why would neglecting to say the blessing before studying Torah cause the loss of Eretz Yisrael?[3] Rashi[4] explains that this failure to make the blessing indicated a lack of true appreciation for the Torah's importance.

However, this does not sufficiently explain the severity of the punishment, especially in light of the fact that the

27
Kislev

27
Adar

27
Sivan

27
Elul

---

1. See Ch. 7, "Finding Answers to Unanswered Prayers."
2. *Bava Metzia* 85a.
3. Especially according to the Ramban, who holds that the blessing is a Rabbinic requirement.
4. *Bava Metzia* 85b, s.v. *Shelo*.

people *were* learning Torah and *were* performing mitzvos. Furthermore, how does one reconcile the cause stated here with the one in Gemara *Yoma*,[5] namely, that the first *Beis HaMikdash* was destroyed because of three great sins — "idolatry, immorality, and bloodshed"? Finally, why did the Jewish people's learning and devotion to mitzvos fail to protect them from falling into these sins?

Rav Itzele Peterberger provides an answer in *Kochvei Ohr*.[6] He explains that the *Beis HaMikdash* was indeed destroyed because the Jews transgressed the three grievous sins cited in the Gemara[7] even though elsewhere in the Gemara[8] it states: "Hashem says, 'I created the Evil Inclination and I created the Torah as an antidote.'"

Thus, according to Rav Itzele, the Sages and Prophets were not being asked the nature of the sin that caused the loss of the Land of Israel. Rather, the question posed was why their Torah learning did not prevent the transgression of these three sins. Hashem then explained that their learning did not protect them from transgressing because of their lack of appreciation for the Torah.

Why did the lack of appreciation for Torah, evidenced by their neglecting to recite the blessing, result in the removal of the natural protection from sin that Torah learning automatically provides? The Gemara[9] says: "He who scorns clothing will eventually be unable to benefit from [it]," and offers the following example. As a young man, David HaMelech ripped the clothing of King Shaul without regard for its usefulness. Later, in David's old age, *he was covered with clothing but it did not warm him.*[10]

The lesson in this episode is that even great individuals who do not demonstrate the proper esteem for items from which they derive benefit will at some point lose access to that benefit. This explains why the generation that neglected the blessing before Torah study, demonstrating

5. 9b. Also see *Bava Metzia* 30b, Tosafos, s.v. *Lo chorvah*.
6. *Siman* 8. See also *Lev Eliyahu, Parashas Tetzaveh*, p. 216, s.v. *V'yesh l'hisbonein*.
7. *Yoma* 9b.
8. *Kiddushin* 30b.
9. *Berachos* 62b.
10. *I Melachim* 1:1.

a lack of reverence for Torah, lost access to the protection that its study normally conveys.

The same concept applies to one who talks during *chazaras hashatz*. Just as David HaMelech lost the benefit of clothing, and the Jewish people lost the protective benefit of Torah learning, one who talks during *chazaras hashatz* loses the benefit of that which he fails to honor. His act displays a great disrespect for prayer and disregard for its efficacy, and thus, he loses his ability to reach Hashem through prayer. It is for this reason that "the sin is too great to bear."

In truth, once one understands the implications of conversation during *chazaras hashatz*, there can be no choice other than maintaining a respectful silence. By choosing our prayer above whatever distractions present themselves around us, we preserve the most valuable asset we have — our personal connection with our Creator.

▸ A person undermines his power of prayer when he speaks during chazaras hashatz.

▸ A person who does not show regard for the value of prayer loses the ability to benefit from it.

**DAY
87**

REBUILDING BURNED BRIDGES

P rayer is a bridge between man and Hashem, and as has been shown, abusing the gift of prayer burns the bridge. Perhaps, however, there may come a time when a person begins to feel the emptiness left by years of spiritual numbness, or perhaps a difficult situation ignites his longing to reach out to Hashem. This person suddenly realizes that after years of neglect and abuse, his bridge to Heaven has been reduced to rubble. Can he repair the damage, and if so, how?

**28
Kislev**

**28
Adar**

**28
Sivan**

**28
Elul**

The Rambam[1] provides an answer: "What is total repentance? The person encounters a possibility to sin in exactly the same manner that he has previously transgressed, and he refrains from doing wrong purely out of repentance, not from fear of being caught or lack of energy. For instance, if he sinned … and later is … in the same situation, but he refrains solely to avoid doing wrong."[2]

A person who talks during *tefillah* can likewise, through complete repentance, repair the damage he has done. To effect this level of repentance, he must face the same challenge in a similar setting, and this time refrain from talking. Obviously, this may be a challenge of great difficulty.

How does one find the courage to undertake such a challenge? To begin the process of change, a person must first internalize the belief that, with Hashem's help, he can succeed. As *Chazal*[3] teach, "Someone who attempts to purify himself will be assisted [by Hashem]."

A sense of optimism and direction is essential to suc-

---

1. *Hilchos Teshuvah* 2:1.
2. *Rabbeinu Yonah* lists twenty components of *teshuvah*, of which two are absolute essentials. They include *charatah al he'avar*, remorse over the past, and *azivas ha'chet*, giving up the sin in the future. Also see *Beis Elokim, Shaar HaTeshuvah* 2:2, who writes that *teshuvah* is not complete without these two ingredients.
3. *Shabbos* 104a; *Menachos* 29b; *Yoma* 38b; *Avodah Zarah* 55a.

cess, for the opposite — feeling defeated and adrift — provides fertile soil for the Evil Inclination. Rav Chaim Shmulevitz[4] illustrated this concept in discussing the episode of the Golden Calf. He asked how the Evil Inclination could have drawn the Jewish people into this sin at a time when they were at a spiritual peak, having just received the Torah on Mount Sinai. His answer provides a valuable lesson on how to respond to the Evil Inclination.

First, the Evil Inclination deceived the Jewish nation into thinking that Moshe Rabbeinu was no longer alive. This caused them to become heartbroken and confused. Rav Chaim explains: "A person who is frightened and lost, without advice, even if he is among the world's greatest people, as was the case with the Jewish nation in the desert, is placed in great jeopardy."

In *Kovetz Sichos Maamar Mordechai*,[5] Rav Mordechai Schwab explains that a person who feels hopeless as a consequence of a sin is likely to feel trapped and unable to improve himself with *teshuvah*. Therefore, the first step in self-improvement is to reassure oneself that success is within reach.

> Rav Schwab[6] relates that a student once cried to Rav Yechezkel Levenstein that he had sinned and was unable to do teshuvah and change his evil ways. Rav Yechezkel advised him not to despair. He assured him that he would succeed by beginning with just one small step and that help from Hashem would surely follow.

Points to Ponder

▸ Complete *teshuvah* enables a person to undo damage caused by talking during *tefillah*.

▸ Complete *teshuvah* entails refraining from sin when a similar situation recurs.

▸ Feelings of hopelessness undermine the motivation to do *teshuvah*, and are baseless, for Hashem helps those motivated to change.

---

4. *Sichos Mussar, Maamar* 14, 5733, p. 49.
5. Vol. 1, p. 87.
6. Ibid.

AN INDIVIDUAL'S RESOLVE

The following letter, written on *Shevat* 14, 5765, provides a glimpse of one businessman's[1] awakening to the immense impact of not speaking during prayer, and of the fruits of his inspiring efforts to improve.

Dear Friends,

Three weeks ago in Eretz Yisrael I had the *z'chus* [merit] to have an incredible and inspiring visit with **Rav Chaim Kanievsky,** which I would like to share with you.

I asked Rav Chaim if he would be *mispallel* [pray] for a *refuah sheleimah* [recovery] for a good friend of mine from our shul. You can imagine my reaction when Rav Chaim asked me, "Do they talk in your shul?" I responded, "Yes, but it's much better lately." Rav Chaim immediately said, "That's not enough. The talking ***must stop completely!***" And with that, he asked his son, Rav Shloime, to take out a *Mishnah Berurah.* Rav Chaim pointed to the *shulchan Aruch Orach Chaim, Siman 124 (Seif 7),* which clearly states: "Lo ya'siach sichas chullin b'shaah she'ha'shaliach tzibbur chozer hatefillah. V'im sach hu chotei, vegadol avono min'so" — One should not speak mundane talk while the *chazzan* repeats the *Shemoneh Esrei.* If one does speak such talk, he is a sinner."

I then said to Rav Chaim, "But that's only during *chazaras hashatz.*" "No!" Rav Chaim said, pointing to the *Mishnah Berurah* that says that one should

---

1. Permission is granted by the author of the letter.

not speak during the ***entire davening.*** "Speak to the people in your shul," Rav Chaim continued, "and tell them that they should be *mekabel* [accept] on themselves, *b'li neder*, not to speak ***at all*** during davening, and in that *z'chus* your friend will have a *refuah sheleimah.* "That's not enough," I said.

Rav Chaim looked at me questioningly and asked, "What do you mean?" I replied, "Nowadays, sometimes quoting the *Shulchan Aruch* is not enough. I need to tell them that Rav Chaim personally requested that there should be no talking in shul." Looking puzzled, Rav Chaim again asked me, "What do you mean?"

I then told Rav Chaim the famous remark of the Kotzker Rebbe, "It is unfortunate that the Ten Commandments were not written by R' Yehudah Ha-Chassid!" At that, Rav Chaim burst out laughing (a very rare occurrence) and said, "All right, you can tell the congregants, **in my name,** that in this *z'chus* your friend will have a *refuah sheleimah* and I will be *mispallel* not only for him but for the success of all the congregants of the Shul as well."

I left Rav Chaim feeling very moved and eager to convey his message … The other night my doorbell rang and my friend who had been ill stopped by for a visit. I was shocked! I knew that as of the day before he still had not been doing well, and there he was in my living room looking wonderful. To my great joy, he told me that he was really feeling much better …

Truthfully, as someone who is guilty of talking in shul myself, I feel awkward writing this letter. But I heard Rav Chaim's *havtachah* [promise] firsthand, to *daven* for our friend — and for all of us — and I have already seen the fruits of his efforts. I could not help but be inspired to try to make a change.

And so with the permission and encouragement of my friend and his family, I am writing to convey this message from Rav Chaim Kanievsky. **It is now up to us to take the next step.** May our sincere effort

> *Rav Chaim Kanievsky's havtachah: Maintaining quiet during prayer brings great merit to us all.*

> *It is up to all of us to take the first step to stop talking during prayer and reignite the power of our prayers.*

in this matter bring *hatzlachah* [success] and *refuos* and *yeshuos* [salvation] to us all.

Sincerely,
M. Hager
Brooklyn, N.Y.

THE FIRST RUNG

The ability of man to overcome his Evil Inclination was elucidated by Hashem Himself, when He spoke to Cain, who committed the seemingly irreparable sin of taking his brother's life:[1] *Surely, if you improve yourself you will be forgiven. But if you do not improve yourself, sin rests at the door, its desire is toward you, yet you can conquer it.*

Rav Shamshon Raphael Hirsch[2] expounds on the words *"yet you can conquer it"* by explaining that Hashem created the Evil Inclination so that man could conquer it, not so that it should control man. However, one might wonder how it is possible for man to conquer the Evil Inclination, which is after all an angel.

Rav Hirsch explains that Hashem created the Evil Inclination solely as a means to challenge us in ways that would build our spiritual strength. Going a step further, Rav Hirsch points to the beginning of the phrase — *its desire is toward you* — to prove that the Evil Inclination's desire is *to help* man. It poses its challenges with the hope of being defeated, since it is an angel created solely for the purpose of prodding man to reach his spiritual potential.

When one applies this concept to the challenge presented by the tempting conversations that arise during *chazaras hashatz* (and during the entire time of prayer), one can see that the temptation is by no means designed to be irresistible. It is a temptation that is waiting to be overcome; in fact, it was created to be overcome by the specific person undergoing the challenge, in the exact time and place in which it occurs.

Even if a person has fallen prey to the temptation many times before, a further attempt can still bring success. Rav

30 Kislev

29-30 Adar

30 Sivan

29 Elul

---

1. *Bereishis* 4:7.
2. Cited in *Kovetz Sichos Maamar Mordechai*, Vol. 1, p. 87.

Schwab[3] explains that a necessary component of true *teshuvah* is recognition of the reason for the failure. Since talking during *chazaras hashatz* indicates a great disrespect for prayer, it follows that a person can achieve true *teshuvah* by recognizing this cause and seeking ways to move himself in a positive direction.

There are those who may recommend taking upon oneself a dramatic change in approach. For instance, even initially having *kavannah* when uttering each and every word, praying very slowly, or perhaps standing during the entire *tefillah*. These recommendations, although admirable, may not be practical for everyone.

What can a person do, then, to signify to himself and to Hashem that he has embarked upon a new, more serious approach to prayer? A surprising and reassuring answer is found in a profound insight into human nature offered by Rav Dessler.[4] He says that the small steps taken by a person — although they may not appear valuable or important — reveal his innermost spiritual reality. The larger steps, however, may merely reflect a superficial enthusiasm disguising a person's actual spiritual level.

Thus, an effective method to demonstrate how greatly one values a particular matter is to make an effort with the "small things." There are many ways for a person to act upon the realization that he values the opportunity to speak to Hashem daily. Many of these concrete actions are the very same ones a parent seeks to impress upon his children: coming on time to pray with a *minyan*, reciting the complete *Pesukei D'Zimrah*, and staying until the end of *Kaddish* after *Aleinu* are just a few small but significant ways to actualize the feeling that prayer is truly important. These acts will reinforce one's effort to refrain from talking and give one the strength to meet each challenge the Evil Inclination presents.

As Rav Segal has said,[5] progress is made moment by moment, day by day. When one focuses on the challenge that stands before him at the moment, and makes the right

---

3. Ibid. p. 86.
4. *Michtav MeEliyahu*, Vol. 3, p. 107.
5. *Yirah V'Daas*, Vol. 1, p. 91.

choice in facing that challenge, he is building the edifice of his own spiritual greatness.

Taking these small steps, armed with the knowledge that with Hashem's help we can succeed, will allow us to repair our special relationship with Hashem. This repair is not just one difficulty resolved; it is the resolution of every trouble and every sorrow befalling our fellow Jews and the Jewish people.

By restoring the power of our prayers, we rebuild the bridge that carries our love, our praises, our hopes, and our desires to our Father in Heaven. May we learn to reach out to Him with our whole heart, and may He heed every tear, and answer every sincere prayer of His beloved nation for good and blessing.

Points to Ponder

▸ *Progress to more powerful prayer is made day by day, moment by moment.*

▸ *The challenges posed during prayer are designed to strengthen the individual.*

▸ *The power of our prayer is our direct connection to Hashem.*

To dedicate a day of learning in future editions of this work, as a zechus in memory or honor of a parent or relative, or as a merit for a loved one, please call (718) 258-2210 or fax (718) 252-3646.

This book,
Praying With Fire,
launches the
"The V'Ani Tefillah Foundation"

The foundation's mission is to increase awareness of the importance and power of prayer and to provide education, inspiration, and tools for more sincere, powerful, and effective prayer.

For further information, please call:
(718) 258-2210 or fax (718) 252-3646.